More Praise for the Second Edition of *The Change Leader's Roadmap*

"Change today is fast and furious. *The Change Leader's Roadmap* covers every phase of transformational change—from preparing for change to lessons learned. It is a must-read blueprint for anyone looking to succeed in the field of change management and organizational development. I highly recommend it—no professional should be without it."

—Darlene Meister, director, Unified Change Management,
United States House of Representatives

"Having a vision and direction for change is one thing, implementing vision is quite another. Linda Ackerman Anderson and Dean Anderson have been there and have done it. This book about implementing the change process is an invaluable guide for how to do it."

—W. Warner Burke, Ph.D., Edward Lee Thorndike Professor of Psychology and Education;
chair, Department of Organization and Leadership; program coordinator, Graduate Programs in
Social-Organizational Psychology, Teachers College, Columbia University

"*The Change Leader's Roadmap* is essential reading for today's organizational leaders. Change is constant in healthcare. This work has been enormously helpful to us in organizing our successful transformational change agenda. I highly recommend this book as a doorway to this valuable methodology."

—Alan Yordy, president and chief mission officer, PeaceHealth

"I cannot imagine a more thorough or useful resource for those involved in leading change than this book. The authors, through their deep experience and knowledge, have made this very complex topic accessible and provided clear direction for those who are charged with considering, planning for, and implementing transformative change."

—B. Kim Barnes, CEO, Barnes and Conti Associates, Inc.; author,
Exercising Influence: Making Things Happen at Work, at Home, and in Your Community

"In this stand-alone companion book to their groundbreaking work on conscious change leadership, the Andersons provide a practical, step-by-step guide for change leaders, managers, and consultants. The book provides conceptually grounded, real world, time-tested tools and guidance that will prove invaluable to those faced with navigating the challenges of leading organizational change in today's turbulent times."

—Robert J. Marshak, Ph.D., senior scholar in residence, MSOD Program,
American University; organizational change consultant

"Every once in a while a book is written for change leaders that deserves more than a simple reading and justifies study. Roll up your sleeves, crack the cover, and you'll have something worth going to work with."

—Mel Toomey, LHD, scholar in residence for Master of Arts in Organizational
Leadership, Center for Leadership Studies, The Graduate Institute

"While the first editions were excellent to begin with, these enhanced second editions of *Beyond Change Management* and *The Change Leader's Roadmap* are even better with age. The additional years of experience deepen the authors' articulation of the links between theory and practice. These books are outstanding resources for both organization change consultants and organization system leaders. Having a roadmap in common promotes the teamwork required for complex adaptive and continually evolving change efforts."

—Charles Seashore, Ph.D., Malcolm Knowles Chair of
Adult Learning, Fielding Graduate University

T0330337

"In every generation there are creative and disciplined mapmakers who provide clear guidance to those whose paths will take them on similar journeys. Dean Anderson and Linda Ackerman Anderson are this generation's mapmakers. Their books are rich, resilient, comprehensive, and innovative guides that enable change leaders and consultants to practice their trades with heightened awareness and skill. Their grasp of the multiple dimensions of leading successful transformation help us recognize both the practical and the wise."

—David S. Surrenda, Ph.D., author, *Retooling on the Run*

"*The Change Leader's Roadmap* is an essential book for anyone attempting to understand and manage complex change, especially today's healthcare leaders. The book offers a comprehensive and practical guide that will help you get change right the first time. It will significantly increase your likelihood of success and lower your risk of costly setbacks. We have used the Being First methodology successfully on a variety of difficult organizational change initiatives including major clinical quality improvement and safety initiatives, as well as technology implementations such as electronic health record and enterprise resource planning systems. Based on over fifteen years of experience successfully managing complex clinical and operational change, I highly recommend *The Change Leader's Roadmap* and its companion text, *Beyond Change Management*."

—John Haughom, M.D., senior vice president,
Clinical Quality and Patient Safety, PeaceHealth

"Once again the Andersons have demonstrated their mastery of organizational transformation. *The Change Leader's Roadmap* is essential reading for any professional who is serious about leading sustainable change in large organizations."

—Rayona Sharpnack, founder and CEO, Institute for Women's Leadership

"Change efforts fail because of haphazard or arbitrary actions. This guide, essential for everyone involved in today's organizational change efforts, is the most comprehensive and systematic guide for change leadership ever created!"

—John Adams, Ph.D., emeritus professor, Saybrook University,
Organizational Systems Ph.D. Program

"I believe Linda and Dean have raised the bar again. The in-depth understanding provided through theory, concept, method, and a roadmap will support anyone leading and managing organizational change to enhance the possibility of immediate results and creating sustained capability."

—John D. Carter, Ph.D. President, Gestalt Center for Organization & Systems Development

"*The Change Leader's Roadmap* provides access to a rare experience: creating real, transformational change in a grounded, easy-to-understand manner. It calls into question our often hidden assumptions about what *should* work, and points us to what *does* work. And, it is refreshingly practical! I kept being surprised by the Andersons' clean approach. This is a must for anyone responsible for or involved in complex, large-scale change efforts. And who isn't these days?"

—Debbie King, organizational development leader, Kaiser Permanente

"The definitive 'how to' guide for change leaders—the Andersons have taken up where the theorists left off, providing practical mechanisms and strategies to build change capability within organizations. They challenge all of us who call ourselves change agents to practice what we preach and build reflexive consciousness into all our change leadership efforts."

—Quentin Jones, Australian Managing Director, Human Synergistics International;
coauthor, *In Great Company—Unlocking the Secrets of Culture Transformation*

"In *Beyond Change Management* and *The Change Leaders Roadmap*, Dean and Linda provide practitioners and executives not only the how (tools) but the why (concepts). If you are looking for a comprehensive treatment of the tricky journey of transformation, this is it."

—Christopher G. Worley, Center for Effective Organizations, University of Southern
California; former director, MSOD Program at Pepperdine University

"If you've been searching for a practical approach to large-scale change and transformation, this is a book worth reading. It presents the ideas and approaches in a way that today's busy leaders can understand and operationalize. In the dialog about what works and what doesn't work, I think readers will recognize approaches they tried in the past that haven't produced the hoped-for results, and will see new directions that offer a reachable place from where to lead and catalyze results."
—Sue G. Murphy, chief operating officer, Kaiser Santa Clara Medical Center

"Linda and Dean are in a unique position to offer such comprehensive thinking, models, and tools for change, because they have devoted more than three decades to working directly with senior leaders and strategic consultants in numerous transformations across a wide variety of organizations. By doing the work, studying the theory, and reflecting on outcomes, they have captured both the basics and the nuances of change and integrated them into understandable models, processes, and tools. These books are essential reads for change leaders as the authors have advanced the theory and practice of planned change to new heights. Kurt Lewin would be proud!"
—David W. Jamieson, Ph.D., practicum director, American University/NTL MS in OD Program; past president, American Society for Training & Development

"The Andersons capture the science and the art of orchestrating organizational change by providing both practical and insightful strategies and tools for leaders who must use strategic change as a thoughtful competitive advantage."
—Jackie Alcalde Marr, director, Organization and Talent Development, North America Oracle USA; coauthor of *Social Media at Work*; founder of Evolutions Consulting Group

"The Andersons bring their tremendous experience in OD to create what is truly a 'roadmap' for change, a road map that effectively translates abstract concepts into a concrete journey for successful change—probably the most critical issue in leadership today."
—Peter F. Sorensen, Ph.D., director, Ph.D. and Masters Programs in Organization Development, Benedictine University

This book is a must-read for anyone seeking to understand the logics and structures of successful large-scale change. It is filled with practical tools and step-by-step guidance that will help you master the complex task of change leadership.
—Diana Whitney, Ph.D., president, Corporation for Positive Change; author, *Appreciative Leadership: Focus on What Works to Drive Winning Performance and Build a Thriving Organization* and *The Power of Appreciative Inquiry*

"*Beyond Change Management* and *The Change Leader's Roadmap* are the best sources I know to learn how to lead and excel at change and business strategy execution."
—Eric Dillon, chief operating officer, Servus Credit Union Ltd.

"When I discovered Being First and their approach to leading transformational change, I knew I had found what I was searching for! The methodology described in this book is very comprehensive, teaching you how to be disciplined in your thinking, and most importantly, how to be a conscious change leader."
—Louise Branch, assistant deputy minister, Service Canada, Atlantic Region

"In *The Change Leader's Roadmap*, Linda Ackerman Anderson and Dean Anderson guide leaders safely through the turbulence of leading change, helping leaders mitigate the dangers of overwhelm, chaos, and uncertainty. Whether you are launching new products, restructuring, cutting costs, or growing, you'll learn how to take effective action with confidence. This is a must-read for any consultant or change leader who wants a clear path to navigate transformational change successfully."
—Faith Ralston, Ph.D., author, *Dream Teams, Emotions@Work*, and *Play Your Best Hand*

"Linda Ackerman Anderson and Dean Anderson are to be congratulated for producing a well crafted and insightful text. *The Change Leader's Roadmap* skillfully combines a range of conceptual insights with practical tools and techniques that will greatly assist educators, students, and practitioners of change. This book is an essential read for anyone interested in leading change effectively."

—David Grant, professor of Organizational Studies, University of Sydney

"*The Change Leader's Roadmap* is a uniquely effective success methodology in the change initiatives I have led. It is at the same time the most comprehensive set of strategies and tools I have come across globally and the most practical in its guidance toward the ones that will work best in each individual situation."

—Christian Forthomme, CEO, RealChange Network, Inc.

"*The Change Leader's Roadmap* is critical reading for leaders navigating organization transformation in times of uncertainty. The Andersons' book provides a powerful and practical toolkit for anyone trying to create a positive pathway to change! You will learn how to navigate and manage change that enhances the performance of your organization. This book provides the roadmap to lead you in the right way."

—Jacqueline M. Stavros, associate professor, director, Doctorate of Business Administration, Lawrence Technological University

"If you missed the Andersons' first editions, you may not know what a terrific contribution they are to the field of Organization Development. Now you have a second chance to read these excellent new editions from these gifted writers. These books are essential reading to those who want to become master practitioners in this field."

—Jane Magruder Watkins, coauthor, *Appreciative Inquiry: Change at the Speed of Imagination*

"*The Change Leader's Roadmap* moves beyond theory and grounds you in practical application. Reading this book will alter how you lead change. It not only informs you, but provides you with a framework for guiding people through transformation to get to your outcomes."

—Zoe MacLeod, director, Centre for Applied Leadership and Management, Royal Roads University

"Significant transformation in an organization is unbelievably difficult, yet this book provides a practical and reliable methodology for those of us who are change leaders. This approach is so useful because it indicates the required steps while keeping a focus on the desired results of the transformation."

—Nick Neuhausel Partner, Senn Delaney

"The perfect companion for any project manager. The detailed tasks and deliverables in this book can be inserted directly into your next project schedule to insure implementation success."

—Ben Snyder, CEO, Systemation

"We've all had those rare experiences where extraordinary results are produced through great teamwork and a commitment to delivering on that which may occur as impossible. And yet the ability to distinguish what made those breakthroughs possible, such that an organization can reliably produce such results again and again, may remain elusive. That is, until you are guided through the paradigm shift and steps of *conscious change* in The Change Leaders Roadmap!"

—Barbara Plumley, vice president regional operations, HealthCare Partners Medical Group

"This book will help leaders at all levels better understand the critical components of sustainable change. Often we focus on just content and neglect the human dynamics to our own peril."

—Katie Holmes, system director change strategy and consulting, PeaceHealth

FREE
Premium Content
▼

Pfeiffer®
An Imprint of

WILEY

This book includes premium content including worksheets and job aids that can be accessed from our Web site when you register at **www.pfeiffer.com/go/anderson** using the password ***professional***.

Instructors are invited to download a free Instructor's Guide with materials and information for using *The Change Leader's Roadmap* (or *Beyond Change Management* in that book) in a workshop or college course. The Instructor's Guide includes PowerPoint slide shows, key points, resources, student activities, helpful teaching strategies, and other supplemental classroom aids. College professors may download the materials at **www.wiley.com/college/anderson**

Corporate trainers, please email **instructorguides@beingfirst.com** to receive your copy for use in your executive and management development programs.

About Pfeiffer

Pfeiffer serves the professional development and hands-on resource needs of training and human resource practitioners and gives them products to do their jobs better. We deliver proven ideas and solutions from experts in HR development and HR management, and we offer effective and customizable tools to improve workplace performance. From novice to seasoned professional, Pfeiffer is the source you can trust to make yourself and your organization more successful.

Essential Knowledge Pfeiffer produces insightful, practical, and comprehensive materials on topics that matter the most to training and HR professionals. Our Essential Knowledge resources translate the expertise of seasoned professionals into practical, how-to guidance on critical workplace issues and problems. These resources are supported by case studies, worksheets, and job aids and are frequently supplemented with CD-ROMs, websites, and other means of making the content easier to read, understand, and use.

Essential Tools Pfeiffer's Essential Tools resources save time and expense by offering proven, ready-to-use materials—including exercises, activities, games, instruments, and assessments—for use during a training or team-learning event. These resources are frequently offered in looseleaf or CD-ROM format to facilitate copying and customization of the material.

Pfeiffer also recognizes the remarkable power of new technologies in expanding the reach and effectiveness of training. While e-hype has often created whizbang solutions in search of a problem, we are dedicated to bringing convenience and enhancements to proven training solutions. All our e-tools comply with rigorous functionality standards. The most appropriate technology wrapped around essential content yields the perfect solution for today's on-the-go trainers and human resource professionals.

Pfeiffer
www.pfeiffer.com

Essential resources for training and HR professionals

The Change Leader's Roadmap

HOW TO NAVIGATE YOUR ORGANIZATION'S TRANSFORMATION

SECOND EDITION

Linda Ackerman Anderson
Dean Anderson

Foreword by
Daryl R. Conner

A Wiley Imprint
www.pfeiffer.com

Published by Pfeiffer
An Imprint of Wiley
989 Market Street, San Francisco, CA 94103-1741
www.pfeiffer.com

Library of Congress Cataloging-in-Publication Data

Ackerman-Anderson, Linda S., 1950-
    The change leader's roadmap : how to navigate your organization's transformation / Linda S. Ackerman Anderson, Dean Anderson ; foreword by Daryl R. Conner. —2nd ed.
        p.   cm.
    Includes bibliographical references and index.
    ISBN 978-0-470-64806-3 (pbk.)
        1. Leadership.   2. Organizational change.   I. Anderson, Dean, 1953-   II. Title.
    HD57.7.A25   2010
    658.4'06—dc22

                                                                                            2010032263

ISBN 978-0-470-64806-3; ISBN 9780470877494 (ebk); ISBN 9780470877920 (ebk); ISBN 9780470877937 (ebk)

Acquiring Editor: Matt Davis
Production Editor: Joanne Clapp
Fullagar Editorial Assistant: Lindsay Morton

Director of Development: Kathleen Dolan Davies
Editor: Julie McNamee
Manufacturing Supervisor: Becky Morgan

PB Printing   10 9 8 7 6 5 4 3 2 1

*To Terra, our lovely daughter, for her precocious pursuit
of conscious awareness, and to
our wonderful parents, for their unconditional
support of our lives and work.*

CONTENTS

FIGURES, EXHIBITS, AND TABLES

Introduction

Chapter 1

Chapter 2

Chapter 3

Chapter 4

Chapter 5

Chapter 6

Chapter 7

Chapter 8

Chapter 9

Chapter 10

Chapter 11

Chapter 12

Chapter 13

Chapter 14

PREMIUM CONTENT FOR
THE CHANGE LEADER'S ROADMAP

Available for download at www.pfeiffer.com/go/anderson

- Ten Most Common Mistakes in Leading Transformation
- Leadership Breakthrough: Topic Options and Methods
- Building Change Capability: Leading Change as a Strategic Discipline
- Upgrade Your Organization Development and Project Management Staff to Strategic Change Consultants
- How Developing Breath Control Can Make You a Better Leader
- How Command and Control as a Change Leadership Style Causes Transformational Change Efforts to Fail
- Identifying Project Briefing Questions
- Selecting the Best Change Process Leader to Oversee Your Transformation
- Ten Critical Actions for Leading Successful Transformation
- A Candid Message to Senior Leaders: Ten Ways to Dramatically Increase the Success of Your Change Efforts
- How to Use Decision-Making as a Tool for Successful Transformation
- Six Faulty Assumptions about Change Communications
- Elements of a Whole System Integration and Mastery Strategy

FOREWORD

Compared with other disciplines, the field of change management is a relative newcomer. As a discrete field of practice, its theoretical roots can be traced back to the late 1940s/early 1950s. Among executive ranks, widespread knowledge of its existence didn't come about, however, until the 1960s—and even then, it was considered an obscure specialty for human resource or organization development types. It wasn't until the 1980s that it developed any real degree of acceptance from the line side of business, and it wasn't until the 1990s that it became an accepted strategic tool for senior officers. Today, change management has come into its own and is considered a must for most organizations engaged in critically important change efforts.

Any business tool that obtains widespread notoriety over a relatively short period of time can become populated with more than its share of academicians who write about it but don't live the experience on a daily basis. The field of change management is no different. There are many well-meaning but inexperienced, novice practitioners and, unfortunately, even some who are willing to peddle smoke-and-mirror "snake oil" that produces little real value. Thankfully, the field has also produced many excellent practitioners who work from the inside to provide genuine value to their organizations or from the outside as they assist the clients they serve. Within this population is a smaller number of individuals who have immersed themselves in both the study and application of organization change to a point where their understanding of the phenomenon far surpasses what others are able to see or do. This book is the product of two such people who have practiced in and contributed to the field as few others have and who have committed their experience to print.

For more than thirty years, the experience base Linda Ackerman Anderson and Dean Anderson have acquired is such that they have forgotten more about orchestrating change than most who claim expertise in it ever learned. They grant much more than exceptional knowledge and skills; they offer wisdom . . . a rare gift in such a young profession.

In this book, Linda and Dean leverage their deep command of the change domain to stretch the reader's perspective to what is on the other side of classic change management . . . the terrain of change leadership.

"Management" of anything is about standardization—maximizing consistency and decreasing, if not eliminating, variations. It is about the technical aspects of a craft. Facilitation of organizational change is still emerging as a distinct profession and has evolved through a period of characterizing itself as being able to *manage* the change process. Doing so allowed the budding profession to offer the hope of taming the change beast and, in the process, gain a degree of legitimacy during an era when many executives still thought anything that wasn't completely predictable couldn't be trusted. This idea of controlling change was useful for launching the profession, but the claim was always an apparition, and it eventually led to the inevitable result of all illusions . . . disillusionment.

Experience has shown that change management could not live up to the promise implied in its name; in this book, Team Anderson points to a new horizon—change leadership. *Management* of something is focused on engaging known variables with predictable outcomes. *Leadership* includes, but transcends, this objective and additionally provides for the art side of a craft. In the case of organizational transformation, leading change encompasses the predictable parts of the process, but it also opens the door to the unstable, unforeseeable aspects of change, where creativity and intuitive judgment are applied to unique circumstances.

Leadership embraces the application of both science and art, and this is a book about leading the transformational change process, written by masters of the craft. I recommend you approach its contents with the proper balance of excitement and caution.

The exciting news: Masters of a discipline don't just know more than most people about the conceptual frameworks and practical application of a subject; they are eager to share their wisdom to aid others in their journey toward excellence. Linda and Dean do just that in this outpouring of insights, guidelines, and specific action steps. By articulating their hard-won lessons from decades of successes and failures, they allow you the opportunity to stand on their shoulders and reach even higher.

The cautionary news: You will see in the pages to follow that, like all true masters, Dean and Linda respect their students too much to mask the truth about what it takes to truly succeed. This book is not for the casual browser or for those looking for bandages and aspirin. *It's a serious read for change practitioners who consider themselves committed students of the craft.* It covers the subject by going deep, broad, comprehensive, and thorough rather than trying to seduce the reader with superficial, simplistic explanations and gimmicks. The authors choose to reflect the true complexity organizational change imposes, instead of placating the reader with the veneer so often applied in the name of change management.

Nothing of *real* value comes without a significant investment. The challenge this book presents doesn't stop with the time and effort you will find necessary to fully absorb what is offered here. The more substantial investment opportunity is the chance to explore your soul in search of whether conscious change leadership is really a path for you. With the re-release of this book, Linda and Dean have done their part in paving the path. The ball is now in your court.

Daryl R. Conner
Chairman, Conner Partners,
Author *Managing at the Speed of Change* and
Leading at the Edge of Chaos
March 2010

PREFACE

Our life's work has always been about change. Dean started his career in the field of personal change, and Linda in organizational change. In 1986, when we met, it became clear that our two professional specialties were meant to be merged into one unified approach to transforming organizations.

Dean was one of the first people doing deep personal mastery work in organizations, having created the Optimal Performance Institute to offer his approach to breakthrough performance (originally developed for world-class athletes) to people in business. Linda was one of the founding leaders of the Organization Transformation movement, focusing on teaching the process of organization change and transformational leadership to executives and consultants worldwide. At the time of our meeting, Dean had realized that his personal and team performance models and interest in culture had to align with the complexities of larger organizational systems, while Linda had recognized that her work required more overt emphasis on personal and cultural change to fortify her large systems work. Both our interests and the requirements of successful large system transformation were moving each of us toward the other's expertise.

In 1988, we brought our specialties, insights, and theories together to create an integrated approach to leading transformation and to form Being First, Inc. In our early years, we mentored and coached one another in our individual specialties; now, we each stand in both arenas—personal and organizational transformation—and consult to senior executives across industries, government, the military, and large nonprofits.

Individually, and then collectively at Being First, we have always considered ourselves thought leaders in the area of transformation, not so much because of what we know, but because of the cutting edges we are willing to explore and the continual learning and development we pursue. We are committed to pushing the envelope of thinking and practice for accomplishing tangible, breakthrough-level results. We created Being First—appropriately named for our bias toward the personal work required to transform individuals and organizations—to offer our thinking and advice to people and organizations around the world.

Being First, Inc. is a full-service change education, consulting, and change leadership development firm assisting organizations to maximize their business results from change, transform their people and culture, and build internal change capability. We provide organizational change capability and change strategy consulting, enterprise-wide breakthrough training for culture and mindset change, change leadership skill development for leaders and consultants, licensing of our change process methodology, coaching, personal transformation training, and transformational team development. We support clients to create strategic disciplines for change so that their organizations can embody masterful change leadership and increase their success from change. We are developing a curriculum for women leaders and managers and are planning a worldwide Change Leadership Institute.

Our style, based on our commitment to walk our own talk, is to co-create a personalized strategy for each client with the appropriate balance of consulting, training, and methodology, integrating personal change and organizational change. We are devoted to our own continuous learning and development through applying our own personal practices and true partnerships with our clients. Our personal and organizational work provides us the opportunity to develop, field test, and write about what we see is required to transform human systems successfully and consciously.

We released the first edition of this book and its companion volume, *Beyond Change Management*, in 2001. Much has happened since then—in the world, in organizations, and in us. The messages of the first edition are as relevant today as they were then, and in many ways, more so. The challenges of change leadership continue to increase. Transformations in organizations are ever more complex, the stakes are higher, and the impact these changes are having on people and culture are more profound now than ever. These challenges are requiring leaders and those that consult to them to advance their thinking and methods. As we develop and evolve ourselves, we see with ever-greater clarity and distinction what is required to succeed at transformation—personally, organizationally, and globally.

In this new edition of *The Change Leader's Roadmap*, we have attempted to capture how our thinking has changed and what is true for us in this moment in time about how to best navigate an organization's transformation. We have reorganized Phases I and II to emphasize the importance of building a conscious change strategy and organizational change capability, respectively; streamlined the work of all nine phases; and shortened titles. We have added several new strategies for leveraging the value of The Change Leader's Roadmap, and we have sharpened our thinking on how to put it to best use.

For three decades, we have thoroughly engaged in the debate of personal change versus organization change, change the people or change the structures, carefully plan change versus let it unfold, manage change versus consciously lead it, and focus on process versus outcomes. The debates continue to drive our investigation and fuel the wisdom we seek to share. In our writing, we have attempted to be forthright about what we see as true, while keeping our mindset and eyes open to what we do not yet understand. We have attempted to denote what we think is factual, what we believe due to our own experiences, and what we are still learning or questioning.

We invite you, our reader, into this exploration with us—into the inquiry—into our attempt to give language, guidance, and incentive to growing the field of *conscious* change leadership. We hope you will participate in the conversation about the issues and propositions in these books, and then put them to the test in your own conscious leadership of change.

Please read on with the spirit of inquiry. Read with your concern for the state of today's organizations. Read to contribute to our collective ability to transform organizations into places in which people love to work and feel regenerated, as well as add value to their customers and stakeholders. Read on with a concern for people and the world, and how to make our lives ever more healthy and meaningful as we collectively co-create a future of greater social justice and environmental sustainability. Read on while honoring how far the fields of organization transformation, change management, and change leadership have come from the first attempts to infuse the values of planned change and human development into organizations. And please read with yourself in mind as a leader or consultant of change. Our message is written for you, and we hope it benefits you personally and professionally.

Dean Anderson
Linda Ackerman Anderson
Durango, Colorado
Spring 2010

ACKNOWLEDGMENTS

We deeply appreciate the wonderful people who supported us while writing these new editions of *Beyond Change Management* and *The Change Leader's Roadmap*.

We received abundant help from our trusty readers, friends, and colleagues all, including insightful input from Anne Polino, Carol Tisson, Jan Christian Rasmussen, and Steen Ruby. Their insights, feedback, and encouragement were invaluable to us.

Our staff was untiring in their assistance and encouragement. We sincerely appreciate Erin Patla and Lindsay Patterson for their dedication and patience.

We appreciate our clients, whose investment and commitment to partner with us produced the many insights and outcomes you read about in these books. Their willingness to work in conscious ways helped to formulate and demonstrate what we are most passionate about—leading transformation consciously. Many are true pioneers, and we feel honored to share in their journey.

We also appreciate one another for partnering in this co-creative process, modeling to the other what we deeply know is true, even when we each forgot. Our voices are stronger, our work is deeper, our lives are richer, and our spirits brighter from the experience.

The Change Leader's Roadmap

INTRODUCTION

Imagine having mastered the leadership of change in your organization. Imagine . . . your mission-critical changes are being readily adopted by your organization and being used to deliver extraordinary results. You are getting the outcomes you need, and your business is reaping the rewards of them. Your change efforts are running smoothly without major disruptions. Your stakeholders and employees are engaged, committed, and pulling their weight. Change work is getting done on time, and your budgets are being met without costing your operations.

For many in organizations, their history with change makes this possibility hard to imagine. For us, it is the possibility that we commit to create in reality.

In this book, we introduce you to The Change Leader's Roadmap (CLR), a change process methodology that will dramatically increase your ability to navigate your organization's changes, and its transformation, successfully. The CLR has been developed through thirty years of application in large organizations across all types of for-profit industries, government, military, and global nonprofits. It will help you plan, design, and implement a comprehensive change strategy and process plan to deliver your results at optimal speed and cost. It will build your confidence in how best to attend to the most challenging aspects of transformation—the human dynamics—helping you design a change process that engenders commitment and engagement of stakeholders and devotes needed attention to mindset, behavior, and culture change. It will help you stay on track when new information or circumstances arise that would otherwise thwart your effort with conflict, chaos, and resistance.

The path of failed change is easy to find because research shows us that the large majority of change efforts fail to produce their needed ROI. Organizational change is pressured, constant, and competitive, and it has become much more complex and dynamic than in previous decades. It is tougher than ever to succeed at organizational change. In difficult economic times—and in our increasingly competitive world—leaders have little choice but to press for more with less, cut corners, try to attend to their highest priority changes while keeping customers satisfied, and get results as fast as possible.

Not only are leaders responsible for more complex changes, but the social, technological, economic, and political terrains they must navigate during change are shifting faster than they can keep up with. The name of today's game is: "Change as fast as you can to stay ahead of your competitors!" With the marketplace operating at hyper-speed, leaders have their hands full, to say nothing of their heads, minds, and hearts. While they intend to do the best they can with what they have, they too often resort to old command-and-control practices that will not get them what they need, while dangerously taxing their workforce. Getting the chaos under control is an understandable instinct, but the current modes of managing change are not working.

Does the following sound familiar?

We see many leaders overloading the workloads of their employees with change on top of change on top of pressured operating requirements. They believe they have no extra resources, yet still need to get the change work done with what they have. We see an over-reliance on standard change practices applied to all projects, even if some changes are more complex and emotionally tumultuous than others. In such changes, traditional approaches such as project management and change management are not always sufficient. We see superficial attention to upfront change strategy, absentee sponsorship, and the drive for quick fixes. We see too much delegation without clear design requirements for what the outcome needs to achieve. We see leaders under-attending to the human dynamics inherent in change—with little patience for people's needs and reactions, ignorance about the cultural implications of the changes they are making, and sidestepping the need to engage people in shaping their futures. An assumption on our part is that, under pressure, leaders believe that all this "human stuff" takes more time and resources, and they don't have them. People will just have to deal with it.

The risk of this—especially in an economic downturn—is the tendency to increase control, speed, and mandate—in many ways doing more of what actually *doesn't* work. However, there is a leadership opportunity here—to step back, pause, gain greater perspective, learn from the past's unsuccessful patterns, and set up your organization to actually achieve the results it needs from change, still with the most expedient resources and pace. When things are most challenging, as they are right now in many markets, the time is right to give serious consideration to what you already have going for you in leading change and to learn specifically what you need to do differently to catapult your results. This assessment is the starting point for recreating your organization's ability to succeed in change. The challenge to leaders is to understand what this renewal of change capability requires.

This book and its companion, *Beyond Change Management* (Anderson & Ackerman Anderson, 2010), provide that understanding. We have written these two books as a set to support the evolution of leaders and consultants to become successful change leaders—knowledgeable of what transformation requires and capable of providing it. These two books are designed to alter your paradigm about organization change, from burden to necessity, from distraction to focus, from checklist to strategic orchestration. They provide the pragmatic approaches to guide organizations realistically through the dynamic river of ever-changing economic, business, and social environments. First and foremost, the change game clearly needs new leadership thinking and approaches. Change is not the enemy; in fact, it is the only road to the future. Leading change successfully requires new perspectives, practices, and ways of treating people as they change. *Beyond Change Management* outlines much of this new thinking.

Without question, the nature and complexity of change has evolved over the past thirty-five years. We are not dealing with the more manageable, controllable types of change that dominated the 1970s and 1980s—developmental and transitional change. The most prevalent type of change in organizations today is *transformation*. Developmental and transitional change can be tightly managed. Transformation cannot. It requires a broader and deeper knowledge of the people and process dynamics of change, a knowledge that stretches beyond change management and project management. It demands a close and intelligent partnership between the tangible requirements of change—organizational and technical—and the intangible human and cultural dynamics of change. Leaders must create the capabilities, infrastructures, mindsets, and behaviors they require. Both leaders and consultants must learn how to masterfully guide transformational change—in style, skill, and strategy. Both leaders and consultants must evolve to become competent *conscious change leaders*—**a new caliber of leader for a new type of change**.

Transformation demands shifts in leadership and employee mindset, culture, ways of relating, and the ability to course-correct. These are not easy shifts to make.

However, over our three decades of consulting, we clearly see that the level of awareness, perceptiveness, and openness of leaders and consultants has direct impact on whether change succeeds. Time and again, our clients' results are directly proportional to the degree that they address their mindsets about people, organizations, and change; shift their leadership style and behavior to be more co-creative and engaging; and transform deep-seated cultural norms to unleash the human potential in their organizations. In the absence of conscious awareness, change processes and their outcomes are disappointing.

We offer these books to compel leaders and consultants to step into the role of *consciously* shaping the transformation of their organizations. We believe they are in need of a comprehensive approach for leading transformation with a greater focus on what it takes to succeed: (1) a meaningful context for transformational action; (2) guidelines for thinking strategically about how to plan the process of transformation so that results are realized in both the bottom line and the culture; (3) knowledge of how to ensure that the people who must make the change happen want to change and can succeed; (4) the infrastructure to support and expedite change; and (5) a methodology for doing so. The context and guidelines for thinking strategically about the people and process dynamics are featured in *Beyond Change Management*. This book provides the methodology—The Change Leader's Roadmap—and the recommended infrastructure.

Beyond Change Management describes the conceptual underpinnings of transformation and what it takes to lead it to become more than a leader—to become a conscious change leader. This book describes the approach to put these concepts into practice. *Beyond Change Management* explores the theoretical foundations, and this book offers the pragmatics. We have written both books simultaneously to blend conceptual understanding with tangible steps and tools. Together, they provide an integrated and balanced approach to this essential evolution in the fields of organization development, project management, change management, and sound management in general.

Building your company's change capability is like building proactive continuous improvement into the fabric of your organization. Being able to lead change better than your competitors is a key strategic advantage in the 21st century. The more organizational change capability you have, the more successful you will be. Having the change leadership skills, tools, mindsets, and methodology to lead change of any magnitude is an essential corporate competency. Take some time to step back and learn about the realities of transformation because, more than likely, your organization is in fact transforming at this very moment. Learn about the CLR's evidence-based best practices of conscious change leadership. Set up the infrastructure, standards, and common change practices with strategic foresight—practices that allow you to hit the ground running with each major change effort your business strategy demands. The more strategic you can be in your change leadership and its supporting methodology and infrastructure, the more likely will be your success. Figure out how to establish in your organization the conditions that drive success—in the operation, the culture, and your leaders and workforce. We invite you to entertain establishing the cutting-edge strategic disciplines for change that we introduce in *Beyond Change Management*. They provide possibilities for enabling your organization to lead all of its changes with much greater intelligence, consistency, and skill. This book provides your toolkit.

In response to the need for conscious change leadership and greater results from change, there is also a new standard for change consultants. No matter what you currently call yourself, or how you perceive your work, we propose that you consider expanding into the new role of the Strategic Change Consultant. These consultants work at the large-scale or enterprise transformation level and are engaged from the beginning, as well as in setting up the change infrastructures their organizations need to succeed at change over the long term. We explore the role of the Strategic Change Consultant in *Beyond Change Management*, describing how it raises the possibility of having much greater impact at the system level from the onset of major change through to results. *Beyond Change Management* and The Change Leader's Roadmap methodology pave the way for this new brand of conscious consulting, addressing the competencies required to master both the people and process dynamics of transformation.

Although The Change Leader's Roadmap (CLR) is crafted for transformational change, it fits all types of change and all sizes. It includes the work relevant to engaging all levels of the organization from executive to the front-line workforce. It is your roadmap, and after you learn it, you will be able to tailor it for any type of change. We will overview the CLR methodology momentarily, and then explore it in depth in the remainder of this book. But first, we will provide an overview of the key points covered in *Beyond Change Management*. Review them as your foundation to understand what underlies the design and content of the CLR.

KEY POINTS FROM BEYOND CHANGE MANAGEMENT

1. **Competent Change Leadership Can Deliver Extraordinary Breakthrough Results from Change.**

   Breakthrough results are outcomes that far exceed what would occur if your organization continued carrying out its changes in the same way it always has. Breakthrough results, by definition, are a level of achievement *beyond* what most people would even conceive as possible.

   Research shows that the majority of change efforts fail to produce their intended outcomes. This is unacceptable! Change leaders can improve—not just a little, but a lot. We know how to lead transformation successfully, and leaders can learn what is required. Not only are intended outcomes achievable, but extraordinary outcomes are also within grasp if leaders develop their change leadership capability.

   Leaders initiate change to improve things. Organizations all have a "normal improvement line"—the level of results they usually get from their change efforts. Few leaders are conscious of this line, but it can be plotted year by year to measure what level of improvement is acceptable in each organization's culture. This line determines the organization's current change capability. If you improve your organization's change capability, the line will go up, and you will achieve greater results.

   Few people pursue real breakthrough results; rather, they unconsciously accept "the territory of the average," the middle of the bell curve. That does not interest us. We are after achieving the extraordinary, and this requires substantially increasing leaders' understanding of transformation, building a new leadership mindset, and applying a new set of approaches and tools.

2. **Creating Breakthrough Results from Change Requires Proficient Attention to Three Critical and Highly Interdependent Areas: Content, People, and Process.**

   Content refers to *what* must change in the formal organization—strategy, structure, business processes, management systems, technology, products, services, culture, and so on. *People* refers to the *human dynamics* that either influence the change or are triggered by it—dealing with people's emotional reactions, turning resistance into commitment, motivation, engaging them in shaping the change, learning new behaviors or skills, changing mindset, dealing with politics and relationships, and addressing cultural implications of the change. *Process* refers to *how* the organization will transform, and the decisions and action steps it will take along the way. Process includes how you govern the effort; how you pace it; how you design the change solution; how you course correct implementation; and how you ensure the level of communication and engagement that will deliver the highest possible outcome.

Leaders focus much more on content than either people or process. This is one root cause of the high failure rate of change. If any one area is under-attended, results suffer.

The greatest possibilities for breakthrough results reside in how you lead the areas of people and process. Integrating organizational and personal change into one unified change process is key. It is your people who unleash the potential within your content solution. It is your people who can make extraordinary things happen, or keep them from occurring. When people understand and believe in the changes, accept their role in achieving successful outcomes, and commit to working together with everyone needed to produce those outcomes, the possibility of breakthrough increases significantly. As a change leader, you create this possibility by designing a change process that engages your stakeholders, frees up cultural limitations to change, and promotes conscious attention and support for people to move through their resistance to full commitment.

3. **Understanding What Drives Change Is Essential to Building a Change Process That Delivers Breakthrough Results.**

Organizational change is catalyzed by a number of forces that first trigger awareness and then action. Understanding what drives change is critical because the drivers establish the overall context within which any change is identified, scoped, and planned. The drivers of change establish a change effort's relevance and meaning for both leaders and stakeholders. Without understanding them, a change effort can be disorganized, poorly planned, and resisted. Figure I.1 shows the Drivers of Change Model. Here is how it works.

Environmental forces (e.g., regulations, economics, politics, social trends, and international relations) drive changes in the marketplace's requirements for success (e.g., customer demands, client/patient expectations). In response, you establish a business strategy—imperatives for change—to meet those new requirements. These new strategies require change in your organization (e.g., its structure, operations, technology, etc.) If those changes are significant, your culture will need to transform to achieve, sustain, and get real value from the organization's changes. Culture

Figure I.1. **The Drivers of Change Model**

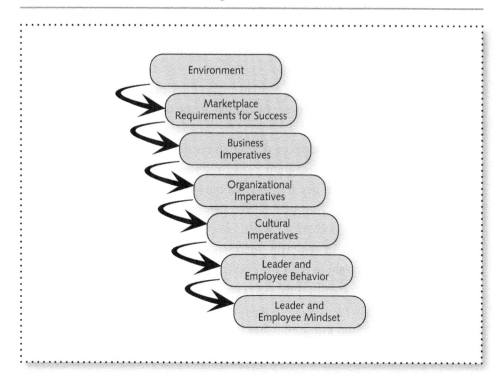

change drives the need to shift leader and employee behavior, and to sustain these, especially if significant, you will need to alter people's mindsets—their assumptions, perceptions, and beliefs about themselves, each other, and the organization.

While the model denotes a linear sequence, do not let this fool you. The drive for change follows this cause-effect path, but all seven areas must get your full attention, not necessarily in the model's order, but as an integrated undertaking. Change leaders must assess the changes required in all seven drivers to accurately scope their organization's transformation. If you leave a driver out, again, results will suffer.

Notice the direction of impact among the drivers. The larger, *external* forces (environment, marketplace requirements, business and organizational imperatives) drive the need to change in the more *internal* areas of people (culture, behavior, and mindset). Leaders are most accustomed to focusing on the external drivers, which generate the content of change. But to lead change competently, they must also attend to the internal drivers and human dynamics. Transformation requires conscious attention to both the external drivers *and* the internal drivers of change, to both content and people.

4. **You Need to Know the Type of Change You Face to Build the Right Kind of Change Strategy.**

Change has evolved over the past forty years. We now recognize three different types of change, each requiring different change leadership strategies and approaches. The three types of change are *developmental* change, *transitional* change, and *transformational* change. The most prevalent type of change occurring in today's organizations is transformation. It is by far the most complex and requires more than traditional approaches such as change management and project management to ensure its success.

Developmental change is an *improvement* in an organization's existing way of operating, such as improving skills, increasing communications, making a business process more efficient, or improving an existing sales process. Because developmental change does not ask people to radically alter their existing way of operating, it triggers fewer human dynamics than transformation and does not affect the organization's culture significantly. People just have to get better at what they already do. Such changes can also be project managed fairly easily.

Transitional change, rather than simply "developing" the current state, occurs when a problem is recognized in the current reality that needs to be solved with a new way of operating. Transitional change involves replacing the old state with a *clearly designed* new state that is formulated to resolve the inadequacies of the old state. Because transitional change entails the implementation of something different from what currently exists, it requires leaders to dismantle the current way of operating and systematically put in place a newly designed desired state. The process of "transitioning" from the old to the new can be planned, paced, and *managed*. Reorganizations, the installation of new computer hardware, and the creation of new products or services are typical transitional changes. Project and change management are quite useful methods for supporting transitional changes.

Transformation occurs when the organization recognizes that its old way of operating, even if it were to be "improved," cannot deliver the business strategies required to meet new marketplace requirements for success. This calls for content changes that are far more radical than in developmental or transitional changes, and require a fundamental shift from one state of being (the organization's old state) to another (its transformed state). These changes are so significant that they require the organization, in addition to changing its operations significantly, to shift its culture and people's behavior and mindsets to implement the transformation successfully and sustain it over time.

A key feature of transformation is that the specifics of the new state are unknown when the change process begins. They emerge as a product of the change effort itself. This makes a transformational change process very unpredictable, uncontrollable, and often messy. It must be crafted, shaped, and adapted *as it unfolds*. Leaders must be alert for the signals that indicate what the new state needs to be, as they engage the organization in moving away from its old way of operating and figuring out how the new reality needs to work. A direction may be set in motion, but the leaders need to actively course correct it every time new information emerges that calls for a shift of direction in either the content or the change process.

The second key feature of transformation is the significant factor of human dynamics and the essential role that mindset, behavior, and culture change play in its success. Because people are required to trust and step in to the unknown, transformation triggers fear and anxiety, which must be managed throughout the process to keep moving people's natural resistance toward greater commitment. In most transformations, the organization's culture must change to support the future state being created. Plus, most transformations require a shift of mindset, or worldview, for both leaders and employees to succeed. This means that transformation demands attention to deeper, internal human dynamics beyond simply changing their behavior or improving their skills. The nonlinear and emergent nature of the change process and the significant human and cultural dynamics make leading transformation very challenging.

The challenges require leaders to do three critical things to ensure success: (1) They must be willing to engage in their own personal change process to shift how they think, lead, and relate; (2) they must engage stakeholders earlier in the change process and to a greater extent; and (3) they must overtly set up the change process to welcome and respond to rapid course correction along the way. These actions are in addition to the guidance that traditional change and project management offer. These services can support transformation but are insufficient to deliver and sustain breakthrough results.

Some significant examples of transformation include old economy organizations moving into e-businesses, globalization, and major information technology implementations such as electronic health records in healthcare.

5. **Achieving Successful Transformation That Delivers Breakthrough Results Requires a *Conscious* Change Leadership Approach.**

Your state of awareness or level of consciousness is the greatest determinant of your success as a change leader. Your level of awareness impacts every aspect of your change leadership capability, experience, and outcome. Nothing is left untouched. Your level of awareness influences your change strategy, plans, decisions, leadership style, interpersonal and organizational communications, relationships, what you model, emotional reactions, willingness to change, and ultimately, your outcomes.

In the simplest of terms, leaders approach transformation with either expanded awareness or limited awareness. We call the expanded awareness mode the "conscious" approach and the limited awareness mode the "autopilot" (or unconscious) approach.

Expanded awareness is like getting the benefit of both a wide-angle lens and a high-powered microscope at the same time. Through the wider view, you can see the broader dynamics at play in transformation, such as cross-boundary impacts, regional vs. enterprise solutions, and how change in one area of the organization will impact operations in another. Through the microscope, you can see the deeper and subtler dynamics that would otherwise go unnoticed, such as how people's emotions influence commitment or how culture stifles implementation. Expanded awareness provides both greater span and greater depth to your view of what needs your attention.

Taking a conscious approach is a requirement of leading transformation successfully. When leaders take a conscious approach, their greater awareness provides more perspective and insight about what transformation demands and better strategic options to address its unique people and process dynamics. They can see more accurately what is occurring and can therefore respond to it more effectively.

When leaders take an autopilot approach, they respond automatically and unconsciously to the dynamics of transformation based on their conditioned habits, existing knowledge, and dominant leadership style. Their lens is filtered by biases and assumptions from their default or historical mental conditioning, causing critical people and process dynamics to go unseen. They apply old management techniques because they do not know of or think about other possibilities. In all fairness, the autopilot approach has sufficed for leading organizations and developmental and transitional change for a long time; it just is not adequate for leading transformation in the dynamic marketplace we operate in today.

Breaking out of autopilot to become more conscious is the primary leverage point for greater change leadership success. Everything else pales in comparison. We cannot overemphasize this point. The success formula is simple: *On average, your results from change will be in direct proportion to the level of conscious awareness you bring to the effort.* Working with your level of awareness requires some foundational understandings:

▶ Leaders who take a conscious approach understand that they and all human beings possess a mindset: values, beliefs, and worldviews that are unique to themselves; mental models from which they operate, interpret the world around them, and produce results.

▶ They understand that "mindset is causative": (1) that values, beliefs, and worldviews determine how people perceive and interpret facts; (2) that facts are different from a person's perceptions and interpretations; (3) that how someone perceives a situation causes the person's thoughts, feelings, and emotional reactions to that situation, which then determines the person's decisions, behaviors, and actions and ends up determining the results the person creates. The initial catalyst or source of outcomes is in the person's mindset.

▶ Conscious change leaders understand that mindset "causes" both their and others' internal states (being excited or threatened, confident or doubtful), as well as their external results (success or failure). Of course, these leaders realize that environmental factors also influence outcomes, often placing limitations on what is possible. But this reality does not diminish for them the primary fact that mindset determines how a person responds inside those limitations.

▶ Conscious change leaders understand that their mindset is "conditioned" by their experience, and that past events and how they perceived, felt, and responded to those events set up habits for how they will respond to similar events in the future. These patterns of perceiving, thinking, and feeling are the basis of a person's leadership style and approach to change. If your conditioned responses get you what you want and need, keep them. But if they do not, become conscious of them, and look for how to change them to generate different, and better, results.

A key differentiator between conscious and autopilot change leaders is that conscious leaders value and attend to *both* inner reality (internal human dynamics) and external reality (organizational factors) in their leadership. They take a whole systems approach. They actively engage with their and others' mindsets, thoughts, feelings, values, and levels of commitment as a part of what is necessary for the change to succeed. They intentionally focus on evolving their organization's culture and increasing employee engagement. These efforts are not nice-to-do's for them; they are must-do's.

Leaders operating on autopilot typically label attention to internal human dynamics as nonessential "soft stuff." They might *say* that they understand that people's reactions have an impact on performance or that culture should be attended to, but they ask someone else, such as the HR department, to handle it. What they do matters, not what they say, and autopilot leaders do not lead in ways that demonstrate a true understanding that mindset is causative and has a direct impact on human dynamics and results. They do not witness their mindset in action or how their conditioning influences how they behave, or how they impact others. They under-attend to culture and do not account for its pervasive force in their change strategies. Leaders on autopilot focus nearly exclusively on external dynamics. Their attention is primarily on content, the design solution, implementation plans, reporting mechanisms, and metrics.

6. **Conscious Change Leaders Are Accountable for All of the Factors Impacting the Organization's Ability to Transform Successfully.**

For thirty years, we have been promoting the idea that leading transformation *masterfully* requires leaders and consultants to design and implement change processes that attend to both internal and external dynamics at the individual, relationship, team, and organizational levels. We have called this a "multi-dimensional, process approach" to transformation to denote all of these different, but interdependent areas of required attention for transformation to succeed. Now, with the rapidly growing global movement catalyzed around Ken Wilber's ground-breaking work at the Integral Institute headquartered in Boulder, Colorado, we can describe our approach as "integral" as defined by Wilber. This alignment is affirming, given the power of Wilber's work.

The full breadth of what conscious change leaders must attend to—the multi-dimensional and process factors at play in successful transformation—is shown in Figure I.2, The Conscious Change Leader Accountability Model. Note that the model includes content (systems), people (mindset, behavior, and culture), and process. It is a lot to pay attention to, and conscious leaders stay as present to these forces as they can.

Figure I.2.   **The Conscious Change Leader Accountability Model**

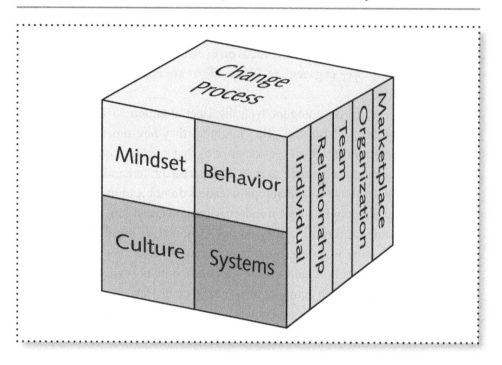

Before we address the individual aspects of the model, let's discuss the way the model is organized. We borrow from Wilber's core work that he calls All Quadrants, All Levels (AQAL) (2000). Notice that the face of the model is a matrix built on an *x* axis (internal and external) and a *y* axis (individual and collective), making four "quadrants." (Figure I.3, The Four Quadrants of Change Leader Accountability, is a section of the overall Accountability Model, and further clarifies this.) The two quadrants on the left describe aspects of internal reality, while the two quadrants on the right describe external reality. The upper two quadrants address the individual, and the lower two address the collective. All together, this simple, elegant, and accurate model depicts all dynamics of reality. (For further explanation, we refer you to Wilber's works noted in the bibliography.)

Conscious change leaders must attend to all four quadrants: (1) mindset (internal, individual); (2) culture (internal, collective); (3) behavior (external, individual); and (4) systems (external, collective).

The **mindset** quadrant includes values, beliefs, thoughts, emotions, ways of being, levels of commitment, and so on. **Behavior** includes work styles, skills and

Figure I.3. **The Four Quadrants of Change Leader Accountability**

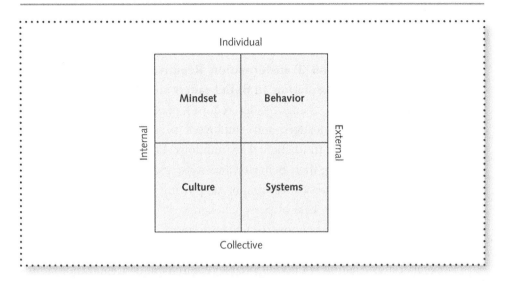

actions, as well as behaviors. **Culture** includes norms; collective ways of being, working, and relating; climate; and esprit de corps. **Systems** include strategy, structures, systems, processes, and technology.

Each of these quadrants must be addressed at all levels of human interaction—individuals, how people relate, how teams function, and interaction with the marketplace itself. Organization transformation is not simply about organizational systems or culture. It demands attention to all levels, as they all will have an influence on your attempt to transform your organization.

We benefit greatly from Wilber's AQAL model to depict this graphically, and we acknowledge his contribution to our improved way of communicating the full scope of required conscious change leader attention. Most importantly, the model makes it clear that conscious change leaders must always attend to internal and external dynamics within both individuals and the collective.

We complete our Conscious Change Leader Accountability Model by capping it all off with "change process." Change processes occur within all the quadrants at all levels. Of critical importance, a successful organization transformation requires a change strategy and process plan that organizes and integrates all of these change processes and the activities within them into a unified organization-wide process that moves the organization (all its quadrants and levels) from where it is today to where it wants to be . . . transformed to something new that produces significantly improved results in its marketplace. In our consulting practice, we accomplish this very challenging and essential outcome using The Change Leader's Roadmap methodology described in this book.

7. **Successful Organization Transformation Requires Significant Personal Awareness and Transformation, in Both Leaders and the Workforce.**

Becoming a conscious change leader requires personal change. Transformational change calls for leaders and employees to transform *themselves*—changing their mindsets and fundamental assumptions about reality; their ways of being, working, and relating; their behavior and style; and their level of personal empowerment and effectiveness at causing or supporting things to happen in the organization. We call this process of personal change *self-mastery*, which implies that the individual leader must choose to change, be aware of what needs to change, and be empowered to do so.

Personal transformation is a nonnegotiable requirement of organization transformation. If change leaders do not overtly model personal change in themselves, they cannot ask it of their people. If they do not demonstrate the new behaviors and work practices that the new state requires, they cannot ask that the workforce engage in them either. Both are essential to the success of transformation, and both must be built into any effective transformational change strategy. For consultants, this level of personal transformation is equally important. Otherwise, they cannot model this type of change nor coach their clients through it.

There are two principal aspects we all share as humans that are essential to understand to make transformative personal change—ego and "being." The ego is a function of the mind, and performs the role of ensuring that we have a personal identity and a sense of individual self, as distinct and separate from everyone else. It makes sure that we know—and maintain—predetermined roles, behaviors, choices, boundaries, and levels of performance. The ego acts consistently in ways that reinforce who it perceives each of us to be, as successfully as possible and protected from the risk of failure. In transformational change, when so much is uncertain, a leader's ego will be actively engaged in maintaining the leader's identity and securing a known outcome, which may not be at all what the organization's transformation requires. Without an awareness of our ego and how it controls our thinking and behavior, we cannot effectively lead transformation for the good of the organization.

Being, or one's higher self, on the other hand, "holds the space" for everything that is happening inside and outside of us, regardless of whether our ego judges it as positive or negative. It brings neutrality to leaders' perceptions and decision making, enabling them to discern an objective response, not a protective or conditioned one, and hopefully a better one. Being lacks emotional reactivity, allowing for the identification of the right actions required for desired outcomes. Leaders operating on autopilot are controlled by their egos and relatively out of touch with their beings. Conscious change leaders are more in touch with their being, which empowers them with more choices in the face of the uncertainty of transformation.

8. **Change Capability is a Twenty-First Century Competitive Advantage, and to Ensure it, You Need to Establish Change Leadership as a Strategic Discipline.**

Change is the essence of innovation, growth, and transformation. Organizations that can change quickly and successfully will win in the dynamic twenty-first century marketplace. Change is no longer a "nice-to-do," but rather, is an ongoing, critical function within organizations. Developing change leadership capability is essential.

Organizational change capability requires investment in change leadership development for executives, managers, and the workforce. But even more importantly, superior change capability requires establishing change as a *strategic discipline* in the organization. Virtually all other key functions in organizations have such strategic disciplines, such as finance, marketing, sales, supply chain, HR, and IT. These disciplines, and the management protocols that go with them, are crucial to these business functions performing effectively on an ongoing basis. Change is now so complex, pervasive, and constant that it requires similar strategic disciplines.

There are five key strategies for building the organizational capability to lead change as a strategic discipline: (1) identifying and managing an enterprise change agenda; (2) having one common change process methodology; (3) establishing change infrastructures—based on best practices—to execute initiatives consistently and successfully; (4) building a Strategic Change Center of Excellence; and (5) establishing a strategic change office (SCO) with its leader, the Chief Change Officer (CCO), on the executive team. Any one of these disciplines will support your organization to better succeed at change. However, establishing all of them sets up your organization with the conscious attention and methods to drive achieving greater results from your changes. These disciplines are the next edge of change leadership and are necessary to achieve breakthrough results from change consistently.

9. **Turning Stakeholder Resistance into Commitment Requires Competent Attention to Deeper Human Dynamics**

Stakeholder commitment is a key to successful transformation. Transformation often triggers people's emotional concerns, fears, doubts, and anxieties, which manifests as resistance. Minimizing resistance and turning it into commitment is a primary role of conscious change leaders and consultants.

People's emotional reactions, or resistance, are caused by their perceiving that the change will not meet their core needs. Universal core needs include (1) safety; (2) inclusion and connection; (3) power; (4) control; (5) competence; and (6) justice and fairness. These core needs are often unconscious; people are not overtly aware of them or the influence they have over behavior and reaction. Whether people's needs are met or not governs their attitudes and actions. Each of us has two or three dominant needs. Change may trigger fears that "I won't be on the new team" (inclusion), or that "I won't know how to succeed with the new system" (competence), or perhaps that "selection for new positions will not be fair" (justice and fairness). Leaders often call these fears resistance, but they are not. This "resistance" is nothing more than these deep-seated issues ruling people's emotions and behavior. In other words, people are not intentionally resisting the change; they—or actually their egos—are simply afraid their core needs won't be met.

Conscious change leaders design their change processes to minimize triggering these core human needs (resistance). Strategies could include (1) making the selection process for new positions overt early (power and control); (2) announcing that everyone will be adequately trained in the new systems before being held accountable to perform in them (competence); or (3) in a merger, announcing that job selection decisions will be made by teams with equal representation from both merger partners (justice and fairness).

Success in transformation requires attention to human dynamics at a far deeper level than that provided by typical change management methods. People go through an emotional transition process to resolve their emotional issues and turn their resistance into commitment. Conscious change leaders must understand this process and instead of attempting to "contain" people's reactions, they must provide opportunities to "invite them out" so that people's reactions can be transformed. They must build steps to allow people to have their experience, make the transformational shift from resistance to commitment, and engage constructively in the change. Leaders must provide personal development opportunities that build conscious awareness of one's internal dynamics—core needs and emotional reactions—in transformational efforts that seek breakthrough results.

10. Culture Change Is a Critical Driver of Transformation.

Culture is to organizations as mindset is to individuals. Culture is the way of being of the organization—its character or personality. Within culture lie the company's core values, its norms and operating principles, its myths and stories. It determines what types of individual behaviors are acceptable or not and shapes the behaviors and style exhibited by the organization in the marketplace. Culture infuses "*how* work gets done around here," and how the organization behaves in relation to its customers.

Culture is a like a universal design parameter. Everything tangible in the organization reflects this template. Culture impacts the state of being of its employees (morale), and sets the tone for people's emotional experience at work. Culture determines the level to which the organization "walks the talk" of its espoused values. Culture impacts the organization's performance and results and determines how much of the human and organizational potential actually gets used in service to the marketplace. If the culture is high performing in nature, then the organization's systems (content) and its people (mindset, behavior, and performance) will be too.

Changing culture is a critical aspect of a transformational change strategy. There are six conditions that must be in place for culture change to succeed. Culture change:

- Must be relevant to business success
- Must be made explicit and legitimate
- Must include and support personal change
- Must have a champion and be modeled by leadership
- Must engage a critical mass of employees
- Must ensure that all aspects of the organization are realigned to the desired culture

The Change Leader's Roadmap methodology calls for the actions that drive culture change while simultaneously designing and implementing business solutions.

11. Leading Transformation Requires a Process Approach.

By "process," we mean the natural or intentional unfolding of continuous events toward a desired outcome. The key word is "continuous." Transformation cannot be achieved solely through isolated, disconnected, or random events. Change leaders must ensure that all change-related activity is purposeful and integrated. Each action or event must build toward the next. In this way, momentum is created, and the change process rolls out toward its desired result.

A process orientation is especially critical in transformation more than any other type of change for two reasons. First, because the future state of the organization is unknown at the beginning of the process, it has to emerge as the transformation unfolds. This requires designing a process that supports this "emergent re-invention" to occur. Second, transformation requires significant personal and cultural change, which only occurs over time.

Transformational change leadership requires *conscious process thinking*, intentionally attending to inputs, outputs, what has occurred historically, and how present actions can best support future steps in the change effort. This is distinct from project thinking and systems thinking, or the use of checklists or cookbooks for change. Through the conscious process thinking lens, leaders see their organizations as multi-dimensional, interconnected, living systems in constant and perpetual motion—all quadrants and all levels. They see them as ever-evolving and constantly seek to advance their development. In designing their transformational change processes, they account for the fact that their best-laid plans will be constantly adjusted to the realities that occur at all levels of the organization as change proceeds.

Conscious process thinking generates a need for an advanced tool for leading transformation. You must have a process model as your guidance system. Change *process models* are very different from change *framework models*, which are more common. Framework models are static depictions of types of change activity requiring attention, such as business case, communications, training, and work redesign. Each of these may be necessary focal points in any given effort, but such frameworks do not provide process guidance (actions to take over time, sequence, pacing, etc.). Process models demonstrate the flow of activity of what has to occur to get from your current state to your desired future state. Given the complexity of change, and how to actually get to a new state, a process roadmap is essential.

12. **Change Leaders and Consultants Must Consciously Design and Facilitate Their Change Processes Using a "Fullstream" Change Process Model.**

The Fullstream Transformation Model (Figure I.4) shows that the process of change has an upstream component, a midstream component, and a downstream component—all of which need to be consciously designed and led for the change

Figure I.4. **The Fullstream Transformation Model**

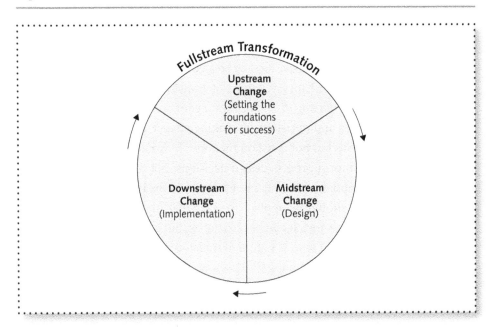

to succeed. The *upstream* stage sets up the foundations for success. The *midstream* stage focuses on designing the desired state, while the *downstream* stage attends to implementation. The Fullstream model helps to graphically and easily understand a high-level overview of the entire process of change requiring conscious attention.

Traditionally, most leaders have thought of "planning for change" as "planning for implementation." If leaders think only of implementation, it is no wonder that their well-intentioned efforts flounder! The seeds and roots of successful transformation are sewn in the upstream and midstream stages. Implementation is essential, yet it is the last of three stages of the change process. Implementation goes smoothly, and typical implementation problems are avoided by getting the upstream and midstream stages right.

Critical upstream activities include communicating a clear case for change and desired outcomes, building an integrated change strategy, clarifying how to engage stakeholders early and meaningfully, establishing a sound communication plan, and shifting leadership mindsets. Skipping these deliverables creates downstream challenges. When leaders rush through the midstream stage and design a desired state with little or no stakeholder involvement, people do not understand the new reality they are being held accountable to create and resent having one foisted on them. If leaders neglect doing an impact analysis of the desired state, they get blindsided during implementation from impacts they did not know existed. If they only engage project management and change management expertise just before implementation, then their previous oversights would have already created serious flaws in their plans.

Given the dynamic and messy nature of transformation, a process model for leading it must be a *thinking discipline*, not a cookbook of prescriptive action. It should inform choices and decisions by making change leaders *conscious* of all key *potential* change tasks but not insist on their use. It should guide action but not mandate it. It should inform process design decisions, not dictate them. It should point to predictable human dynamics, not trigger them. It should organize the plan, not rigidify it. It should be applied in ways that make it easily adapted as new dynamics emerge. In short, it can be structured, but it must accommodate the evolving, multi-dimensional *process* nature of transformation.

The Change Leader's Roadmap (CLR), shown in Figure I.5 and described in this book, is such a thinking discipline. It is designed as a process model, with attention to the past, the current reality, and the future. It is multi-dimensional, attending to mindset, behavior, culture, and systems at all levels of the organization. It is flexible, providing options and considerations as a navigation system. You, as the change leader or consultant, must choose the right actions to take. With conscious awareness, infused with your experience and wisdom, the CLR will guide you to achieve a successful transformation.

THE CHANGE LEADER'S ROADMAP METHODOLOGY

The CLR model outlines a fullstream roadmap for getting an organization from where it is to where it wants to be, from its current state to its desired future. It delivers your business results in ways that your people are able and willing to engage in the change and succeed. The CLR is a true process methodology that helps you decide which change tasks are critical, the order in which to take them, and how to execute them for optimal impact. The CLR enables you to consciously design your change process so that each task flows into the next, building momentum toward your desired outcomes.

The model portrays nine phases of activity that represent generically how transformation—and all change—takes place in organizations. As a process roadmap, it can't tell you which destination to pursue or which turns to make to get

Figure I.5. **The Change Leader's Roadmap Model for Leading Conscious Transformation**

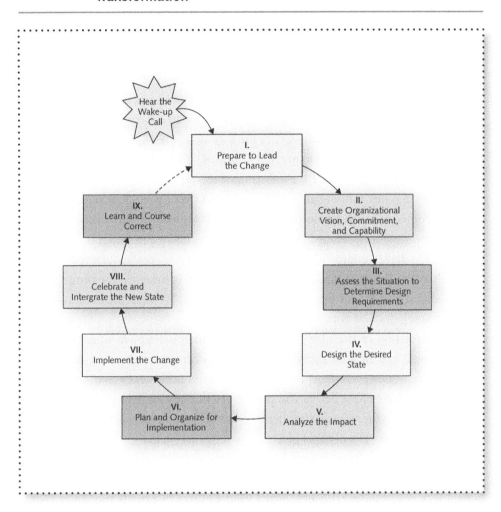

there, but it does provide guidance regarding the whole terrain that lies ahead. It outlines the general process you will take to discover your destination, how to set up the organization and the people who must change to be successful, and how to achieve results as expediently as possible.

We have been applying and developing the CLR for more than thirty years. Every task in the model is there because it served a significant people or process requirement in one live case or another. In some of our experiences, a task was officially added because its presence or absence was a make-or-break factor in a client's success. Any of the tasks in the CLR may be that critical for you. We encourage you to become familiar with all of the tasks so you can decide which are central to your effort's success. At the same time, we encourage you to make your change process as streamlined and efficient as possible. *Include as few tasks as you can but always what you need to succeed.* Most transformations will require at least 40 percent of the tasks outlined. Many require closer to 70 percent. You choose which tasks you will need to undertake based on your understanding of your organization's need, readiness, and capacity, and the results you are trying to achieve.

Although designed for transformational change, the CLR can be tailored for all types of change, as well as for any magnitude of change effort. Smaller, less complex changes will require selective tailoring of the tasks in the model. Remember that the model is just a model until you tailor it to fit your particular situation. Then the work comes to life and becomes your particular transformational change plan.

The most highly leveraged experiences we have had using the CLR are in organizations that have declared it as their *one common change methodology*, driving all major changes. They use it as their "Change Operating System," the program that stands behind and shapes the execution of all change. We describe the advantages of this strategy in more detail in Chapter Fourteen.

The depiction of the nine phases of the model is designed to represent the inherent logic and flow of the activities of transformation on any given change effort. You may, however, interpret the model's sequential nature to mean that you must complete one phase before you proceed to the next. In reality, you may be in two, three, or even four phases simultaneously. You may do the work of some phases in parallel with the work of other phases, as your situation allows. Different levels of the organization may be in different phases at the same time, and you may need to cycle through all nine phases several times until all aspects of your transformation conclude. Understanding the logic of the model makes this multi-tracking easier.

The graphic representation of the CLR may also cause you to think mistakenly that the roadmap portrays change as circular, where you end a cycle only to start over again from the same place. The graphic is rendered to clearly show the sequence of the Phases I to IX and back to I, yet in reality, the model is a spiral. When your change effort is complete, you are likely to continue on your journey with another change effort. After each "cycle" of change, you end at a future state that is transformed and improved—an advancement from where you started. Hence, the accurate message of the model is that change is a spiral going continuously upward, as our organizations continue to evolve.

As we describe the model, we refer frequently to "the transformation of your *organization*." It is important to note that not every organizational transformation is enterprise-wide. Transformation can occur in a business unit, function, department, plant, group, or any intact part of the organization. Any of these segments of the whole organization is a system in and of itself. The model still pertains to its transformation, just at the smaller boundary of that subsystem. The transformation, even in these smaller systems, must attend to the *whole* of that system. Thus, when we refer to the "organization," it means whatever is within the boundary of the system that is undergoing the transformation.

In enterprise-wide transformations, many change initiatives occur to support the overall transformation. The organization goes through an overarching nine-phase process, as do the individual change initiatives within the larger effort. Therefore, different change initiatives, business units, or areas of the enterprise may be in different phases and will likely need integration so that all initiatives support the overarching transformation. When each change effort is using the same process model, language, and tools, integration becomes much easier. We offer strategies for integrating various initiatives in Chapter Three.

It is also important to note that, while we focus in this book exclusively on the organizational application of the CLR, it also guides transformational changes in systems other than organizations. Communities, social movements, national policy, and multinational issues are examples of arenas that also undergo transformation and would benefit from the application of this roadmap.

Structure of The Change Leader's Roadmap Methodology

Each of the nine phases of the model accomplishes a specific body of work. Together, they generate the activities required to complete a full life cycle of transformation. In the Fullstream Transformation Model, each of its three stages covers three of the nine phases of the CLR: Phases I to III are the *upstream* stage (setting the foundations for success), Phases IV to VI comprise the *midstream* stage (design), and Phases VII through IX denote the *downstream* stage (implementation). Figure I.6 shows this graphically.

Depending on your need, you can customize the model to any level of detail. The most conceptual level is the general description of the nine phases as shown earlier in Figure I.5. Each phase is divided into major activities, as shown in Figure I.7. The activities are achieved through focused tasks, all of which have deliverables.

Figure I.6. **The Change Leader's Roadmap as a Fullstream Process**

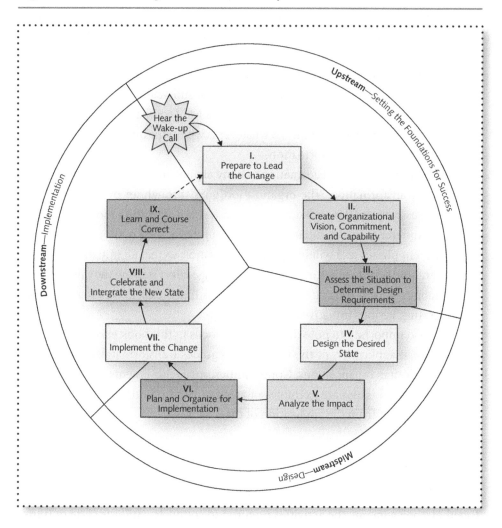

The deliverables of each task, at the most operational level, are accomplished through a series of suggested work steps.

We have structured the material in this way—phase, activity, task, work step—for ease of use for line managers who are familiar with similarly structured project management methods. The structure also provides the greatest versatility for the various people who use it, be they executives who need only the conceptual phase level or change process leaders, project managers, or consultants who benefit from the greater detail of the activities, tasks, and work steps.

Figure I.7. The Change Leader's Roadmap—Activity Level

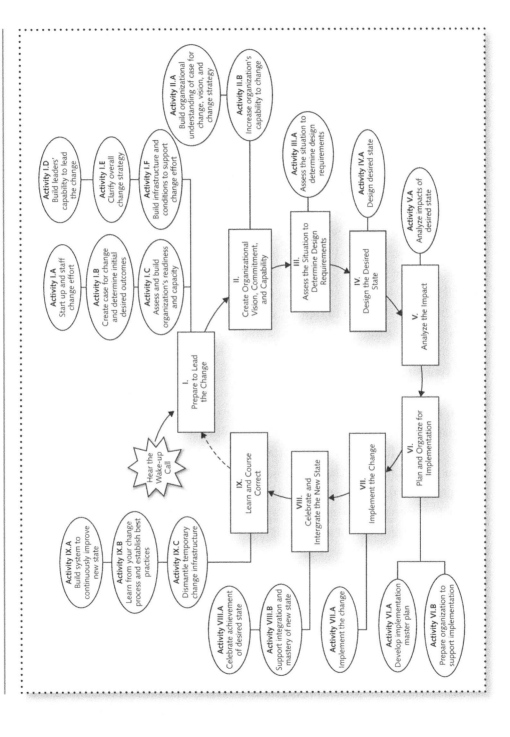

In this book, we present the purpose of each phase, its major activities, and its tasks. A listing of the task deliverables for each activity is included at the beginning of each chapter. In the overview of each phase and activity, we point out several of its predictable underlying people and process dynamics so that change leaders and consultants will become conscious of these forces at play and attend to their causes or resolutions when planning their change processes.

A complete outline of the phases, activities, and tasks is included in the Appendix. The work steps are not included because this book is not intended to serve as an operational manual. More in-depth information about the work steps within each task, additional consulting guidelines, and detailed application tools and information are included in The Change Leader's Roadmap online application available from Being First, Inc. Go to www.changeleadersroadmap.com for more information.

We have designed the CLR to be as comprehensive as possible, including all that we have found necessary to support transformation. *This does not mean you will have to do all of the activities the model suggests.* In all its comprehensiveness, the model is designed to support you to ask which of its many tasks are critical for *your* transformation's success. The application of the model must *always* be tailored to the outcomes, magnitude, style, pacing requirements, and resource constraints of your situation. Remember, the model is a thinking discipline, not a prescription for action. Keep in mind that there is a recognized learning process for mastering the breadth of the CLR. We describe the typical phases of learning the CLR in Chapter Thirteen. Your reading of this book starts your development process!

The CLR provides an important strategic advantage regarding capacity when you are planning for change across your organization. Every change task requires capacity, borrowing it from operations. You must understand the magnitude and criticality of the work needed to accomplish your changes so that you can make an intelligent determination of how much *capacity* your organization has—and needs—to successfully accomplish them. The more robust your change process plan, the more capacity you will need to carry it out, which will pull from operations. Make your change process as streamlined and efficient as possible. Taking on more than you and your organization can realistically handle is a formula for failure. The clarity of the CLR tasks will enable you to develop a more accurate assessment of your capacity needs. Keep your capacity requirements in mind as you learn what each task entails.

No two change efforts are ever alike. Their desired outcomes or content may be similar, but the presenting organizational and cultural circumstances are always different. Tailoring the CLR is a given. We recommend that you be selective about the work you include in any particular change strategy and plan. For each change effort, we suggest that you consider all of what is offered here and then select *only* the work that is appropriate to your transformation and only what will help you guide and accelerate your effort. You should skip activities or tasks that you have completed already or are irrelevant. You will likely combine tasks to achieve multiple deliverables and accelerate progress.

We hope that the information presented here will help you understand what work you must include in your plans and also see the implications of omitting or skimming through key tasks. Again, we recognize that there is a development process to feel confident in your decisions about what to include or not. As you proceed in your learning, this work will become more obvious. Read this book with an eye toward understanding first, then expediency and strategic impact of each task. And, to make your planning decisions easier, we have included "The CLR Critical Path" in Chapter Fourteen, which lists thirty tasks to consider first.

How The Change Leader's Roadmap Methodology Is Unique

There are many models for how to manage change in organizations. The CLR stands out in several ways. First, it is designed to be comprehensive, giving you a thorough overview of the terrain of change from which you will design your right path to achieving results. The CLR is a multi-dimensional methodology, guiding the work required at the organizational level, within teams, relationships, and individuals. It spells out the change tasks to shift mindset, behavior, culture, and systems at each of these levels. The CLR integrates classic project management and change management with cutting-edge approaches to human performance and culture. Simpler models may be appealing, but they are not effective for transformation. What the CLR offers is essential for delivering breakthrough results from transformation.

You can use the CLR to plan, design, and implement change solutions for any "content" of change, including technology implementations such as ERP, CRM, or electronic health records; restructuring; process reengineering; systems changes; job redesign; culture change; or mergers and acquisitions. The CLR raises awareness of the need to simultaneously attend to the content of the change, the people dynamics triggered by that change, and the process requirements to get you to your intended outcomes. It guides you through developing a high-level change strategy to initiate each change effort with aligned attention to all people, resources, and change work for the most expedient and positive action from the start. Of great importance is that it provides you the tools with which to accomplish each and every task. We have included a sampling of those tools in this book, and the remainder are available from the online application offered from Being First, Inc. at www.changeleadersroadmap.com.

The CLR includes actions to ensure that your organization has the capacity and builds the capability to succeed in change, and it guides you in how to minimize the negative impacts on people and operations while optimizing engagement and rapid course correction throughout the entire journey. Importantly, it helps you to change the mindset and culture of your organization while you achieve your new business outcomes. Each activity begins with the recommendation that you design the process of that activity's task-level work before you begin. This allows you to take a more conscious approach to how you plan and implement the change, keeping in mind the many people and process implications that will affect your outcome.

Achieving tangible business results from change, transforming culture, and building organizational change capability are often seen as separate goals, but the actions required to achieve all three are built directly into the CLR. In other words, you can use the CLR to transform your culture and build your organization's change capability while you achieve maximum results from your change efforts.

Our Audience

This book is written for change leaders and consultants who are responsible for designing and implementing complex change processes. This includes line leaders who run change projects and their executive sponsors. It also includes directors and middle managers because they are responsible for seeing that change happens successfully in their organizations. We also write for all change practitioners—change management consultants; organization development practitioners; HR specialists involved in change; project managers; all students of organizational theory, business management, and change; and MBA candidates.

We provide useful information about what it takes to both *lead* transformation and *consult* to transformation consciously. Separating the two audiences is, in our opinion, one of the conditions that can impair the success of transformation. Leaders must understand more about the nature of transformational change and all of its dynamics—organizational as well as personal—that are required to guide it effectively. Change consultants must understand more about the business realities of the organizations they are supporting. We hope that consultants will have their line clients read both this book and its companion, *Beyond Change Management*, and discuss their insights and impressions of both as they strive to lead their actual transformations. We also hope that line leaders who read these books will share them with their consultants or will hire consultants who aspire to this level of work. If your intention is to produce breakthrough results from your change efforts, these books are your springboard.

How This Book Is Organized

The book is organized into four sections. The first three reflect the three stages of the Fullstream Transformation Model—upstream, midstream, and downstream. The chapters in each of these sections present the three phases of the CLR within that stage, as described earlier. Each chapter begins with an overview of its activities and a list of task deliverables. At the end of each chapter is a list of high-leverage consulting questions to help you apply and tailor the work of that phase. The questions can be used to help you determine whether your transformation requires the tasks within a phase or activity. Worksheets and tools are also included to assist you.

Beyond the pages of this book, we provide Premium Content in various places throughout the book. Premium Content is additional information that supports the topic being discussed and is identified by an icon in the margin. You can access the Premium Content at www.pfeiffer.com/go/anderson. A list of all of the Premium Content is provided at the beginning of the book. For use in their courses, college and graduate school professors can access an Instructor Guide for both this book and *Beyond Change Management* at www.wiley.com/college/anderson. Corporate trainers can access the Instructor Guides for use in their executive and managment development programs by sending an email request to instructorguides@beingfirst.com.

Being First, Inc. also offers free change tools and articles at www.beingfirst .com and the complete online CLR methodology at www.changeleadersroad map.com. Explore the Being First Web site for specific training and development programs, consultant certification, and partnership opportunities.

The fourth section in the book, "Leveraging The Change Leader's Roadmap," consists of three chapters. The first chapter describes the developmental stages of learning to master the CLR, and the most common initial reactions leaders and consultants have after being introduced to it, which we find helpful to raise awareness for how best to present and pave the way for its use. The second chapter discusses the opportunities for gaining the greatest value from the methodology, and provides a listing of the CLR Critical Path—the thirty most important tasks—which can be used as your first step in tailoring your change roadmap. This chapter also offers a guide to using the CLR as your roadmap for culture change and discusses how to embed it as your organization's common change methodology or phase gate system. It also discusses acceleration strategies and how to consult using the CLR's breadth in a "just-in-time" fashion. The last chapter gives personal guidelines and questions for leaders and consultants to make the most of the insights and motivation you have gained from your reading.

Using This Book to Your Advantage

Before you begin exploring the CLR model, we have a few suggestions. First, we suggest you read *Beyond Change Management* if you have not already done so. It provides valuable and necessary context for applying the CLR. Just as a painter's brush is only as useful as the competency of the artist who holds it, the CLR delivers its greatest value to change leaders who understand critical concepts introduced in *Beyond Change Management.*

A useful way to expedite your understanding and application of this material is first to read the chapters in their entirety for general understanding and reaction, at the 30,000-foot level. Compare the content and structure of this model with other models or approaches to change with which you are familiar. Then review the model again with a real transformational change effort in mind, now at the 5,000-foot level. Identify which activities or tasks you need to perform and how you will tailor them to fit your change effort. You might start with the CLR Critical Path tasks in Chapter Fourteen. Remember to be selective. Consider the consulting questions at the end of each chapter as they relate to your initiative. Review the CLR phases and activities periodically as your change effort proceeds. Then apply the model on other change efforts to broaden your skill in tailoring it.

Also, consider the information requested on the worksheets. The worksheets within this book are intended to provide you with a representation of the type of tool you might use or tailor for your live change effort. All of the worksheets in this book are available to you as Word documents at www.pfeiffer.com/go/anderson. You can download, customize, and reproduce these.

No matter how great or comprehensive a change model is, it is only valuable when it is put into use. Imagine how many good change plans lay gathering dust on the shelf! Your thinking and skill in tailoring and applying this model to a real transformation brings it to life. Theory is one thing; pragmatic application is another. Remember, the map is not the territory, especially for transformational change!

Lastly, think about how to build greater change capability into your organization. Think about how to embed the CLR as your common change methodology, and how to train the appropriate leaders and consultants in its use. Think about creating best practices and change infrastructures that would make your organization's successful leadership of change much more predictable. And think about how to create a community of practice or center of excellence in conscious change leadership so that your organization grows its mastery while it produces greater results. It is one of the smartest investments you can make in your future.

Our Challenge to You

Learning to master the conscious leadership of transformational change is a monumental challenge. We have spent our careers building and testing approaches, strategies, and tools for supporting leaders and consultants to lead transformation strategically and proactively. Our body of evidence for the success of these approaches is in some cases thirty years deep and, in other cases, still in its infancy. The more we learn, the more we realize there is to learn.

Both this book and *Beyond Change Management* are products of our consulting and training experience. Writing these books has been a major step in our continual process of learning about transformational change. Putting our ideas into words makes them appear so permanent! But, because we understand the transformational process, we know that we will continue to evolve ourselves and the ideas and approaches captured in these pages. This second edition is evidence of that. We build on what we know works, and challenge ourselves to seek out ways to address what we have not yet figured out.

We want to share this challenge with you. We challenge you to deepen your learning about transformation and its unique people and process dynamics. We challenge you to create a breakthrough in your ability to lead and consult to transformational change. Build on what you know to be useful and true. We encourage you to expand your role in helping organizations and your peers to achieve greater results from change. Rebrand yourself. Get repositioned to do more strategic change work. Help set up your organization's change infrastructure and strategic disciplines to succeed in change from its inception. And bring personal transformation into the scope of your organization's executive and management development aspirations.

We challenge you to design and develop the organizations you serve to be change-ready, change-capable, and change-healthy. And we invite you to take on the personal development required for you to truly be a masterful conscious change leader.

Upstream Change

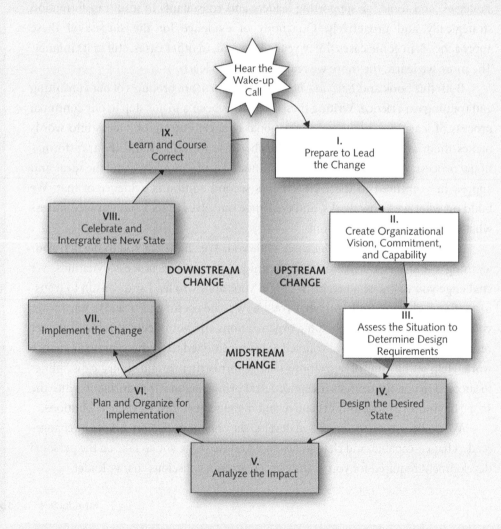

Hear the Wake-up Call

IX.
Learn and Course Correct

I.
Prepare to Lead the Change

VIII.
Celebrate and Intergrate the New State

II.
Create Organizational Vision, Commitment, and Capability

DOWNSTREAM CHANGE

UPSTREAM CHANGE

VII.
Implement the Change

III.
Assess the Situation to Determine Design Requirements

VI.
Plan and Organize for Implementation

MIDSTREAM CHANGE

IV.
Design the Desired State

V.
Analyze the Impact

PHASE I   PREPARE TO LEAD THE CHANGE

PHASE II

PHASE III

CHAPTER

1

PHASE I

Prepare to Lead the Change: Start Up, Staff, and Create Your Case for Change

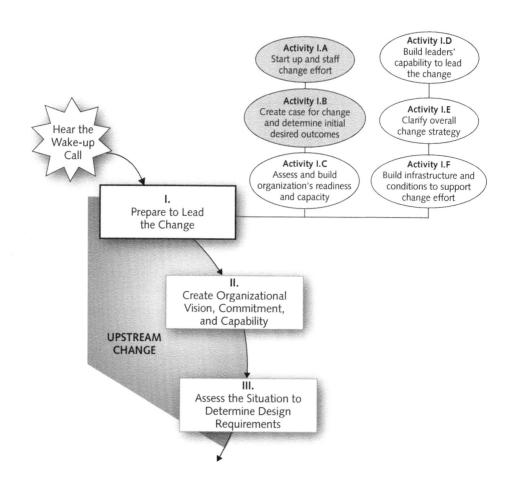

Activity I.A
Start up and staff change effort

Activity I.B
Create case for change and determine initial desired outcomes

Activity I.C
Assess and build organization's readiness and capacity

Activity I.D
Build leaders' capability to lead the change

Activity I.E
Clarify overall change strategy

Activity I.F
Build infrastructure and conditions to support change effort

Hear the Wake-up Call

I.
Prepare to Lead the Change

II.
Create Organizational Vision, Commitment, and Capability

III.
Assess the Situation to Determine Design Requirements

UPSTREAM CHANGE

ACTIVITY I.A AND I.B: TASK DELIVERABLES

I.A.1: A project briefing has been obtained, shared, and agreed to by all key leaders.

I.A.2: Change leadership roles have been defined, and the change effort has been staffed with qualified people.

I.A.3: Effective working relationships have been established among all change leaders, and between all of the change leaders and change consultants.

I.A.4: Your project community has been identified and mobilized to support the change.

I.A.5: Your Phase I roadmap has been determined.

I.B.1: The process for creating your case for change is clear and has been staffed appropriately.

I.B.2: The drivers of your change have been determined.

I.B.3: The type of change has been clarified.

I.B.4: Leverage points for making the change have been identified.

I.B.5: An initial analysis of the organizational and human impacts of the transformation has been done.

I.B.6: The target groups of the change have been identified, and the scope of change is clear.

I.B.7: The degree of urgency for making the change has been assessed.

I.B.8: Your initial desired outcomes for the change have been determined, and the complete case for change has been prepared for communication.

The process of change actually begins the moment a person or group recognizes that there is a reason to alter how the organization and its people operate. This awareness triggers a decision process, ending in the leaders agreeing to proceed. By the time leaders decide to formally mobilize a change effort, work has already begun and information has surfaced that will affect how the leaders start up the effort. Phase I is designed for leaders to clarify where the effort is, what they are trying to accomplish, and how best to get it launched. They need to understand what is known, who is doing what, and how far along the work has progressed. Early speed and effectiveness depend on the leaders being as aware, aligned, and informed as possible.

The overall purpose of Phase I, covered in Chapters One through Four, is for the leaders of the change to establish a conscious, shared intention and strategy for a successful transformation and to prepare to lead the effort through the following:

- Clarifying change leadership roles and the status of the change effort, and staffing the effort with the right people
- Creating a clear case for change and determining their initial desired outcomes to use to inform and compel people to support the change
- Assessing the organization's readiness and capacity to take on and succeed in the effort given everything else going on
- Strengthening leaders' capability—individually and collectively—to understand, commit to, and model the behaviors and approaches required to lead this change successfully
- Clarifying the overall change strategy
- Designing the optimal conditions and structures for supporting the change strategy to be successful

These efforts represent the six activities of Phase I. This chapter covers the first two activities, *Start Up and Staff Change Effort* and *Create Case for Change and Determine Initial Desired Outcomes*. Before we address the work of these two activities, let's start the action where it actually begins, with the first notion of the need for change.

HEARING THE WAKE-UP CALL

Wake-up calls are "aha moments," awareness of an opportunity to be pursued or a threat to be removed. They can surface anywhere in the organization, at any level. At times, there is grass-roots awareness of the need long before executives take notice. However, for an organization-wide transformation to mobilize, the leaders of the organization affected must ultimately hear the signal clearly enough to warrant attention and discussion, if not action. In change-resistant organizations, executives typically do not get or heed wake-up calls until the signals become so painful and dangerous that they threaten the organization's very survival.

The wake-up call may come in the form of a dramatic event, such as the competition beating you to market with a similar or better product; or it may be the accumulation of many small indicators that finally culminate in a loud and meaningful message. Examples of the latter include loss of market share, new technological advancements in your industry, mergers of your key competitors, the required closure of a once valuable factory, the initiation of a hostile unionization effort, or an increase in turnover of critical talent.

At this very early stage in the transformation, it is important to identify and understand what wake-up calls exist, what they mean, and what is being done with them by those in position to initiate a change effort. The mindset of the leaders has a major impact on the meaning they make of the information in the wake-up call. If the leaders are conscious and open to learning and changing, they will deal with the wake-up call differently than if they are not.

If you are consulting to the change, your initial responsibility is to assist leaders to acknowledge and respond to their wake-up calls in depth. This is the first moment of truth in the change effort; it can mean the difference between a reactive, superficial change and one that is conscious, purposeful, and able to achieve breakthrough results.

Let's assume that, at some point, the leaders receive the right signals and have acknowledged the need to change. They will automatically create an initial case for change and scope in their minds. These informal impressions will be used later as the starting point for designing the official case for change. After the leaders have committed to launch a change effort, the process is underway, officially beginning Phase I.

PHASE I: PREPARE TO LEAD THE CHANGE

Establishing clear foundations for a successful change effort from the beginning increases the organization's likelihood of success. Phase I and its six activities accomplish the majority of this work. Many of the tasks of these activities can be done in parallel.

Phase I is *critical work* for the leaders. It covers 50 to 60 percent of the decisions that will inform your change strategy and plan. It does not take that same percentage of time, but it requires that amount of upfront decision making. The leaders cannot delegate this work, although other people can be involved to help lay the groundwork for the change leaders.

Remember the television commercial where a car repairman removes himself from under the hood of a car and says to the viewer, "Well, you can pay me now, or you can pay me later." He is referring to the fact that work *must* be done. You can do it now, or you can do it later; but you cannot skip it. Doing this required work upfront will undoubtedly be easier and less costly than neglecting it and dealing with the problems its absence creates downstream. In our experience, conscious leadership attention to the work of Phase I is the most powerful of all change acceleration strategies. It models the principle "Go slow to go fast" and is well worth the time and effort.

ACTIVITY I.A: START UP AND STAFF CHANGE EFFORT

Task I.A.1: Obtain Project Briefing

After the leaders decide to formally initiate their change process, it is imperative to gather and coalesce all of the existing information and opinion about the effort. The leaders need a clear picture of what is known, who has been doing what, and what the current reactions are. Without this, attempting to lead the change can be like herding cats. They need this early project briefing to ensure alignment, leverage progress, and minimize surprises.

You may find it useful to interview the various people or groups that know about the change and are going to be impacted by it to assess how they view the effort. Questions to these people usually include their knowledge of the content or focus of the change, people issues, political dynamics, or process expectations. You can ask about their knowledge about the drivers of the change, the history of the effort, perceptions of the current change events and activities underway, key issues that have arisen, and future directions. (See Premium Content: Identifying Project Briefing Questions, www.pfeiffer.com/go/anderson.) Once gathered, you would prepare this information to brief everyone who needs to know the status of the change effort at this early stage, including all consultants in the effort.

Briefing data usually reveals whether key stakeholders, including the leaders, see the change effort through the same set of lenses or whether there are potentially confusing or conflicting discrepancies in people's perceptions. How people are talking about the change effort at this early date can be a significant predictor of how well it will be received after it gets underway. And, if leaders are not aligned, they will not be able to lead the effort effectively. Their alignment is essential.

Task I.A.2: Clarify and Staff Initial Change Leadership Roles

The second task in this activity is to determine how the transformation will be led—who is sponsoring the effort, who is designing and leading the change strategy and process design, and who is involved in various other ways. Clear roles and responsibilities are needed for all of the change leaders to minimize redundancy and ensure full coverage of change leadership responsibilities and decisions.

Because taking on a change leadership role is usually considered an addition to one's existing duties, there are two predictable issues in staffing. The first is when these roles are assigned to people who have the most available time. Caution! Roles should be given to the people who are the most *competent* and *best positioned to successfully lead the effort*. These selections must be very strategic because your effort will either be enhanced or encumbered by these staffing selections. The second issue is that your best people are already over-committed and cannot give the change leadership role the time and attention it needs. If your best people are that busy, then you must ask yourself whether their current activities are more important than achieving the outcomes of the change. If these people are the right leaders for the change, they must free up the time to fulfill their role adequately. "Lip service" will not work.

The following sidebar presents a list of six typical change leadership roles and their deliverables. You can use all of them as described, or you may tailor them to fit the magnitude of your change effort and the resources available for it. To tailor

CHANGE LEADERSHIP ROLES

SPONSOR

The individual with highest line authority over the change effort, "executive champion," has primary influence over desired outcomes and breakthrough results: inputs significantly to change strategy; supports change process leader; is a member of change leadership team; sets boundary conditions and design requirements; approves desired future state solution, including cultural imperatives; ensures conditions for success are named and supported; keeps the transformation in alignment with overall business; delivers major communications; requires key course corrections to be surfaced and made; acknowledges benchmark successes during the process and sets standards for breakthrough results; maintains ongoing links with major stakeholders; models the desired culture, mindset, and behavior required by the transformation.

DELIVERABLES:

▸ Achievement of the organization's business strategy through the creation and oversight of the change strategy, initiatives, and conditions required to produce business outcomes and breakthrough results

(continued)

- Mobilization and alignment of entire organization undergoing change

- Clear direction and path for change, clear expectations for results

- Sustained well-being in the organization during and after change

- Being a model of the mindset, behavior, and cultural changes required for success and breakthrough results

EXECUTIVE TEAM

The executive leadership team of the organization within which the change effort is occurring (may be the entire company or a segment): responsible for determining desired outcomes and breakthrough results of the transformation as required by business strategy and supporting their achievement; runs the business and inputs to change strategy; ensures right fit and priority of overall change effort within the other priorities underway in the organization.

DELIVERABLES:

- Clear expectations for change results required within organization

- Effective operations of the business while the change is taking place

- Being a model of the mindset, behavior, and cultural changes required for success and breakthrough results

CHANGE LEADERSHIP TEAM

Leaders (cross-functional, initiative leaders, or key stakeholder representatives from entire system being transformed) with delegated authority to create change strategy and high-level process plan to execute it: This includes refining desired outcomes, breakthrough results, and conditions for success, as necessary, prioritizing and integrating initiatives, and identifying milestone events and realistic pace; led by change process leader; core team that oversees and course-corrects change strategy, initiatives, change process, and conditions for success as the overall effort unfolds; ensures resources, right pace, and cultural imperatives. Depending on scope of change, this team may be same as executive team, in which case it has responsibilities for combined functions of both teams. If a separate team, it runs change effort while executive team runs current operations, with some executives likely having dual membership—"two hats." If large, this team may have a small subset that functions as a nimble "strategic navigation team"—max three to five most influential/knowledgeable people.

DELIVERABLES:

- A change strategy and change process plan that will produce desired outcomes and breakthrough results
- Continuous oversight and realignment of change strategy, initiatives, and process to meet emerging needs of change effort during continued operation of the business
- Successful integration and alignment of all change initiatives
- Adequate resources and pacing for change effort
- Being a model of the mindset, behavior, and cultural changes required for success and breakthrough results

CHANGE PROCESS LEADER

A line manager or executive as high as possible in the organization being changed: has delegated authority from sponsor to lead change effort and produce its results; oversees design and execution of change strategy, initiatives, and each phase and activity of overall change process; leads change leadership team and project integration teams; responsible for clarifying scope, desired outcomes, pace, conditions for success, constraints, infrastructure, and metrics; provides advocacy for and integration of change initiatives; obtains resources for transformation; oversees communications and information management, and ensures course correction; models mindset and behavior changes; provides feedback and coaching to all change leaders, initiative leads, and stakeholders.

DELIVERABLES:

- A change strategy and change process plan that will produce the desired outcomes of the change effort
- Creation of conditions for success
- Continuous oversight and realignment of the change strategy, initiatives, and process to meet the emerging needs of the change effort during the continuing operation of the business
- Successful integration and alignment of all change initiatives

(continued)

▸ Building a critical mass of support for the change through employee engagement

▸ Being a model of the mindset, behavior, and cultural changes required for a successful change

CHANGE INITIATIVE LEAD

A line or project manager who is in charge of an initiative within the overall change effort: may have own sponsor, yet also reports to change process leader and change leadership team; responsible for setting their initiative up for success according to the overall transformation's content and cultural outcomes, values, and guiding principles; ensures that best solution is designed, and oversees planning and implementation so that results are achieved and people are engaged in positive ways; ensures timely course correction and coordination with interdependent initiatives; leads change project team for this initiative; models the desired mindset, behavior, and cultural norms.

DELIVERABLES:

▸ A change strategy and change process plan that will produce the desired outcomes of this initiative

▸ Continuous oversight and realignment of the change strategy, project teams, and process to meet the needs of the overall change effort

▸ Successful integration and alignment of this initiative with all other change initiatives and events

▸ Being a model of the mindset, behavior, and cultural changes required for a successful change and breakthrough results

CHANGE PROJECT TEAM

Cross-functional representatives, sub-initiative leaders, and/or specially skilled individuals who help the change initiative lead in day-to-day activities of carrying out a particular change effort: completes work of various change activities for this change effort (e.g., design and impact analysis); pursues feedback and information for course correction and communicates with all stakeholders;

invests in change required to produce cultural changes and breakthrough results.

DELIVERABLES:

- Fulfillment of requirements of each major phase of change process for an initiative
- Continuously gather new information about change effort that may influence how it rolls out
- Being a model of the mindset, behavior, and cultural changes required for success and breakthrough results

CHANGE CONSULTANT

Change process expert and coach: key support to sponsor, change process leader, and change leadership team in building and carrying out best overall change strategy and change process; acts as sounding board, third party, and advocate for conscious awareness and breakthrough results; educates about transformation and strategies for how to proceed and achieve breakthrough results; helps plan change strategy, major events, communications, trainings, and meetings; assesses progress, problems, concerns, political and cultural issues; helps facilitate change in culture, mindset, and behavior; facilitates course corrections to change strategy and process; provides feedback and advocates for conditions for success; interfaces with other consultants working on the transformation. You may have a change consultant for each major sub-initiative to guide the process and participate in integrating all interdependent change initiatives.

DELIVERABLES:

- Advice and support to produce change strategy and change process that will deliver the results of overall change effort and/or sub-initiative
- Guidance to make change initiative integration successful
- Improved competency and knowledge transfer to organization about effective and conscious change leadership
- Timely course corrections on any aspect affecting success
- Being a model of the mindset, behavior, and cultural changes required for success and breakthrough results

the roles, you can use different titles and determine expanded, reduced, or different responsibilities and deliverables for each role.

We have labeled the role of the person in charge of planning the change effort as the change process leader, rather than change project manager. This title conveys the required shift from project-oriented thinking to process thinking, as described in *Beyond Change Management*, and emphasizes that the person in this role is responsible for designing and overseeing the transformational change *strategy* and the transformational change *process* in ways that make the possibility for breakthrough results most likely. This person may provide input to the content of the change, but the priority of this role is to shape *how* the change is led, designed, implemented, and course-corrected throughout.

The person selected as the change process leader will represent the degree of importance the transformation has for the organization. The more well-respected the person is, the more important the change will be perceived as being. In most cases, our bias is that a high-level line executive should fill the role of change process leader. This role should not be filled by a consultant or a staff person, unless the change is occurring primarily in a specific staff function, or the staff person is well-respected by the leaders and the organization. It is critical that the entire workforce respond positively to the leaders of the change, especially this one. The person selected to fill this role is one of the first clear signals you will send about the magnitude and priority of what is to follow. (See Premium Content: Selecting the Best Change Process Leader to Oversee Your Transformation, www.pfeiffer .com/go/anderson.)

The change process leader should be selected not only for the respect he or she commands from the line organization but also for three other critical competencies—the ability to demonstrate conscious process thinking and design skills, being sophisticated about dealing with the human dynamics of change, including culture, and having a facilitative (versus controlling) change leadership style. In addition, the more dedicated this person is to personal development and building awareness in nonthreatening ways, the better, for all the reasons discussed in *Beyond Change Management*. Change process leaders stuck in the autopilot, controlling, need to be "right," or project thinking modes will severely limit the probability of a successful transformation. This role works best when filled by a leader capable of working with all of the dimensions of the Conscious Change Leader Accountability Model.

One more note of caution: We frequently find that the individuals named to this critical role are the primary content experts, such as the IT guru in charge of implementing a new technology system, or worse yet, the external IT content consultant. This is extremely dangerous! The more invested the person is in a particular content outcome of the change, the less effective—or more complicated—his or her influence will be on the process of change and understanding the intricate people and cultural issues. More often than not, these people are not knowledgeable about the process or people dynamics—they are the protective owners of the content. Because there are so many process and people issues that IT implementations trigger, an objective change process leader is required—an internal person who understands how the organization operates. This role can then make sure that the content expertise of the IT guru is used in the right ways in the right tasks to produce the best content outcome for the change.

The most current example of this is in the healthcare space, for all hospital systems implementing electronic health records (EHRs). The vendors that offer the IT solutions to this critical change in healthcare are typically the least able to perceive and influence the organization's unique cultural, mindset, and behavioral requirements that a successful EHR implementation demands. EHR implementations are transformational changes—they have a direct and heavy impact on the culture, relationships, communications, and emotional needs of physicians, nurses, and support staff. They need an internal, culturally smart change process leader to shape the strategy and process plan, meet the people needs that inevitably surface, and work closely with the EHR vendor and internal IT experts when their knowledge is required.

We have experienced one creative way of dealing with the requirements of the change process leader role when an IT or other content expertise is critical to a successful outcome. It is to create a "project/process" partnership between an individual who has the technical or business expertise and a consultant with process design, people, culture, and organization development expertise. The benefit of this scenario is that the technical leader learns how to design a complex change process, and the consultant learns how to make the process relevant and timely to the business and workable for the people who must make the change happen on the ground. This joint strategy requires that the two leads have clearly defined "decision rights" and work in true partnership. Its cost is that it requires the focused attention of two people who must regularly share data and perceptions and work closely on behalf of achieving a sustainable outcome.

After change leadership roles have been defined and staffed, a common dynamic that surfaces is the confusion or tension created when leaders are asked to wear two very distinct hats—a functional executive hat and a change leadership hat. Most often, the functional hat takes precedence because it is most familiar and immediate. Plus, leaders' compensation is often tied only to their functional performance. Without support to balance leaders' drive to keep the business running *and* to change it, this conflict can sandbag the change effort before it gets off the ground.

Under normal circumstances, leaders' tendency to take care of daily crises in their functional organizations first is a good thing. However, when an organization is undergoing major transformation, the functional leader mindset is not sufficient. Change leaders must focus on *doing what is good for the overall organization as it transforms* while keeping it operational, especially at start-up. There is no formula for the percentage of time a leader will spend wearing each hat. We do know, however, that keeping full-time functional responsibilities without making real space for change leadership duties is a formula for failure. Therefore, you will need to set clear priorities and expectations for how and when the leaders should be wearing each hat, and how much time they will need to give to their change responsibilities. The resolution requires a shift of both mindset and behavior because there is only so much time available for both roles. Make the change focus a conscious one!

Ensuring that the right people are in key change leadership roles and that core responsibilities are fully covered is essential to mobilizing the quality of leadership required for conscious transformation. Our definition of "right people" here means the best match of mindset, behavior, expertise, leadership style, and time with the magnitude and type of change you are facing.

An exploration of your change leadership roles may reveal that the wrong people are in key roles. This task is an opportunity to correct your change leader selection and role expectations. Although this can be politically ticklish, making these changes now is far less costly than doing it later. You will have another opportunity to do this when you confirm your governance structure for leading the change in Task I.E.3.

Task I.A.3: Create Optimal Working Relationships

Building and sustaining effective working relationships is an important condition for success. When people take on special change leadership roles, it is essential to clarify the working relationships among them and with their peers who retain existing functional roles. Too often, old political struggles will surface and hinder the change leaders from doing what the change effort requires. By addressing and clearing up past history, conflicts or political dynamics, the leaders ensure the cleanest, clearest leadership thinking and behavior to support the overall transformation.

Having the leaders model the healing of broken relationships and the creation of effective partnerships is a powerful cultural intervention, one that is absolutely required to make your change effort expedient and to produce breakthrough results.

When key change leadership roles, such as the change process leader or the top change consultants, are filled by people from lower levels in the organization, you must re-establish effective working relationships among all of the change leaders and the executives. Everyone who has a key role must be clear about who has responsibility and authority to do what so that everyone can pull in the same direction. It is especially critical that people from lower in the hierarchy be given the authority they need to succeed in their new roles.

The relationship between the executive team running the business and the change leadership team changing it has to be crystal clear. The business must continue to operate effectively during the transformation, and it must also be enabled to change so that it can better serve its customers' new needs. This requires negotiating clear decision authority and responsibilities between these two teams. Make the predictable tension between these teams overt and clarify how both teams can best serve the overall good of the organization. Organization development consultants can assist with this work, which should begin when the change leadership team is established and be revisited periodically, or when issues surface throughout the transformation.

Because most enterprise-wide transformations use multiple external consultants, make sure that all consultants know who is responsible for what and how to work among them and with in-house resources to do what is best for the organization, versus their own individual agendas. Set the expectation for addressing the quality and effectiveness of their working relationships in advance, and then hold them to it.

Task I.A.4: Identify Project Community

It is important to be clear about whose realities the change effort is affecting and who needs to be involved in some way. Who has a vested interest in it producing its results? Who has something to offer it—knowledge, skill, resources? Who is going to be seriously impacted by it? Whose voices should you be seeking out and listening to as you plan it? At start-up, identify everyone—internally and externally—who has a stake in the effort and is engaged in or affected by it. This identification will provide you an easy reference for thinking through various stakeholder needs as you shape your change strategy, process plan, communications, and engagement strategy. It will also help identify the critical mass of support required for the transformation to succeed.

Some change management approaches refer to this exercise as building a "stakeholder map," which they use to identify resisters to the change. We call this group the "project community," preferring this language to convey the intention of this group to share a common vision of the change and to work together for the collective good of the organization, which provides much more use than just resistance-mapping. Figure 1.1 shows a sample project community map.

When you map your project community in detail, consider the categories of people to include: those with knowledge, skill, resources or influence to offer; those who need to be on board politically or emotionally, or buy in to the change to implement it; and those who will be impacted by it but not involved in execution,

Figure 1.1.   **Sample Project Community Map**

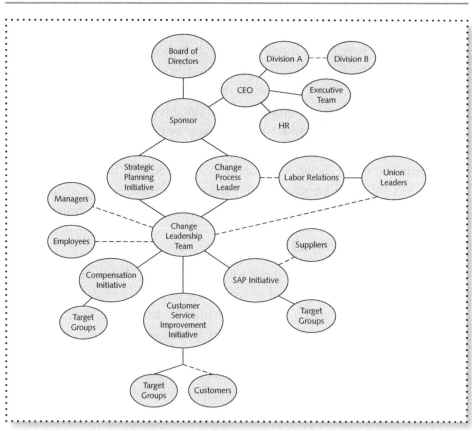

Note: Solid lines represent direct reporting relationships, and dotted lines indicate influence and/or partnership or cross-boundary relationships.

such as partners, vendors, customers or patients, or other departments dependent on what you are doing.

Your project community map should graphically reveal the relationships among its members. This will enable you to leverage these relationships strategically—and politically—throughout the change process. You may also want to identify any relationships within the community that need improvement because you will be counting on these relationships to function effectively to support the overall transformation. Use this information as input to Task I.A.3, *Create Optional Working Relationships.*

You can work with your project community in many ways—in person, by e-mail, or as an electronic discussion community. Your primary intention for the community is to create the conditions among all of the members to support the transformation actively as it unfolds. We are not advocating that you make this group into a formal structure. You will likely have greater impact by allowing it to operate organically, working with parts of it as your change process requires. Your strategies for this group may include the following:

- Keeping these people informed of the status of the change effort; as references to help shape your change communication plans

- Assigning them key roles in major change activities or events

- Establishing shared expectations for how they can add value to the effort; working with them to create a critical mass of support for the vision and desired state

- Shaping your engagement strategy over the course of the change process; interviewing appropriate members to gather pertinent input or using them as sounding board advisors on various strategic, operational, or cultural choice points during the transformation

- Identifying resistance and political dynamics in advance

- Training them in the unique requirements of your desired culture, mindset, and ways of relating

- Positioning them as change advocates, models of new behavior, information generators, and so on

Exhibit 1.1 presents a worksheet to assist with identifying your project community.

Now that you are clear about who is doing what and what the current status of the change effort is, you can proceed with the important work of creating your official case for change.

Exhibit 1.1. **Identifying Your Project Community**

WORKSHEET

Identify the members of your project community for your project. Name the key players from the following groups:

CHANGE LEADERSHIP:

▸ Sponsor:

▸ Change process leader:

▸ Executive team:

▸ Change leadership team:

▸ Change initiative lead:

▸ Change project team:

▸ Change consultants (internal and external):

STAKEHOLDER GROUPS OR INDIVIDUALS:

▸ Board of directors:

▸ Executives:

▸ Upper management:

- ▶ Mid-management:

- ▶ Employee groups:

- ▶ Stakeholders:

- ▶ Unions:

CUSTOMERS:
- ▶ Internal:

- ▶ External:

SUPPLIERS/VENDORS:

AREAS OF THE ORGANIZATION (FUNCTIONS/PROCESSES):

LOCATIONS WITHIN THE ORGANIZATION:

OTHER IMPORTANT CHANGE OR IMPROVEMENT INITIATIVES:

RELATED CHANGE PROCESS LEADERS OR PROJECT MANAGERS:

OTHERS:

Task I.A.5: Determine Phase I Roadmap

Phase I of your change effort is extremely important to a successful start-up and requires a plan of its own. This task creates your roadmap for this work. At the end of Phase I, you will create a roadmap for Phases II through V. In Phase V, you will develop your Implementation Master Plan, which will be your roadmap for the remaining execution of your change effort.

In planning your Phase I roadmap, only select the tasks that you deem essential from each of the activities in this phase. Consider having your change leadership team review the Phase I tasks in their entirety, or from the CLR Critical Path offered in Chapter Fourteen, for general understanding, and then decide which they need to invest time and resources to complete. The next three chapters discuss the remaining work of Phase I.

ACTIVITY I.B: CREATE CASE FOR CHANGE AND DETERMINE INITIAL DESIRED OUTCOMES

No one, leader or employee, will give heart and soul to such a complex and challenging effort as transformation unless he or she understands why the change is necessary and what benefit it promises—personally and organizationally. This activity answers the basic questions: "Why transform?" "What needs to transform?" and "What outcomes do we want from this transformation?" "What is 'in game' or 'out of game'?" Frequently, people have many different views of why change is needed, what is driving it, and how big it is. Until your desired outcomes are clear, people will not know why they should invest the effort it will take; until they do, they will not support it. Creating your case for change and determining the results you want from it creates a common view for the change leaders and gives their stakeholders meaning, direction, and energy for aligned action. Without a clear case for change, the transformation will lack relevance for employees, causing resistance, confusion, and insecurity. The case for change includes the following:

▶ Why the transformation is needed

▶ What is driving this change

▶ Type of change

▶ Leverage points for change

- Initial impacts on the organization and its people
- Target groups
- Scope of change
- Urgency for the change

In addition, this task clarifies your initial desired outcomes for the change.

Although we have positioned this work as a part of leader preparation for the transformation, many other people may be involved in shaping the case for change and its outcomes. The marketplace, as the primary driver of the transformation, dictates the content focus of the case for change. Marketplace requirements for success can be sought by anyone who has a perspective on what your customers need and your competitors are doing. When front-line employees and middle managers participate in creating the case for change, they add credibility to the assessment of need, leverage points for transformation, and impacts. Their participation is an enormous catalyst for their understanding and commitment. No matter who generates the data for the case, we believe the leaders are responsible for putting all of this information into a clear picture that they agree with and will communicate to the organization during Phase II.

The information for your case for change may already have been generated through the organization's business strategy efforts. If so, take your exploration of the business strategy to the next level of specificity: How does the strategy require the organization to change? Use the business strategy as input to the tasks of this activity to ensure that you have a complete picture and that your case for change and your business strategy are aligned. If they exist, your case for change can also identify boundary conditions—what is okay to change, and what must stay the same. Boundary conditions may be shaped by a number of factors, such as (1) the leaders' expectations for the vision or desired outcome of the change, (2) pre-existing conditions such as strategic business imperatives or political dynamics, (3) risk mitigation needs, (4) the organization's current state of performance or financial condition, or (5) any other driving force affecting the situation. Your case for change will be strengthened by clarifying your desired outcomes for this effort—what you need to produce going forward and/or what breakthrough results you are striving to create. The statement of your outcomes should also include the benefits your organization will reap and a picture or definition of success. In simple terms, this activity describes the cause and effect of the change—what is causing it to happen and what will be achieved when it has occurred successfully!

Task I.B.1: Design Process for Creating Case for Change and Initial Desired Outcomes

Who builds the case for change, and how is it best produced? Who should be involved in defining your desired outcomes, the vision, and boundary conditions for the change? Your decision criteria for these questions should include: (1) people who have a big-picture understanding of the systemic and environmental dynamics driving the need for change; (2) people who understand the need for a new culture and mindset; (3) the level of urgency you face; (4) the degree to which your case and vision have already been formulated by your business strategy; and (5) people's content expertise in the areas within the predicted scope of your transformation.

Design your process for creating the case and your desired outcomes by reviewing all of the tasks of this activity and then determining how to accomplish them and the timeframe for doing so.

Task I.B.2: Assess Drivers of Change

As a change leader or consultant, you must determine the catalysts driving the changes in your organization to design an effective case for change and change strategy. *Beyond Change Management* introduces seven drivers of change which, taken together, expand leaders' typical view of the scope of change. All seven drivers must be addressed to accurately scope your change effort and plan its roll-out strategy—especially if it is transformational. The Drivers of Change Model is shown in Figure I.1 in the Introduction to this book, and the following sidebar briefly defines each driver. Each provides essential data for the determination of what must change in the organization and why. They might also inform what must not change. Remember, explore all seven drivers; do not stop at organizational imperatives. A full scope for transformation must include culture, behavior, and mindset.

Keep in mind that all seven drivers of change must be clarified to understand the full scope of your change. Your responses to them can tell a story, making your full case and scope easy to understand. Your story should include what will be required of leaders and managers to model and mobilize change in themselves and the organization.

Exhibit 1.2 provides a worksheet to assess what is driving your change. Use your responses as input to the scope of your change and case for change story.

- **Environmental Forces:** The dynamics of the larger context within which organizations and people operate. These forces include social and demographic trends, business or economic pressures, political dynamics, government regulations, technological advances, demographic patterns, legal issues, and the natural environment.

- **Marketplace Requirements for Success:** The aggregate set of customer requirements that determine what it takes for a business to succeed in its marketplace. This includes not only their actual product or service needs but also requirements such as speed of delivery, access to information, customization capability, cost limits, level of quality, need for innovation, level of customer service, and so forth. Changes in marketplace requirements are the result of changes in environmental forces.

- **Business Imperatives:** Business imperatives outline what the company must do *strategically* to be successful, given its customers' changing requirements. This can demand systematic rethinking and change to the company's mission, strategy, goals, products and services, e-commerce position, pricing, the need for merger or acquisition, or branding. Business imperatives are usually identified through the organization's strategic planning process.

- **Organizational Imperatives:** Organizational imperatives specify what must change in the organization's structure, systems, processes, technology, resources, skill base, or staffing to realize its strategic business imperatives. Examples include reengineering, new technology, restructuring, new knowledge management practices, new engagement vehicles, or new sales approaches.

- **Cultural Imperatives:** Cultural imperatives denote how the values, norms, or collective way of being, working, and relating in the company must change to support and drive the organization's new design, strategy, and operations. Some change efforts are driven by a need to change the culture, such as the need for a new leadership style, teamwork, or cross-boundary work practices. If so, this driver is given more detailed attention, and ideally is still positioned as being in support of the organization's imperatives to change and its business imperatives.

- **Leader and Employee Behavior:** Collective behavior creates and expresses an organization's culture and performance. Behavior is more than just

(continued)

overt actions; it describes the style, tone, or character that permeates what people do and how their way of being must change to create the new culture. Leaders and employees, both individually and collectively, must choose to behave differently to transform the organization's culture.

▸ **Leader and Employee Mindset:** Mindset encompasses people's worldview, assumptions, beliefs, and mental models. Mindset causes people to behave as they do; it underlies behavior. Becoming aware that each of us has a mindset and that it directly impacts our feelings, decisions, actions, and results is often the critical first step in building individual and organizational awareness and willingness to change. For instance, leaders and employees must shift their thinking from "What we do has always worked for us, so let's keep doing it" to "We need to look for how to fulfill our customers' needs in different ways."

Mindset change is often required to catalyze and sustain new behaviors in both leaders and employees. A shift of mindset is usually required for organizational leaders to recognize changes in environmental forces and marketplace or customer requirements, thereby being able to determine the best new strategic business direction, structure, operation, or culture. Mindset change in employees is often required to understand why the changes being asked of them are necessary, and certainly for what they must do to carry it out. Mindset is always included in culture change efforts.

Task I.B.3: Clarify Type of Change

The drivers of your change reveal the primary type of change you are leading—*developmental, transitional*, or *transformational*. The more culture, behavior, and mindset change required, the more it is transformational. In our writing, we frequently refer to your change effort as transformational. That is because the CLR is designed to serve the unique needs of transformation, as well as the other types of change. Because your change effort may not actually be transformational, you will still need to determine the right type of change you are leading.

The type of change has direct implications for the change strategy and leadership your effort requires. The consequences of not defining the type of change accurately can create costly havoc, or failure, for the effort. Too often, when leaders learn of the three types, they choose developmental or transitional change because these

Exhibit 1.2.   **Determining What Is Driving the Change**

WORKSHEET
▸ Environmental Forces:
▸ Marketplace Requirements for Success:
▸ Business Imperatives:
▸ Organizational Imperatives:
▸ Cultural Imperatives:
▸ Leader/Employee Behavior:
▸ Leader/Employee Mindset:

types appear to be easier to manage. If your change is actually transformational, however, you cannot change that fact by calling it something else. If it is transformation, it is transformation; you will still need to build a change strategy and plan that fits transformation. As a conscious change leader, your challenge is to determine the *actual* type of change occurring and plan from there. Figure 1.2 graphically portrays the three types, discussed in depth in *Beyond Change Management*.

Although you may have multiple types of change present within your overall effort or your composite initiatives, one type is always primary. That is the one

Figure 1.2. **Three Types of Change**

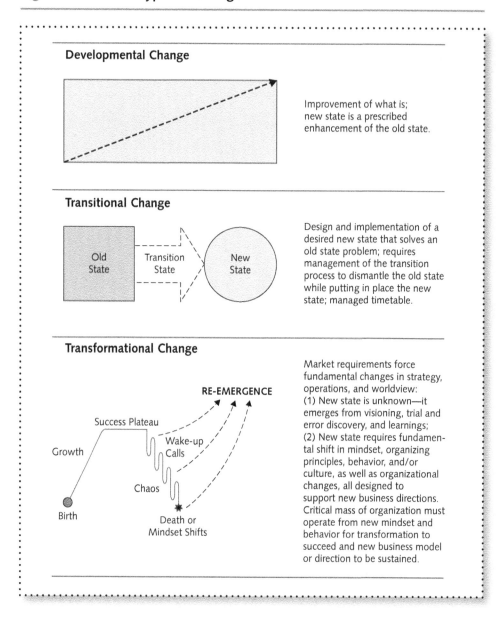

Developmental Change

Improvement of what is; new state is a prescribed enhancement of the old state.

Transitional Change

Old State — Transition State → New State

Design and implementation of a desired new state that solves an old state problem; requires management of the transition process to dismantle the old state while putting in place the new state; managed timetable.

Transformational Change

RE-EMERGENCE

Success Plateau

Growth

Wake-up Calls

Chaos

Birth

Death or Mindset Shifts

Market requirements force fundamental changes in strategy, operations, and worldview: (1) New state is unknown—it emerges from visioning, trial and error discovery, and learnings; (2) New state requires fundamental shift in mindset, organizing principles, behavior, and/or culture, as well as organizational changes, all designed to support new business directions. Critical mass of organization must operate from new mindset and behavior for transformation to succeed and new business model or direction to be sustained.

that will most influence the design of your change strategy. For instance, you may need to develop better marketing skills and systems (developmental change), and you may need to consolidate several functions to improve efficiencies (transitional change), but the primary change is a radical transformation of your business model to e-commerce. Such a change is transformational because it calls for a significant shift in direction *and* requires major culture, behavior, and mindset change in your leaders and people.

Task I.B.4: Identify Leverage Points for Change

Most change efforts have one or two critical things that must change; this work will prompt or catalyze shifts in other aspects of the organization. These few things are called leverage points for change. Frequently, they are the content focus of the change. For instance, your leverage point may be to employ a human resources information system to gather and integrate all data about every employee, for every HR need. That is a leverage point to process large amounts of HR data for policy and performance purposes, and to streamline and standardize all HR transactions across a complex or dispersed organization. Or, a different leverage point is to consolidate supply chain and purchasing across an entire system so that costs and efficiencies can be more vigorously managed. A third example is to change the culture of the organization to be more entrepreneurial, more team-based, or co-creative. These types of cultures are essential to innovation, efficiencies, and the level of cross-boundary work required to serve diverse customer or patient needs. For each of your leverage points, make sure that all change leaders agree on its primary importance and the benefits it will produce toward your desired outcomes.

These examples name the primary work that will catalyze needed changes. They do not, however, define the total scope of your change. That comes from several of the tasks in this activity, culminating in a full scope of change in Task I.B.6. Your case for change, however, will feature your leverage points to help clarify the purpose and focus of the transformation.

Task I.B.5: Perform Initial Impact Analysis

As you become clearer about what your change effort's scope entails, it is important to identify the types of impacts that making this change will create throughout the organization. The earlier in your change you clarify those impacts, the better your planning will be. At this point in the process, an assessment of impacts can only be done at a generalized level. When you have designed the actual future state, you will be able to do a more thorough analysis. That is the purpose of Phase V. For now, this general assessment focuses the leaders' attention on both the business/organizational elements and the personal/cultural impacts. A general impact analysis at this stage may also reveal impacts that challenge the leaders' expectations for what needs to stay the same.

A helpful tool to perform this assessment, the Initial Impact Analysis Audit, is provided in Exhibit 1.3. This tool lists many typical impact areas affected by change in the organization. The Initial Impact Analysis Audit is a powerful way to expand the change leaders' view of the amount of attention, planning, time, and resources the change will require. It is designed to create a systems view of the organization and the transformation. These topics will tell you, at a high level, how broad and how deep the impact of making the transformation will go. This information, in addition to your determination of the drivers of change and your leverage points, is critical to understanding what your change strategy needs to address for the transformation to succeed. This information will be used as input to determining the scope of the change and may also inform your decision about needed capacity for change.

To fill in the Initial Impact Analysis Audit, consider the change effort as you currently understand it. Review each item in the tool, checking it if it will be affected by your change effort during design or rollout. Each item checked requires more detailed planning and attention as a part of Phases V and VI in your change process plan. For now, noting the areas requiring more focus will help you clarify your scope of change.

Task I.B.6: Clarify Target Groups and Scope

Your case for change must accurately identify the target groups of the transformation as well as the scope of change required in the organization. Targets are the groups and people who will be directly impacted by the change or who are essential in carrying it out. If you created a Project Community map in Task I.A.4, you have likely identified your target groups. It is essential that you consider the various needs of your target groups as you plan your change, your communications, and your engagement strategies.

Scope is the breadth and depth of the change effort, including your target groups and initiatives. It determines what you will pay attention to and plan for. One of the most common mistakes leaders make in leading change is to misdiagnose its scope, typically making it too narrow. If it is too limited, repercussions will be occurring outside of your view of things, creating all kinds of unpleasant surprises. If your scope is not accurate, you may be missing key leverage points for

Exhibit 1.3. **Initial Impact Analysis Audit**

WORKSHEET

What aspects of your organization will be impacted by making this change? Check any of the following areas that will be affected by your effort.

BUSINESS/ORGANIZATIONAL IMPACTS

_____ Purpose/Vision/Mission

_____ Business Strategy

_____ Market Posture

_____ Organizational Structure

_____ Management Systems and Processes

_____ Technology/Equipment

_____ Tasks/Job Definition/Job Levels

_____ Products and Services

_____ People: Numbers/Skills/Systems

_____ Policies/Procedures

_____ Resources Needed/Resources Available

_____ Space Requirements/Layout/Moves

_____ Image/Brand (How we are perceived by others)

_____ Identity (Who we are; how we see ourselves)

_____ Customer Service

_____ Vendor Relationships

_____ Union Activity

_____ Response to Government Regulations

_____ Merger or Acquisition

_____ Splits/Divestitures

_____ Downsizing, Consolidation

_____ Standardization

_____ Growth/Expansion/Start-Ups

_____ Talent Management/Management Succession

_____ Work Flow

(continued)

Exhibit 1.3. **Initial Impact Analysis Audit**

WORKSHEET (continued)

_____ Governance and Decision Making

_____ Team Structures

_____ Technical/Professional Skills

_____ Current Skills Training

_____ Communication and Engagement Systems and Methods

_____ Other:

PERSONAL/CULTURAL IMPACTS

_____ Resistance and Anxiety

_____ Sadness at Letting Go of Old Ways

_____ Motivation and Commitment

_____ What People Are Recognized for

_____ Loss of Control

_____ Inclusion/Exclusion Issues

_____ Political Dynamics and a Change in the Balance of Power

_____ Perceptions of Fairness

_____ Values

_____ Norms

_____ Leadership Style/Executive Behavior

_____ Leader Mindset, Attitude

_____ Employee Behavior

_____ Employee Mindset, Attitude

_____ Expectations/Psychological Contract

_____ Need for Learning and Course Correction

_____ People or Relationship Skills

_____ Changes in Relationships (e.g., cross-boundary)

_____ Team Effectiveness

_____ Management Development/People Effectiveness Skills Training

Other:

getting the change to happen or expending energy on the wrong things. The classic misperception is to define scope in exclusively organizational, technical, or business terms, neglecting the cultural and people changes required for success. For transformation to work, scope must attend to all of the change required. Both the Drivers of Change Model and the Initial Impact Analysis Audit outline both types of initiatives required in scope. Use them as input to your scope.

Task I.B.7: Determine Degree of Urgency

Another output from your drivers of change is the conscious determination of the degree of urgency for making the transformation. The degree of urgency you assign at this point in your change effort will set the stage for success or failure, so being aware of what is accurate is essential. Being overly urgent will create panic and unfocused action. Low urgency will create complacency. What is really true about the urgency of your change?

A common error in leading transformation is the automatic assumption that the change needs to occur faster than is humanly possible. Our society assumes urgency; we live in the face of the tidal wave of speed. Urgency, in and of itself, is not a bad thing. It is an important motivator for focused action. However, when leading transformation, a *realistic* sense of urgency is essential. It is one of the key determinants of how well the organization will respond to the change.

Keep in mind that urgency is not the same thing as your timetable. *Wanting* speed is not the same as the marketplace absolutely dictating a deadline. Employees will understand a true need for speed but will disregard fabricated urgency and label it one more reason executives cannot be trusted to tell the truth. Don't make this mistake. Executives who unconsciously push transformation into unrealistic timetables without thinking through their internal motivations or the state of their people usually cost the organization in damaged morale, lost productivity, or impaired quality, all of which inevitably take more time to repair.

This task helps you consider the factors influencing your level of urgency, which is the first step in determining the timing and pace of your change.

The sense of urgency you establish here will become input to Task I.E.12. In that task, you will identify your critical milestones and general timeline as part of developing your change strategy.

Then, in Phase VI, *Plan and Organize for Implementation*, you will be able to develop a more informed timeline. At that point in the change process, your work will be based on a detailed impact analysis of external factors (environment, marketplace, and organization), internal factors (culture, time for skill development, personal change, and people's capacity), and the actions required to resolve all impact issues. Then the real work of the change, compiled into your Implementation Master Plan, can better indicate how long the effort will take if done well. However, at this early Phase I stage, the change leaders can only guess at the timetable, using their initial assessment of the scope of change and their impression of people's capacity to do what is required. Therefore, in communicating time pressures at this early stage, it is smarter to focus on urgency and present your desired timetable only as an initial estimate.

Task I.B.8: Determine Desired Outcomes and Compile Case for Change

The results of the first seven tasks of this activity produce your initial stance on why you need to make this change and what you want it to accomplish—your outcomes. You may have identified desired outcomes for any of the drivers of change as you worked on them. In addition, you will need to clarify any boundary conditions that must be respected as the change proceeds as well as your overarching outcome for the whole transformation.

Desired outcomes can take many forms. We typically see high-level aspirations that comprise a vision or set of compelling expectations. We see goals, objectives, and metrics, all of which are more concrete than aspirations. At this point, your intention is to shape a motivational vision for this transformation. If you have enough data to get more specific, you can also do that. If your change effort is primarily cultural, make sure to develop your outcomes in terms that speak to the *positive effect* of the new culture—what it is intended to enable in the organization. Use this information to provide the workforce with the motivation, rationale, and inspiration for taking on this effort, or provide the information as input to the stakeholders you want to engage in a larger visioning process. In Task I.F.3, you will design your visioning strategy and establish whether it will be primarily leader-driven or participatory.

Beyond Change Management discusses five different levels of success, which are also ways of defining your desired outcomes: (1) New State Design Determined, (2) New State Design Implemented, (3) Business Outcomes Achieved, (4) Culture Transformed, and (5) Organizational Change Capability Increased. This task

Exhibit 1.4. **Sample Case for Change**

PROJECT: CREATING AN INTEGRATED MEDICAL GROUP WITHIN A HEALTH SYSTEM

Vision

ABC Medical Group will be the practice of choice for patients and providers in every community we serve. We will consistently deliver safe, evidence-based, high-value care. Our physicians and nurses choose us as their optimal work environment and are loyal to us and the patients we treat.

The first step in achieving this vision is to unify all medical groups from across our ten hospitals. We will create a medical group division that will be a single operating unit (one medical group) serving every hospital. As a unified group, we will have the infrastructure needed to achieve our vision, including standard, reliable, evidence-based care; effective IT support for patients and providers, and a comforting patient experience. Our single division will give us an aligned payment model for all physicians. We will also obtain significant operational efficiencies from standard practices. In addition, we will have an active forum for sharing clinical and business data, and create an environment of community and shared responsibility to our patients and each other.

Drivers of Change

ENVIRONMENTAL IMPERATIVES:

- "Baby boomers" are aging and needing more care, putting greater pressure on the healthcare system.
- There is an industry shift from acute healthcare needs to chronic disease and population management.
- The explosion of scientific knowledge and capability creates more expensive technologies and medicines, and an industry expectation to use them when they make a difference.
- There is a shift from in-patient services to out-patient services due to improved technologies such as minimally invasive procedures and remote care.
- There is a shortage of caregivers—especially primary care physicians and nurses—just when the demand for care is rising.
- Malpractice insurance rates make cost containment very difficult.
- The current model of healthcare delivery and its costs are not sustainable.

MARKETPLACE REQUIREMENTS FOR SUCCESS:

- Patients need more care and have less insurance to pay for it.
- In the current reimbursement climate, we need exceptional financial performance.
- Healthcare resources are finite, and payers expect value for the dollars they spend.

(continued)

Exhibit 1.4. **Sample Case for Change (continued)**

- Patients expect more from doctors and hospitals—they want better service, access to care that fits their lifestyles, support for preventive care, more access to their medical records, more information, and more opportunity to make their own decisions. They also expect a positive experience across the continuum of care.
- There is an expectation of transparency related to the quality of our performance.

BUSINESS IMPERATIVES:

- The leadership strategy and structure for the medical group must support our overall system strategy, which is to create an integrated health system across all of our hospitals.
- The systems put in place must demonstrate cost savings and consistency of care.
- This integrated medical group must deliver reliable and quality care across all hospitals, no matter where physicians reside or practice.
- We must realize a return on our investment.
- Efficiencies in accounting, pay, and administrative practices must be tangible and measurable, as well as in our supply chain process.

ORGANIZATIONAL IMPERATIVES:

The unified medical group must do the following:

- Use the enterprise's EHR system to capture all information on patient treatment and plans.
- Use the enterprise's integrated HR systems, policies, and procedures.
- Use the enterprise's integrated IT systems and procedures.
- Use the enterprise's integrated financial systems and procedures.
- Use the enterprise's integrated supply chain process.
- Align the medical group's operations to match the operating requirements of the enterprise.
- Be structured to use 100 percent of our existing hospital physicians and 90 percent of our contracted physicians.
- Enable us to maintain and service our medical specialties and acute care facilities.
- Enable us to optimize our ambulatory care services and locations.

CULTURAL IMPERATIVES:

- Physicians must work together effectively to fulfill the medical demands of our ten hospitals. There needs to be willingness and flexibility in scheduling to handle the demands of providing quality and safe care. Physicians need to operate within the construct of being a part of one integrated medical group.

(continued)

- Our nursing staff must be more flexible in supporting physician needs on behalf of achieving required efficiencies. Physicians must be more open to nursing input because nurses will remain on location.
- Patient safety, reliability, and quality of care must come before efficiency, and efficiency is also essential to our success.
- We encourage physician-driven innovation, yet must reduce variation of care. Care should be planned and evidence-based wherever possible. However, continuous improvement must be in our culture.
- We stand for more aware, compassionate healing partnerships between patients and their caregivers.

Behavioral Imperatives:

- Physicians and nurses must input their treatment notes and plans into the EHR in a timely way for all other caregivers to access.
- Physicians must share information across specialties on behalf of an integrated plan of care for patients.
- Physicians must work in teams with other specialists and nursing staff to ensure efficient, integrated, and safe care.
- Nurses, physicians, and administrators must learn and master the relevant integrated systems and procedures, and use only those systems and procedures.
- Nurses and physicians must speak about others in only positive ways, or by offering constructive input to improve care and deepen relationships.
- Collaboration, decisiveness, and personal accountability are essential.
- Physicians must travel to other hospitals to accommodate variations in workload and emergencies.
- Recommendations for improvements in how the medical group operates must be taken directly to the administration, not the water cooler.

Mindset Imperatives:

- Think efficiency.
- Think about what is best for the patient and the whole health system.
- Put patient safety first in the context of timely and compassionate care. Everyone is empowered to do what is best for the patient.
- Physicians and nurses must respect each other and hold each other in a positive light when planning for and delivering care.
- Understand that this will be a learning process for everyone. Every incident is an opportunity to make things better and move forward.
- Stop the use of "against" thinking; we are all in this together.

(continued)

Exhibit 1.4.   **Sample Case for Change (continued)**

TYPE OF CHANGE

Transformational

There will be some components of the change that are transitional, and some developmental.

LEVERAGE POINTS FOR CHANGE

▸ Ten autonomous medical groups cannot function efficiently and provide consistent quality of care. One medical group is required.

▸ Integrating HR, IT, supply chain, finance, and EHR technology is essential to the unified medical group working.

▸ A trusting and supportive relationship between the unified medical group's administration and its practitioners is essential to this working.

▸ Physician input to the design of the group's operational practices is required.

TARGET GROUPS

▸ Physicians within the ten hospitals

▸ All independent physician service providers

▸ Nursing staff within the ten hospitals

▸ Headquarters office administrative and support service providers (e.g., HR, IT, finance, supply chain)

▸ Patients now served by different medical groups and locations

SCOPE

▸ All medical services, administrative, and operational functions, systems, and procedures

▸ All IT platforms being standardized and integrated

▸ The entire organization's culture, especially the culture among the physicians and nurses

▸ All working relationships

▸ The compensation and reward system

▸ All HR systems and policies

DESIRED OUTCOMES: BENEFITS OF ONE MEDICAL GROUP

▸ Having a unified medical group will increase our ability to react nimbly to the public health environment and to patient and provider needs, without increasing bureaucracy. We will be better positioned to respond to competitive pressures in the marketplace.

(continued)

- We anticipate a 7 percent improvement in operating performance of our medical group within three years. We will achieve this by improving our cost structure and by our improved ability to negotiate contracts with payers.
- We'll be better positioned to counter competitive threats and changes in the marketplace.
- Patients will be able to go to any one of our hospitals and receive consistently high-quality, personalized care. This promise will contribute to our becoming the definitive practice of choice in every community we serve.
- Individual providers will benefit from a highly desirable work environment that provides the tools, infrastructure, and resources to deliver high-quality care.
- Recruitment and retention of providers will be enhanced.
- We'll be able to offer a team approach to care within and across settings. This will occur through the redesign of our processes so that physicians spend most of their time providing services they uniquely can provide, and the team is trained and empowered to do the rest, including population management, protocol-driven care of acute and chronic conditions, patient education, and support. This will move us significantly in the direction of successful planned care.

benefits from leaders considering what level of success they are after, because most leaders think of outcomes as only Level Three, Business Outcomes Achieved. The other levels are also outcomes, if you consciously choose them and build them into your change strategy. Each level increases the return on investment from your change.

All of the information generated in this activity forms the basis of your case for change. The earlier introduction to Activity I.B lists all of the elements of your case for change. Review them, refine the results of all of the tasks of this activity, and write your case for change. Exhibit 1.4 provides a sample case for change.

The case for change is critical input for your change strategy, which is compiled in Activity I.E. At the beginning of Phase II, you will communicate the case for change, your change strategy, and any input to your vision for the change to the organization. With this in mind, tailor your case for ease of communication, making it concise, informative, accessible, and inspirational.

SUMMARY

You have now formed a realistic picture of the current status of the change effort and staffed its leadership. You have identified all of the stakeholders of the change and have begun to align all of the key players to support the transformation. In addition, you have clarified your initial assumptions about your case for change, desired outcomes and vision, scope, and pace of the transformation. The next chapter continues with more Phase I work, addressing the organization's level of readiness, capacity, and capability to proceed with what you are currently planning.

CONSULTING QUESTIONS FOR ACTIVITY I.A: START UP AND STAFF YOUR CHANGE EFFORT

Task I.A.1: Obtain Project Briefing

- Who has to be briefed about the status of the transformation (leaders, key stakeholders, consultants)?
- What information will you gather about the history, current reality, and future plans of the effort?
- What methods will you use to gather briefing information, and who will you interview?
- What will you do if you surface conflicting data about what has been happening and how it is perceived? How will you secure leadership alignment with your current reality?

Task I.A.2: Clarify and Staff Initial Change Leadership Roles

- Who is currently in charge of the change effort?
- What roles are needed for this effort to be led effectively?
- How will you select the best people to staff each of the change leadership roles you need?
- How will these people be informed and introduced to the expectations and deliverables of their roles? How will you ensure that they will give their change role the attention it needs?

- How will you address the conflict or time pressures for individuals who are asked to wear both a functional leadership hat and a change leadership hat?
- What will you do if someone currently in a change leadership role is not the best person for the job?
- What is your role in this change? Is it what you think it needs to be to make your greatest contribution? If not, what will you do to reposition your responsibilities?
- What consultants (internal and external) are being used in the transformation and for what purposes? How will you interface with the consultants involved, integrate their activities, and bring them up to speed regarding current plans?

Task I.A.3: Create Optimal Working Relationships

- What is the current condition of the relationships among all of the people filling change leadership roles? Between those in change leadership roles and those in operational leadership roles? Do any of these relationships need to improve? How can you help?
- How can the relationship between the executive team and the change leadership team be clarified and strengthened? Between the sponsor and the change process leader?

Task I.A.4: Identify Project Community

- Who are all of the stakeholders and target groups of this change effort? Is everybody who must have a voice in this transformation identified and able to have input as the change is being planned?
- How will this change effort interface with other groups or projects underway in the organization?
- How will you inform the stakeholders that they are an important part of this effort's project community?
- What will you ask the various members of the project community to do over the course of the change process?

- How will you use your project community to inform your change communications and engagement strategies? To support the overall good of the transformation?

Task I.A.5: Determine Phase I Roadmap

- How will you determine your Phase I roadmap? Who will participate in this exercise?
- What tasks will you engage in to fulfill the requirements of Phase I?
- How will you ensure that the senior change leaders commit to this work?

CONSULTING QUESTIONS FOR ACTIVITY I.B: CREATE CASE FOR CHANGE AND DETERMINE INITIAL DESIRED OUTCOMES

Task I.B.1: Design Process for Creating Case for Change and Initial Desired Outcomes

- Who are the best people to determine the transformation's desired outcomes and create its case for change? Should the people who created the organization's business strategy be included? How?
- What process will be used to accomplish this work? How will you use your business strategy to inform your case for change?
- How will you capture the leaders' input to the vision for this change?

Task I.B.2: Assess Drivers of Change

- What process will you use to assess the drivers of this transformation?
- What is driving this change? (Consider environmental forces, marketplace and customer requirements for success, strategic business imperatives, organizational imperatives, cultural imperatives, leader and employee behavior changes needed, and leader and employee mindset changes needed.)

- How can you use these drivers to shape your full scope of change?
- What boundary conditions are known for what needs to stay the same or not be impacted by the change?

Task I.B.3: Clarify Type of Change

- What is the primary type of change happening in this effort?
- What other types of change are also involved in it?

Task I.B.4: Identify Leverage Points for Change

- What leverage points for change will you focus attention on to catalyze your transformation?
- Why are these the most important things you can do to prompt the greatest amount of needed change?

Task I.B.5: Perform Initial Impact Analysis

- What is the change leaders' initial assessment of the business and organizational impacts of this transformation?
- What is the change leaders' initial assessment of the personal and cultural impacts of this transformation?
- How can you use this exercise to broaden the leaders' understanding of the scope of this transformation?

Task I.B.6: Clarify Target Groups and Scope

- How will you integrate the drivers of change, leverage points for change, and your initial impact analysis data to determine an accurate scope for this transformation?
- What is the scope of the effort?
- Who are the target groups of this transformation?

Task I.B.7: Determine Degree of Urgency

- What is the realistic degree of urgency for this transformation?
- What are the operational and people implications of this degree of urgency? What implications do you see for the organization's readiness, morale, and stamina?

- Have you made a clear distinction in the minds of the leaders between the degree of urgency and the timetable for making this change?

Task I.B.8: Determine Desired Outcomes and Compile Case for Change

- What are your initial desired outcomes for this transformation? Have you considered the levels of success in determining your desired outcomes? If so, what level are you after achieving?
- How can you use this information to shape your vision for what this change might produce?
- If your change effort is primarily cultural, how can you frame your desired outcomes so that the value of the new culture is clear and compelling?
- How would you summarize the case for change in a way that can be effectively communicated to the organization?

CHAPTER

PHASE I
Prepare to Lead the Change: Assess and Build Your Organization's Readiness and Capacity, and Build Leaders' Capability to Lead the Change

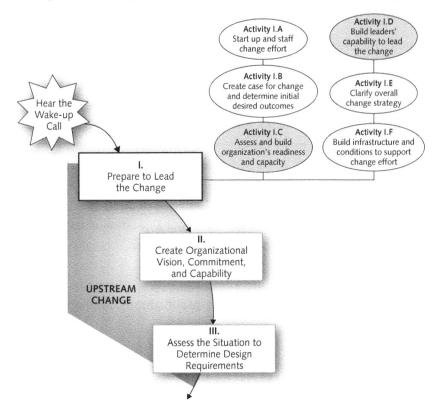

Activity I.A
Start up and staff change effort

Activity I.D
Build leaders' capability to lead the change

Activity I.B
Create case for change and determine initial desired outcomes

Activity I.E
Clarify overall change strategy

Hear the Wake-up Call

Activity I.C
Assess and build organization's readiness and capacity

Activity I.F
Build infrastructure and conditions to support change effort

I.
Prepare to Lead the Change

II.
Create Organizational Vision, Commitment, and Capability

UPSTREAM CHANGE

III.
Assess the Situation to Determine Design Requirements

ACTIVITY I.C AND I.D: TASK DELIVERABLES

I.C.1:   The organization's levels of readiness and capacity to succeed in this change have been accurately assessed and determined.

I.C.2:   Stakeholders' levels of readiness for change are being built, and the additional capacity needed for making this change is being generated.

I.D.1:   Leaders' capability to lead this change has been assessed for each area relevant to their development.

I.D.2:   Leaders understand that their mindset and behavior must overtly model the future state's requirements and are taking steps to do this.

I.D.3:   Leader commitment to and alignment with the transformation have been established.

I.D.4:   The executives and change leaders have the change knowledge and skills to consciously lead this transformation successfully.

I.D.5:   The executive team and change leadership team are operating as high-performing, aligned, co-creative teams, and are able to lead the transformation in a unified way.

I.D.6:   Individual leaders of the change are being trained and/or coached as needed to increase their ability to lead and walk the talk of this change.

One of the most costly mistakes made in leading change is to impose it on an organization that is not ready, able, or wanting to proceed. Many executives, so focused on the need for change, overlook whether or not the workforce has the capacity to change or is capable and willing. This is the number one pattern we see in leaders who do not understand the people or process requirements of transformation. Not many athletes would consider running two marathons without adequate time in between to recuperate. However, leaders frequently ask their organizations to make change after change with little space in between. Leaders must take readiness, capacity, and ability—all internal factors—into consideration when they plan for change. This is not a question of having the luxury of time or the convenience of having a happy workforce. It is a matter of necessity and long-term stamina.

With your case for change and scope identified, you have a fairly clear idea of what your transformation is going to require of both the organization and its leaders. Consider these questions:

- Are people ready and willing to make this change?
- Do people have the time and ability to carry out the work of the change on top of their current workloads?
- Are the leaders prepared to lead the transformation, individually and collectively?

The accurate answers to these questions are essential to formulating a sound change strategy. These two activities proactively address readiness, capacity for change, and capability to lead and succeed. Activity I.C assesses and builds the organization's readiness and capacity, and Activity I.D builds the leaders' capability to lead the effort.

ACTIVITY I.C: ASSESS AND BUILD ORGANIZATION'S READINESS AND CAPACITY

Leaders can gain a great deal of credibility from showing concern for and taking into consideration workforce morale, stamina, or residual emotions from past changes. For example, people's readiness, their emotional states, or people's ability to handle all workload demands, that is, their capacity to take on the change, will all have an impact on the success of the change. Readiness and capacity are separate but related issues. Assessing readiness is fundamentally about determining the emotional, psychological, and energetic state of employees regarding the change. Assessing capacity focuses on whether people have adequate attention, resources, and time to stay on top of their operational workloads as well as the demands of change. When people are emotionally ready for change, they can often take on more work. But if they are overwhelmed with work, that will undermine their emotional readiness to change. If leaders fail to notice and address serious lacks in either readiness or capacity, they add to the problem exponentially, and consciously or not, lose stature in the eyes of the workforce.

The issue of increasing people's readiness to change can be a sticky one and is worth further exploration. A low receptivity to change may be the result of a number of factors, some of which can be addressed and some of which cannot. People may be complacent, bored, or resistant. You can impact these states pretty quickly. However, if people are tired, overwhelmed, or burned out from moving at mach speed for too long or from dealing with too many changes at once, you cannot alter this condition overnight.

Do you proceed with haste anyway, ignoring their state? Do you pressure people to get on with the work or find another job? Do you put them on a shelf, fire them, and replace them with new blood? These can be difficult moral decisions for leaders if they recognize that people are tired because of years of giving so much to an insatiable organization. If leaders don't recognize this, or if they don't care, the usual tactic is to get rid of anyone who cannot keep up with the ever-accelerating pace, despite their years of service. This is no way to retain talent. There is no easy answer in this age of high-pressured change. However, the question cannot go unaddressed and must be reflected in your change strategy and pace.

This activity proactively assesses readiness and/or workload capacity, and builds both if needed. Use the data to demonstrate that you understand people's realities, and respond to it responsibly in your change plans by taking action to strengthen readiness or capacity.

Task I.C.1: Assess Readiness and Capacity

In this task, the executives examine the readiness and capacity of their organization to determine if it can do what is required to succeed in the change. Because change is so disruptive, people need to be ready and able physically, emotionally, and mentally to take it on. They need to have the time and space in their day to take action on change activities. Any lack of readiness or capacity may slow your transformation, especially if the lack is widely shared. Let's look at each dynamic.

Change Readiness

A thorough assessment of readiness includes a variety of topics critical to planning a conscious change strategy. Exhibit 2.1 lists many of the factors that affect readiness. Scan it to determine which topics are relevant to your assessment.

Consider the various audiences whose readiness you need to study. These might be any of the groups in your project community, especially your target groups—people who must implement the change on the ground. In the next task, you will build your strategy for increasing readiness, and initiate it where needed.

Exhibit 2.1. Factors Affecting Readiness

- Emotional residue left over from past changes, especially recent changes
- Degree to which people understand the marketplace forces that are driving the change
- Perceived value of the change: whether people understand and agree with its importance to the organization
- People's willingness to let go of the status quo or their past successes in order to commit to a new future
- The degree of influence people feel they have over making this change, as opposed to feeling that the change is being done to them
- People's beliefs about how much support they will get from leaders
- People's perceptions about how capable and credible the leaders are in leading this change effectively
- The degree of competence people feel they have to be able to succeed in making the change a success and in fulfilling its requirements
- The degree of fear people have about failing at either their operational duties or the change
- People's feelings about whether they think the organization has adequate resources and skills to succeed
- People's feelings about the level of urgency communicated about the change, and their ability to respond effectively in the given timetable
- The number and pace of recent changes people have undergone and the personal toll these created
- People's feelings about whether or not decisions regarding the change will be made fairly and justly
- People's assumptions about whether or not they will lose power as a result of the change
- People's comfort with chaos; their need for order and knowing how things will unfold

Capacity for Change

Even if people want to make a change, if they have too much work already, or feel the risk of failing at their normal duties, they will not have the capacity they need to add the demands of change as well. Figure 2.1 defines the organization's capacity graphically.

Remember, any capacity that you need for change must be subtracted from or added on top of the capacity you need for ongoing operations. Consider the factors affecting capacity, shown in Exhibit 2.2.

You can assess capacity for change by performing a change capacity review to understand the real demands you will be adding to the organization's workload.

In one utility organization, we assisted the leadership team to develop a major change strategy affecting the organization's overall structure and culture. Before completing the strategy, we encouraged the change leaders to assess the readiness and capacity of their primary target groups of the change. Although they were pleased with the support and enthusiasm in their middle management ranks, they were shocked to uncover serious problems with their first-line supervisors.

Apparently, the supervisors were still infuriated about the last change effort, which had affected their role authority, performance measures, and compensation. They felt angry and distrustful, wary of any hint of more change.

We convinced the leaders of the need to address this emotional residue before rolling out the new changes. We created a process for the leaders to listen to the supervisors' concerns in a safe and caring way through an approach called "listening circles." The leaders worked with the supervisors to express their concerns, explore their various points of view without judgment, and clear the air. The leaders learned a lot about the realities of the supervisors and acknowledged their concerns as well as their importance. This process enabled the leaders to build even greater readiness in the organization. Had they not assessed the true emotional state of the supervisors, they would have had to struggle with inordinate resistance, with failure an almost certain result. As it turned out, the supervisors got on board and championed much of the change.

Think about the scope of your change and the number of initiatives it entails. Consider the resources, time, and attention these efforts will require of your various stakeholder groups for each change. Ask the people closest to the current workload, or most knowledgeable about the changes, to generate accurate data about required capacity. In the next task, you will determine and carry out your strategies for freeing up more capacity to ensure that your changes will succeed.

As we mentioned earlier, inadequate capacity for change is consistently the most painful, critical risk our clients name—when asked. Most leaders have never addressed readiness or change capacity issues in preparation for a major change effort. Some may resist delving into such matters. Assessment of these issues

Figure 2.1.   **Capacity for Change**

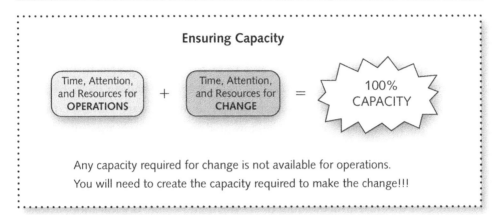

Ensuring Capacity

Time, Attention, and Resources for **OPERATIONS** + Time, Attention, and Resources for **CHANGE** = 100% CAPACITY

Any capacity required for change is not available for operations.
You will need to create the capacity required to make the change!!!

Exhibit 2.2.   **Factors Affecting Capacity**

- Current business goals and priorities
- The number and pace of current changes being asked of people and the burden these create
- The level of people's current operating workload and the degree to which it must accommodate additional work required by the change
- Current commitments and responsibilities, and people's ability to alter them
- Resources available to people
- Current operational due dates/timelines and people's ability to adjust them
- How people are measured and rewarded: only on operational performance or also on change?
- Degree of understanding and buy-in to the change by the functional leader who controls people's operational workloads
- How mistakes and missed deadlines are handled in the organization
- Cultural norms about saying no or setting limits

surfaces information that, although uncomfortable for leaders to acknowledge, is key to aligning their change strategy with the true condition in the organization. At the very least, raising these topics will start many conversations among leaders and employees that you would never otherwise have, all in the name of building awareness for leading change more effectively. This is one issue worth taking head-on.

Use your assessment data to shape your strategies to build both the organization's readiness and capacity for transformation, which occurs in Task I.C.2.

In a ten-hospital healthcare system, we assisted the leadership team to address a change capacity crisis. They had smartly recognized that they had initiated too many changes—nearly 200!—and were risking being able to provide quality and safe care. Before they called us for help, they had cut their change agenda down to 60 initiatives, which was an admirable start. However, they still felt they were at risk of failing and wanted to get on top of their situation once and for all.

We first provided a two-day overview to the executives, physician and nurse leaders, and their internal change consultants about what leading change of this magnitude required—of them and of the organization. They learned about the CLR as a fullstream process essential to them achieving real outcomes from their changes. That alone was incredibly important to their understanding of how much work they were asking of the organization. Achieving their outcomes from change took more than delegation and "checking the box." From this place of greater awareness, the leaders devised criteria for selecting the most strategic of initiatives to include in their change agenda. They were much more discerning.

For each of the change efforts they agreed on—30 the next cycle—they had specific guidelines and templates for how the efforts were to be planned and paced. They paced the initiatives according to the readiness and capacity of their staff, and coordinated much of the work across the multiple efforts to minimize additional burden on physicians and nurses. They combined educational requirements, pilots, and communication events, and involved stakeholder physicians and nurses to input to the change plans and timetables.

Task I.C.2: Build Readiness and Capacity

Based on the results of your readiness and change capacity assessments, this task creates and carries out your plans to raise the organization's level of readiness and capacity for the change. Strategies for building readiness vary widely. Remember that you cannot force anyone to become more ready and willing to change when they are not. *You can only create the conditions within which they can face, heal, or release whatever it is that is holding them back, or identify what would inspire them to move forward.* You may have to address people's mental states, physical states, emotional condition, or sense of meaning and purpose about the transformation. Consider training, breakthrough programs to shift mindset and resolve old emotional issues, communication sessions, dialogue meetings, large group events or rituals, time off, or any other bold actions. Acknowledging people's true condition without judging or condemning it goes a long way to facilitate their ability to advance their state of readiness. This bears repeating: Listen without judgment or blame!

Some of your strategies for building readiness and capacity should be implemented immediately. For example, you will likely need to free up capacity now to attend to the change work of Phase I. Some strategies will need time to implement or are best initiated in later phases of your change.

Consider the following strategies in Exhibit 2.3 for adding capacity for change, once you have named all of the major change efforts you have underway. You can use this exhibit as a worksheet.

ACTIVITY I.D: BUILD LEADERS' CAPABILITY TO LEAD THE CHANGE

The Change Leader's Roadmap is designed on the premise that successful change requires competent—and conscious—change leadership. However, not all change leaders have the awareness, knowledge, behavior, skills, or strategies to effectively plan and orchestrate major change, especially transformation. Leaders so often dive into transformational change full steam ahead, calling for action and decisions without strategically understanding the dynamics they are facing or creating.

Because transformation calls for an essential shift in mindset, behavior, and culture, leaders must look first at themselves rather than automatically ask the workforce to make all of the changes. Leaders must model what they are asking of the organization to be able to compel the workforce to take on the challenge. There is no worse condition when initiating change than to have leaders espouse one set of norms for the organization and then behave according to an obviously different set of norms for themselves.

This activity requires leaders to acknowledge that they have to change personally and collectively. This is not comfortable work, and in many organizations, it has been forbidden from executive development curricula as too personal. As yet, it is rare to see leaders actively pursuing their own personal change and expanding their

Exhibit 2.3. **Strategies to Add Capacity**

WORKSHEET

_____ Determine which change efforts must *continue as is*, which can be *stopped*, and which can be *modified*.

_____ For items that can be modified, consider how to modify them, such as:

　　_____ Reprioritizing

　　_____ Altering start or due dates and/or expanding timelines

　　_____ Changing performance measures

　　_____ Redefining scope

　　_____ Outsourcing work

　　_____ Reallocating resources

　　_____ Combining or integrating change work with other activities

_____ Reprioritize operational goals and work requirements.

_____ Reduce current workload to overtly make time for change.

_____ Create cross-functional teams to collaborate on how to work more efficiently.

_____ Deliver change leadership development programs so your leaders can design and implement more efficient change efforts.

_____ Renegotiate operating performance goals and timelines to include your change effort's requirements.

_____ Provide adequate resources to accomplish the change.

_____ Hire outside resources.

_____ Place a moratorium on new projects.

transformational change leader knowledge and skills. However, because this is so essential, this activity is designed to crack the barrier that keeps these topics "undiscussable." It makes explicit the imperative of personal transformation and positions it as a nonnegotiable part of the organization's overall change strategy. *Leaders must engage in their own development as a core part of the transformation.* Clearly, this work is in the forefront of the internal work, individually and collectively, as referenced in the Conscious Change Leader Accountability Model. Our companion book, *Beyond Change Management*, delves into much of this work in depth, setting the stage for more visionary leaders to show up.

This activity builds your change leaders' awareness and capability to lead this change, and all subsequent changes, successfully. In this activity, you will attend to change leadership skills and knowledge, change methodology and best practices, as well as leadership mindset, behavior, and culture change.

A primary change knowledge area is The Change Leader's Roadmap. Make sure that everyone working on your change effort has an adequate understanding of the model and how to use it to drive change. Rather than having many competing change approaches working within your effort, align everyone to the CLR as the one approach to use. This will help project team members easily share resources, expertise, best practices, and work products.

Task I.D.1 assesses your leaders' awareness and capability to lead change. There are five interdependent development tracks that you may assess, each represented by the five remaining tasks in this activity. Exhibit 2.4 describes the five tracks.

These five tracks reveal that the magnitude of development required for a manager to grow into a conscious change leader is significant. To ensure relevance to the leaders, frame all of this work in the context of achieving the results of your actual transformation.

A number of critical paradigm shifts are required as a leader moves from the classic command-and-control mindset to the co-creative mindset of a conscious change leader. Here are a few of them:

- From being responsible for a discrete function of the organization to looking out for the entire enterprise
- From focusing solely on external dynamics to also attending to the inner issues of "being"—in themselves, others, and the organization's culture
- From trying to remove dissonance by solving problems to looking into dissonance for signs of root causes and unconscious dysfunctional operating patterns
- From delegating change implementation to others to fully embracing what is required to play a significant role in leading change

Exhibit 2.4. **Five Tracks in Building Change Leadership Capability**

LEADERSHIP BREAKTHROUGH

This track ensures that leaders have the conscious awareness, mindset, emotional intelligence, and behavior required to personally lead transformation successfully. It addresses how they view the world, people, and change. It opens the topics of personal change, team development, and how to model the desired culture of the organization. It explores the human dynamics behind command-and-control leadership and the shift of mindset and behavior required to lead co-creatively. It delves into the values and norms espoused by the organization, their fit with the future, and the behaviors and work practices that reflect them. It focuses heavily on interpersonal communication skills, healing of past issues and relationships, and trust-building. This track establishes the power of conscious change leadership.

LEADERSHIP COMMITMENT AND ALIGNMENT

This track ensures that the leaders, individually and collectively, understand the full implications of what the organization's transformation entails, how to lead it, and what is required of them to ensure success. It helps them get through their own resistance and collectively align in support of common desired outcomes. It also addresses how to sustain leadership commitment over time.

CHANGE EDUCATION: KNOWLEDGE AND SKILLS

This track educates the leaders about the Conscious Change Leader Accountability Model, the CLR, and the skills, tools, and templates for planning, overseeing, and course-correcting a complex change effort. Where the Leadership Breakthrough track focuses on the internal dynamics of how the change leaders need to "be" to succeed, this track teaches them what they need to "know" and "do" to be successful. It covers the three types of change and how to create a sound change strategy, process plan, and timetable. It also addresses how to tailor The Change Leader's Roadmap to fit your organization's process needs.

EXECUTIVE AND CHANGE LEADERSHIP TEAM DEVELOPMENT

This track ensures that key teams—especially the change leadership team and executive team—are functioning in ways that will produce extraordinary results from change while simultaneously modeling how to work together in pursuit of enterprise change goals and ongoing performance. It builds alignment for the change within each team and ensures that they each have the mutual support and high level of performance required for success.

INDIVIDUAL LEADER DEVELOPMENT

This track optimizes the development of each key change leader. It may include further education, coaching, or mentoring for any of the leaders in support of each of the other four development tracks. Each leader identifies and acquires the support needed to sustain his or her personal change, skill development, relationship skills, and team performance so each can model the transformation and desired culture, and lead critical change activities successfully.

- From managing and controlling a single, linear change project to facilitating multiple, multi-dimensional, and interdependent change processes, all as one unified effort

- From treating people as cost structures who serve leaders' demands to showing concern for people—their feelings, personal needs, capacity, and choices

- From thinking that any change project will end and go away, to realizing that change is a ongoing reality that needs formal support and disciplines

- From attempting to fix any problem "for good" to building the organization's capability and mindset for ongoing change, course correction, and continuous self-renewal

Task I.D.1: Assess Leaders' Capability to Lead the Change

This task has you establish the importance of this work in the minds of the leaders and then assess the five tracks of change leadership development. Before you can proceed, you must ensure that the leaders agree to be assessed, and that the data you generate may show that they need development to become more effective change leaders of their transformation. The leaders must see the value of this development and be willing to engage in it over time. The material contained in Premium Content can be used to raise the awareness, interest, and invest-ment of the change leaders for ensuring their greatest capability to succeed. (See Premium Content: (1) Ten Most Common Mistakes in Leading Transformation, (2) Leadership Breakthrough: Topic Options and Methods, (3) Ten Critical Actions for Leading Successful Transformation, and (4) A Candid Message to Senior Leaders: Ten Ways to Dramatically Increase the Success of Your Change Efforts, www.pfeiffer .com/go/anderson.)

Task I.D.2: Ensure Leaders Model Desired Mindset and Behavior

If the change effort is truly transformational, you must address whether the leaders' mindsets and behavior fit the future requirements of the organization and its culture. If they do not, you must decide how to change them and develop the leaders to become real models of what is actually required. They must first explore what mindset is, how it impacts results, and how it is a central driver of the orga-nization's transformation. We discuss all of this in depth in *Beyond Change Mana-gement*, emphasizing that, unless leaders address these factors directly, current state mindsets will continue to impact their ability to lead the organization and the transformation. *We cannot underscore the importance of this task enough! It is the source of making your organization's transformation conscious.*

To engage people successfully in the transformation, minimize resistance, and maximize commitment, leaders must learn how beliefs, assumptions, and feelings influence motivation and behavior. To build the organization's trust, they will need to demonstrate the new mindset and behaviors themselves. They will need to relate authentically to employees—identifying and speaking honestly about their own feelings and assumptions—and listen empathetically to others. They certainly won't influence culture change if they do not understand people at the most basic personal levels and model what the new culture requires in practice.

After leaders understand the definition and power of mindset and behavior, they will need to self-reflect and explore the degree of fit or change required in any of the following areas:

- Their leadership and behavioral styles, and the impact they have on others
- Their underlying assumptions about what makes people tick, and how to motivate them
- How their mindset and behavior may contribute to or help resolve challenges the organization is facing
- How their current mindset and behavior may have to change to support the organization's transformation and future
- Their interpersonal skills; how they relate to one another and the workforce; how well they give and receive constructive feedback
- Their communication style and the underlying assumptions they hold about information sharing
- Their personal issues surrounding topics such as power and control, competence, inclusion, relationship, security, or justice and fairness

This exploration will help leaders determine how they must be different to be more successful. They must commit to undergo the personal development required of them and demonstrate the importance of this depth of change to the rest of the organization. They must become models of personal change.

How do you change mindset and behavior? Discussing the concept of mindset and behavior as an agenda item in an executive meeting won't change a thing.

In fact, doing so often creates the trap of executives thinking they have "handled" the issue. Even if leaders agree that shifts in mindset and behavior are needed, these changes cannot be forced on them or mandated. Both leaders and employees have to *experience* the benefit of shifts in mindset and then choose to change themselves. This is accomplished through personal transformation or breakthrough training. Competent facilitators are required to teach leaders how to use transformative personal change approaches.

There are many strategies for addressing leadership mindset and behavior. In our consulting, we begin all transformation efforts with a very powerful systemwide intervention we call the "leadership breakthrough" process. Briefly, the leadership breakthrough process is comprised of a four-day training session preceded by pre-session interviews and reinforced with follow-up sessions and ongoing coaching. In the main training session, participants experientially come to understand what mindset is and the power it has over their performance and results. They explore if and how their own mindset and behavior fit the world they are striving to create. They address the topics listed earlier and learn a systematic personal transformation process, complete with tools, techniques, and daily practice.

Transformational experiences such as the Leadership Breakthrough process provide leaders with a mirror in which to see both the positive and negative effects of their current mindset, style, and behavior. The sessions create a safe environment for leaders to explore and commit to the personal change required of them to be more effective in the new reality they face, and they build sustainable teamwork. To be effective, leadership breakthrough trainings must address the leaders as individuals, the quality of their relationships with others, and the level of their team performance and learning ability.

We can best describe the Leadership Breakthrough strategy by sharing how one company used it (see sidebar).

Transformational change strategy must attend to changing mindset and behavior across the entire system, as this case illustrates. However, beyond the breakthrough training rollout, examples of interventions that catalyze and reinforce mindset and behavioral change include the following:

- Sharing the case for change featuring mindset and behavioral change as primary drivers of the change and recognized as a part of the formal scope of change
- Determining the desired culture as a reflection of the new mindset and style

The transformation of DTE Energy from a regulated to a "fiercely competitive" business was mindset-driven. When we began supporting this effort, both the CEO and president realized that even though they could not yet specify all the changes required in their business strategy and organization, they could and must begin shifting their culture from entitlement to an entrepreneurial, service-oriented style. Early on, they realized that this responsibility began with them.

The strategy for dealing with the leaders' mindsets was developed in partnership with DTE Energy's internal change leaders. We agreed to provide the top executives with a four-day breakthrough experience aimed at "walking the talk of change." This session was designed to wake up the leaders to the limitations of their old mindsets and style of leading and introduce them to new ways to see themselves, one another, their role in the organization, and the opportunities in deregulation. Motivated by the results and power of this experience, the executives decided to provide the same session to all 300 of their top leaders over the next six months, including the leadership of their unions. The positive impact of these sessions then motivated the executives to offer this session to their remaining 1,200 leaders over the next two years. In the third year, the remaining 8,000 employees were also introduced to the principles of the training through an abbreviated one-day program.

The overall strategy went far beyond the four-day workshop. Our experience of delivering breakthrough training has demonstrated to us that, although the multi-day workshop is a central component, the tangible results required to support the organization's transformation come from a much larger, integrated process. For DTE, this included pre-session interviews of each of the participants by the facilitators to establish clear personal objectives, follow-up sessions, pre- and post-session meetings between bosses and subordinates, large group "mobilization" meetings, executive coaching, on-the-job feedback, and team development. Each of these components reinforced and extended the insights from the initial program.

Every follow-up session included the executives, who shared with their managers their own personal development experiences from the program.

The executives modeled telling the truth, being vulnerable, and openly correcting their relationships with one another, various management groups, and the unions.

During these sessions, vital information was shared in a safe environment, the healing of old wounds began, and movement toward greater collaboration was established. Over time, a number of leaders began to see the importance of operating openly and "consciously" with one another if they were to create a vastly different future. Both the CEO and the president felt strongly that the values and principles "taught" in the breakthrough training were to be modeled overtly in the organization. As feedback for the leaders increased in real time, they set better conditions for the overall organization to become faster acting and more entrepreneurial—and to be a healthier place to work. They created a positive union-management partnership that had profound benefits for operations. This established a valuable foundation for the organization's transformation.

Their results? The leaders committed at the beginning of the process to produce at least $100,000,000 of net profit from their new entrepreneurial businesses within five years. They achieved $108,000,000.

- Creating high engagement in revisioning the organization's future
- Having the senior leaders openly talk about their own mindsets and behavior and how they need to change for the organization to succeed
- Employing large group meeting approaches to design the future state
- Building the teams required to implement the future state into high-performing teams that openly address their mindsets, behavior, and relationships as a part of how they operate
- Performing an impact analysis comparing the desired state scenario and the current organization using the new mindset and culture criteria

Each of these can be delivered through a cascade or large group approach.

We have outlined a five-step process for designing an organization-wide mindset change strategy, which is summarized in the sidebar. It can be fully

THE PROCESS FOR CHANGING ORGANIZATIONAL MINDSET

1. **Set the Foundation and Motivation for Changing Leaders' Mindsets.** This step creates the case for changing the mindsets of the leaders and secures their commitment to do so in the most positive and unified way. The results of your exploration of the drivers of change and your change readiness and capacity assessments can provide helpful input, as can the findings from benchmarking admired or visionary companies. Your goal here is to establish that changing leaders' mindsets is critical to their ability to lead the organization's transformation consciously and model personal change to the organization.

2. **Get the Attention of Individuals and the Organization.** This step establishes the nonnegotiable reality of changing the organization's collective mindset and culture as key to transforming it successfully and begins to demonstrate what the change will mean for people and the system as a whole. The executive team engaging in the Leadership Breakthrough process is a great launch. Highly visible executive decisions—driven by obvious changes in mindset and culture—about business strategy and personnel changes, communications, and other bold actions can help accomplish this. A culture assessment can also get people's attention that change is coming and that they are a key part of making it happen, from the inside out.

3. **Build Organizational Momentum for the Change in Mindset.** This step creates a critical mass of support, activity, and energy for the personal and organizational mindset shifts needed. It usually includes the cascade of the Leadership Breakthrough training, or something similar, to accelerate personal growth for a critical mass of the organization's influential leaders and employees. Ongoing communications celebrating mindset, culture changes, and organizational wins driven by the new mindset also help.

4. **Reinforce and Sustain the Change in Thinking and Behavior.** This step deepens and further establishes the changes happening in people and the organization. Follow-up sessions to reinforce learnings from the Leadership Breakthrough process and how they have helped the

organization to change are essential. Executive coaching, 360-degree feedback, continuous communications, and focused large group meetings and celebrations are common strategies.

5. ***Align and Integrate the Changes in the Organization with the New Mindset.*** This step ensures that the organization can effectively operate from the new mindset and culture, and sustain its performance throughout the transformation. Changes in business processes, norms, decision making, structure, policy, and systems must all be aligned to the new mindset. It is important to keep the conversation about the importance of mindset active, relevant, and safe.

integrated into your change strategy and will likely occur throughout the entire transformation.

Task I.D.3: Build Leader Commitment and Alignment

The principle underlying this task must be made explicit: The leaders of the organization must act as a unified team, modeling their collective commitment to the future in both words and action. Examples abound of executive groups not being aligned behind the major changes they face. The majority of these cases occur because the change leaders or the change consultants do not think to assess or actively require real leadership alignment. Perhaps it is too politically sensitive to make this internal dynamic overt. The executives proceed anyway, and the change inevitably falters or self-destructs. Lack of alignment is one of the biggest slow-down factors in the speed of change. There are two conditions you are after here—to overtly acknowledge that sustained executive commitment is *essential* to success, and to make it *safe* to address any commitment issues openly as a team. Achieving these conditions takes time and may require skilled facilitation.

The first step in this task is to assess the current degree of common understanding, alignment, and commitment to the transformation and its outcomes. Alignment does not mean that everyone has to be in lockstep before proceeding. Diverse views can be highly beneficial as long as they do not coun-teract forward progress or set up the conditions for political battling or outright sabotage. If the change leaders have engaged in the earlier activities of Phase I, there will likely be significant alignment and commitment already. If not, a strategy for dealing with disparate levels of alignment and commitment must be created and carried out.

Strategies vary widely. The vast majority of commitment strategies rely on open and honest dialogue. Superficial conversation, filled with false declarations, empty "head nods," defensiveness, accusation, and steadfast posi-tions will not work. Examples of good strategies include directly addressing the issue and exploring people's reasons for withholding their commitment, creating face-saving but sideline positions for those opposed to the change, medi-ating diverse positions, and direct removal of an individual who refuses to get on board.

The best strategy is dialogue. Dialogue is a communication tool that we use heavily in our Leadership Breakthrough process. Dialogue is a simple communica-tion structure and process through which executives discover and tell their per-ceptions of the truth to each other about any relevant issue. The participants in dialogue reflect on their own feelings and thoughts, including their hopes and fears, and listen deeply to one another. This process usually uncovers and helps resolve what has previously blocked alignment. Good facilitation of dialogue is essential until a team feels capable to do it on their own.

We must note that squelching a resister's or naysayer's voice is the worst strategy and almost always generates negative repercussions. The only time such heavy-handed approaches should be used to build alignment is after dialogue and other exploratory strategies have proven unsuccessful. Then it simply is time to say, "Get on board or move out of the way."

A major advantage of offering breakthrough training early in the change process is that it builds leaders' ability to understand and share what is true for them. They learn to really listen to each other. Often, this in itself produces most of the commitment and alignment needed for the transformation.

Task I.D.4: Develop Leaders' Change Knowledge and Skills

Most executives have engaged in major change for most of their careers, and therefore assume they know how to do it. Yet more than 60 percent of change fails!

Leading transformational change, as noted in the Introduction, is a very different animal from leading developmental or transitional changes, both of which require less knowledge and leadership skill. The point here is that most executives and change leaders do need some education and skill development. You have a range of options for what to provide your leaders and various users of The Change Leader's Roadmap methodology.

Essential change education topics that must be understood by leaders are listed next. *Mastery of these subjects means the difference between traditional leadership and conscious change leadership.* The first five are discussed in our companion book and represent the foundation of conscious transformational leadership. These and the remaining topics constitute what change leaders do to lead transformational change successfully.

1. The drivers of change (i.e., environmental forces, marketplace requirements for success, business imperatives, organizational imperatives, cultural imperatives, leader and employee behavior changes, and leader and employee mindset changes)
2. The three types of change (development, transition, transformation)
3. The importance of changing mindset and behavior and overtly modeling this personal change
4. Project thinking, systems thinking, and conscious process thinking; conscious process design and facilitation
5. How to develop a comprehensive change strategy
6. Being able to use and customize the CLR and its tools and resources to fit the organization
7. How to determine and create a comprehensive change infrastructure and conditions for success
8. How to establish the need for rapid course correction and a system to accomplish it, and ensure course correction happens throughout the change
9. How to change culture to support your desired outcomes

You can use the information in both books as a template to assess your leaders' understanding, knowledge, and skills, and to create development plans to build their capability to lead transformational change. Development plans will likely be long-term processes and will require the full commitment of the leaders and managers they are designed for. These plans should be integrated into your executive, management, and supervisory-level development curricula offered in the company.

Task I.D.5: Develop Executive and Change Leadership Teams

The goal of this task is to develop the executive and change leadership teams to be capable of leading both the current organization and the transformation to deliver intended business results. Leaders' inability to work well together—within or between teams—can be one of the earliest and most costly factors in their performance in leading transformation. Until the leaders are able to function as unified teams, politics notwithstanding, their chances of planning and orchestrating transformation are painfully low. Two prior tasks help with team effectiveness: leadership commitment and alignment, and participation in the Leadership Breakthrough program. If you engaged in this work, the core issues blocking the team's success will likely have surfaced and begun to be resolved. This task can then enable the teams' development to continue as the change proceeds. We often provide executive and change leadership team development in the Leadership Breakthrough follow-up sessions.

If you have not done this prior work, it would be helpful to generate data on exactly what areas of team performance need to be strengthened. Exhibit 2.5, Worksheet: Team Effectiveness Assessment, covers important topics for high-performing teams. Each individual on a team can fill it out, and the entire team can then discuss the results and plan for its development. If the change leadership team is just beginning, the topics in the assessment can be used to guide its start-up goals.

Task I.D.6: Support Individual Executives and Change Leaders

This task develops personal mastery in individual change leaders and reinforces the desired personal changes begun in Task I.D.2, *Ensure Leaders Model Desired Mindset and Behavior*. It provides for individualized training and coaching of leaders. This task also creates plans for individuals who may be disrupting the change or are not in alignment with it. Coaching them can reduce their negative impact. In some cases, you may need to offer hard choices about keeping the difficult person positively engaged in the change. At worst, you will need to replace people who do not get on board.

Exhibit 2.5. Team Effectiveness Assessment

1. The team charter is understood and agreed on by all team members.

1	2	3	4	5
Agree	Tend to Agree	Don't Know	Tend to Disagree	Disagree

2. Conditions for success for high performance are developed and agreed to by all team members.

1	2	3	4	5
Agree	Tend to Agree	Don't Know	Tend to Disagree	Disagree

3. Team member roles are clearly defined and accepted.

1	2	3	4	5
Agree	Tend to Agree	Don't Know	Tend to Disagree	Disagree

4. Task processes (goal or outcome oriented) for the team are in place and effective.

1	2	3	4	5
Agree	Tend to Agree	Don't Know	Tend to Disagree	Disagree

5. Group processes (interaction oriented) for the team are in place and effective.

1	2	3	4	5
Agree	Tend to Agree	Don't Know	Tend to Disagree	Disagree

6. The team has the time and resources it needs to function optimally.

1	2	3	4	5
Agree	Tend to Agree	Don't Know	Tend to Disagree	Disagree

7. The team has a high degree of diversity and uses it well.

1	2	3	4	5
Agree	Tend to Agree	Don't Know	Tend to Disagree	Disagree

8. The team has a clearly defined decision-making process and uses it effectively.

1	2	3	4	5
Agree	Tend to Agree	Don't Know	Tend to Disagree	Disagree

9. All team members are highly committed to the success of the team and its charter.

1	2	3	4	5
Agree	Tend to Agree	Don't Know	Tend to Disagree	Disagree

(continued)

Exhibit 2.5. **Team Effectiveness Assessment (continued)**

10. All team members are skilled in two-way coaching and facilitating others' learning.

1	2	3	4	5
Agree	Tend to Agree	Don't Know	Tend to Disagree	Disagree

11. All team members are skilled at giving and receiving feedback.

1	2	3	4	5
Agree	Tend to Agree	Don't Know	Tend to Disagree	Disagree

12. The team is able to identify and resolve conflicts well.

1	2	3	4	5
Agree	Tend to Agree	Don't Know	Tend to Disagree	Disagree

13. The team has and uses a well-defined course-correction process for both behavior and results.

1	2	3	4	5
Agree	Tend to Agree	Don't Know	Tend to Disagree	Disagree

14. The team is able to change directions or practices quickly once it recognizes the need to do so.

1	2	3	4	5
Agree	Tend to Agree	Don't Know	Tend to Disagree	Disagree

15. The team has a clear accountability process and actively uses it to hold team members accountable for behavior and results.

1	2	3	4	5
Agree	Tend to Agree	Don't Know	Tend to Disagree	Disagree

16. The relationship between this team and other teams supporting the organization and the change is effective.

1	2	3	4	5
Agree	Tend to Agree	Don't Know	Tend to Disagree	Disagree

17. Team members have a high degree of trust in each other.

1	2	3	4	5
Agree	Tend to Agree	Don't Know	Tend to Disagree	Disagree

18. The team has good spirit and energy.

1	2	3	4	5
Agree	Tend to Agree	Don't Know	Tend to Disagree	Disagree

In some cases, this task is fulfilled through one-on-one executive coaching. In other cases, the leaders actually form two-way coaching partnerships with each other to support one another's development. The two-way coaching partnerships are often formed as a part of the Leadership Breakthrough strategy. The partners can focus on the mindset, behavior, language, knowledge, and/or skills required by the change effort. The tools learned in the Leadership Breakthrough training can be employed in partnership coaching. This work continues as long as it adds value to the individuals involved and benefits their participation in the change effort.

SUMMARY

Through these Phase I activities, you have assessed the organization's readiness and capacity to succeed in the transformation being planned. You have also designed your strategy for building the leaders' capability to lead the change, individually and collectively. As accelerators of change, the organization's readiness, capacity, and capability are high-return investments in the creation of your desired outcomes and are well worth the time and energy.

 CONSULTING QUESTIONS FOR ACTIVITY I.C: ASSESS AND BUILD ORGANIZATION'S READINESS AND CAPACITY

Task I.C.1: Assess Readiness and Capacity

▶ Will you assess the organization's readiness for making this transformation? If so, how?

▶ Will you assess the organization's capacity for handling the change on top of its operating priorities? If so, how?

▶ What aspects of readiness and capacity will you assess?

▶ Are the change leaders prepared to hear *and use* the results of each assessment to shape their plans for the change?

Task I.C.2: Build Readiness and Capacity

▶ What strategies will you use to build either readiness or capacity in your key stakeholder groups?

▶ How will you know when you have built readiness? Freed up adequate capacity?

▶ How will you monitor these factors throughout the change effort?

CONSULTING QUESTIONS FOR ACTIVITY I.D: BUILD LEADERS' CAPABILITY TO LEAD THE CHANGE

Task I.D.1: Assess Leaders' Capability to Lead the Change

▶ How will you position the value of doing leadership assessment and development with the change leaders and executives in the organization?

▶ How will you obtain both their understanding and commitment to proceed with this work now and throughout the change effort?

▶ How will you assess the need for leadership development in each of the five areas in this activity?

Task I.D.2: Ensure Leaders Model Desired Mindset and Behavior

▶ How will you initiate the topic of leadership mindset and behavior with the executives? Of becoming models of the new mindset and behavior?

▶ How will you engage leaders in identifying their prevailing mindsets and behavior, and the fit of both with the future the leaders want to create?

▶ Will you use a Leadership Breakthrough process? Will you design and deliver it yourself or bring in specialists in this type of work?

- How will you reinforce and sustain personal change work throughout the change process?
- How can the leaders model the changes they have made in mindset and behavior in the organization? How can you monitor that this is done? Will the leaders self-monitor?

Task I.D.3: Build Leader Commitment and Alignment

- How will you address the issue of commitment and alignment among the change leaders and the executives?
- What is the current level of commitment among the change leaders and the executives for making this transformation successful?
- What meaning do you make of any insufficient commitment and/or alignment?
- How will you increase commitment to where it needs to be?

Task I.D.4: Develop Leaders' Change Knowledge and Skills

- What new knowledge and skills do the executives and change leaders need to know about change, transformation, and The Change Leader's Roadmap?
- Do the leaders understand and buy into the new standard of conscious change leadership?
- How will you provide them what they need to develop into more capable leaders of change?
- How can you tie this education to your content changes to make it relevant and results oriented?

Task I.D.5: Develop Your Executive and Change Leadership Teams

- What is the status of team effectiveness in the executive team and the change leadership team?
- How will you strengthen each team's functioning and the relationship between them so that they can lead this transformation in the most conscious and effective way?

Task I.D.6: Support Executives and Change Leaders

▶ Which individuals on the executive team and the change leadership team need personal coaching or development to ensure they are able and willing to contribute their best to this change effort?

▶ Does each person recognize his or her need? Is each open to receiving support?

▶ How will you engage these people in a personal development process? Does a senior leader have to request that they pursue this development? Should their development be attached to their incentive program? Should it be voluntary?

▶ Who is best to provide this support to each individual?

PHASE **I**
Prepare to Lead the Change: Clarify Your Overall Change Strategy

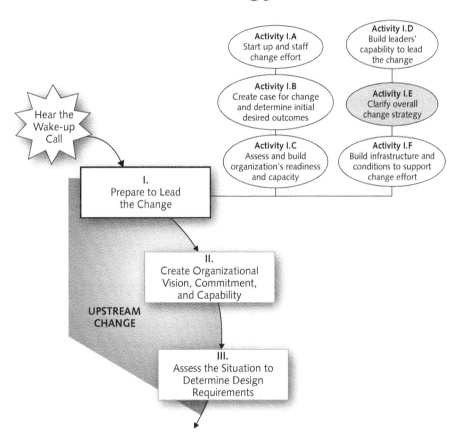

Activity I.A
Start up and staff change effort

Activity I.D
Build leaders' capability to lead the change

Activity I.B
Create case for change and determine initial desired outcomes

Activity I.E
Clarify overall change strategy

Activity I.C
Assess and build organization's readiness and capacity

Activity I.F
Build infrastructure and conditions to support change effort

Hear the Wake-up Call

I.
Prepare to Lead the Change

II.
Create Organizational Vision, Commitment, and Capability

UPSTREAM CHANGE

III.
Assess the Situation to Determine Design Requirements

I.E: TASK DELIVERABLES

I.E.1: The process for creating the change strategy is clear, and the effort has been staffed.

I.E.2: The values and guiding principles for shaping the change effort have been identified.

I.E.3: Governance and decision making for the change have been determined and initiated. Your change leadership team and executive team understand how the two teams will interface to simultaneously optimize running the business and orchestrating the change.

I.E.4: The initiatives required to produce your desired outcomes have been identified. The change leaders are clear about how to integrate all change initiatives into one unified change effort.

I.E.5: The executives and change leaders understand how your change effort fits within and links to the larger changes occurring in your organization, and agree on its priority.

I.E.6: A Multiple Project Integration Strategy has been created to manage both the interfaces among sub-initiatives within your change effort and those outside of it.

I.E.7: Initial bold actions for demonstrating that a major change is happening have been identified.

I.E.8: Engagement strategies for gaining a critical mass of commitment among the stakeholders and target groups of the change are clear.

I.E.9: A communication plan has been created for the transformation, and the change leaders are clear about how they will launch the effort in the organization.

I.E.10: Strategies to accelerate the pace of change have been identified.

I.E.11: The resources required to make the transformation have been estimated, and the leaders are committed to providing adequate resources throughout the change process.

I.E.12: Critical milestones and general timeline of the transformation have been determined. The integrated change strategy has been completed.

ACTIVITY I.E: CLARIFY OVERALL CHANGE STRATEGY

Your change strategy is the ultimate deliverable of Phase I and will influence all remaining phases of your change process. It demonstrates your clarity about what needs to change, sound leadership thinking about how to achieve your outcomes, and concern for the people who must make the change a reality. All of your work to date in Phase I is input to building your change strategy. In Activity I.A, you clarified the current reality of your effort as your starting point, determined your change leaders, and identified stakeholder groups. The case for change (Activity I.B) determined the content and people drivers of your change effort and its scope. You also identified your initial desired outcomes. Your change readiness and capacity assessments from Activity I.C provide significant information for your people strategy going forward. In Activity I.D, you designed your change leadership development strategy to ensure that leaders' mindsets, knowledge, and skills are what they need to be to lead this change. Keep all of this work in mind as you complete your change strategy. The inputs to change strategy and its elements are listed later in Exhibit 3.2.

Building a change strategy consists of determining twelve elements. It makes the following explicit:

- Your values and guiding principles for leading this effort
- Change governance and decision making
- Key initiatives and how you will integrate them to deliver your outcomes
- The priority and positioning of your transformation in the organization
- Your multiple project integration strategy
- Bold actions to get people's attention
- Your engagement and communication plans
- Acceleration strategies
- Resource estimates
- Milestone events and your proposed timeline for the change.

Guided by the change process leader, building a change strategy is the work of senior leaders, by either your executive team or change leadership team, if you have one. Much of the work to plan your change can be delegated. *This work cannot!* Just as your senior-most executives are responsible for business strategy, they also must do the hard thinking to figure out and determine your change strategy. While a lot of the input to each of the elements of the strategy can be generated by informed support staff, decisions about what defines your strategy belong to the leaders. If you are working on a change that does not impact the entire enterprise, apply this principle to the leaders in charge of the part of the organization changing.

After you have compiled your change strategy, you will be ready to more fully develop the conditions and infrastructures needed to support it. This work is also guided by the change process leader and occurs next in Activity I.F.

Task I.E.1: Design Process for Building Change Strategy

Given the wealth of information that is input to your change strategy, it is important to be very clear about the process to pull it all together. Read the remaining tasks of I.E for the key decisions required to create your strategy. Remember, the top change leaders must engage enough in this work to ensure the knowledge and commitment they need to launch and lead the transformation. Change consultants and other resources can help facilitate and manage the development of the strategy, overseen by the change process leader.

Create the process for building your change strategy by determining the following:

▶ How much authority the change process leader has to shape the change strategy for the sponsor and change leaders

▶ Who will input to various elements of the change strategy

▶ The elements of the strategy you will focus attention on

▶ Timeline for its completion

▶ Medium and format for recording the strategy

▶ How to ensure the strategy meets your conditions for success and reflects or furthers your desired culture

▶ How you will summarize, update, and course correct the strategy throughout the change process

▶ How you will communicate your change strategy to the organization

Task I.E.2: Define Values and Guiding Principles

The purpose of this task is to define the values and guiding principles of your desired culture to use to shape your change effort. Values and guiding principles are closely related. Values are the inherent qualities that lie at the essence of a behavior or action. Guiding principles are high-level rules of conduct that guide behavior and action. They are "values in action." To illustrate how to use them to shape how you lead your change, an organizational value of *high involvement* may get translated into a guiding principle of, "Input will be sought from all stakeholder groups." A value of *openness* might generate a guiding principle of, "We will communicate frequently the status of the change, even if we do not have the answers or conclusions."

Once identified, you can consciously design your change strategy, leadership style, and process plan to model your values and guiding principles. In your earlier visioning work for this change, you may have identified desired values. If you did, bring them directly into this work.

If your organization's current values and cultural norms fit your future state, use them to influence how this change takes place. They might impact decisions about structure, systems, and processes; the level of engagement and autonomy your employees enjoy; and your organization's general leadership style.

If your organization's stated values and culture are very different from the real behavior and actions of leaders and managers or do not support the future state, you will need to change the organization's culture. Caution! If you roll out your change based on your old culture, employees will say, "See, nothing has changed." But if your change strategy and leaders overtly model the new culture, employees will see direct evidence that your organization's culture is in fact changing. After you define your values and guiding principles for your change effort, be sure that your change leadership development programs expressly reinforce them.

If needed, culture change should become a formal part of your scope of change. You will be designing your new culture in Phase IV, so for now, generate the values and guiding principles you need for your change effort to be successful. Consider this task as input to the change process for the culture element in the Conscious Change Leader Accountability Model.

Task I.E.3: Clarify Governance and Decision-Making

Leading your change effort effectively requires good governance. This entails defining roles and authorities, a governance structure, and clear decision making for the change. Because the project will be implemented while normal operations continue, you must also agree on how to handle the interface between governing the change and operations. Inevitably, there will be pinch points around resources and timelines that need attention. Engage both the executive team and the change leadership team to overtly decide how to deal with questions and issues when they arise.

In Task I.A.2, *Clarify and Staff Initial Change Leadership Roles*, you began naming the people you thought were appropriate to fill the seven change leadership roles we recommend. Now that the majority of Phase I has been completed, this task asks you to reassess your choices and roles, and formalize the full governance for your transformation. With the insight you now have about what is required, you can make more informed decisions about who and how to govern your change effort.

Figure 3.1 shows two sample governance structures, one hierarchical and one network structure. Either can work, depending on the needs of your change and

Figure 3.1. Sample Change Governance Structures

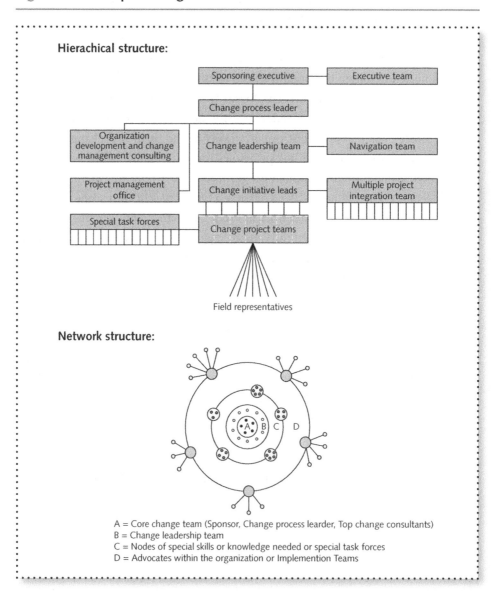

A = Core change team (Sponsor, Change process learder, Top change consultants)
B = Change leadership team
C = Nodes of special skills or knowledge needed or special task forces
D = Advocates within the organization or Implemention Teams

your organization's culture. The hierarchical structure names and organizes both existing teams and functions that will support the change as well as new roles, teams, and functions tailor-made to the change. While the structure may appear bureaucratic on paper, it should be designed to function as nimbly as possible. Make sure you have the right people on the right teams—those who have the expertise, authority, and time to devote to the change.

The network structure is unique and requires skilled oversight to operate effectively. You can name any number of resources to each of the concentric circles and activate them as needed during the change process. We informally call this structure "Dial-a-Team," in honor of transformation being so emergent and dynamic in its needs over time. The right people from each circle would be tasked to work on appropriate change activities and then go back into their normal roles until they are needed again.

Design your change structure to run in parallel with operations and to best meet the needs of your change. Your governance structure will become an integrated part of your overall change infrastructure, which you will complete in Activity I.F.

After you have determined your change leadership roles, make sure that your decision-making roles, style, and process are clear. Clarifying the decision-making style and processes *before* heated issues surface expedites decisions tremendously and prevents change leaders from falling back into habitual or positional behavior patterns that don't support your culture change.

The change leaders may need some education about various decision-making styles, as well as initial facilitation in their use until they master each style. Figure 3.2 shows a continuum of decision-making styles to consider, keeping your desired culture in mind as your leaders select from these options.

The six style options represent a continuum of shared commitment and participation. The more the engagement of stakeholders, the more commitment they will have. (See Premium Content: How to Use Decision Making as a Tool for Successful Transformation, www.pfeiffer.com/go/anderson.)

INDIVIDUAL OWNER

- **Tell:** I make the decision without input.
- **Sell:** I have a position and try to get others to agree before making the decision.
- **Input:** I make the decision after hearing your input.

Figure 3.2. **Decision-Making Continuum of Styles**

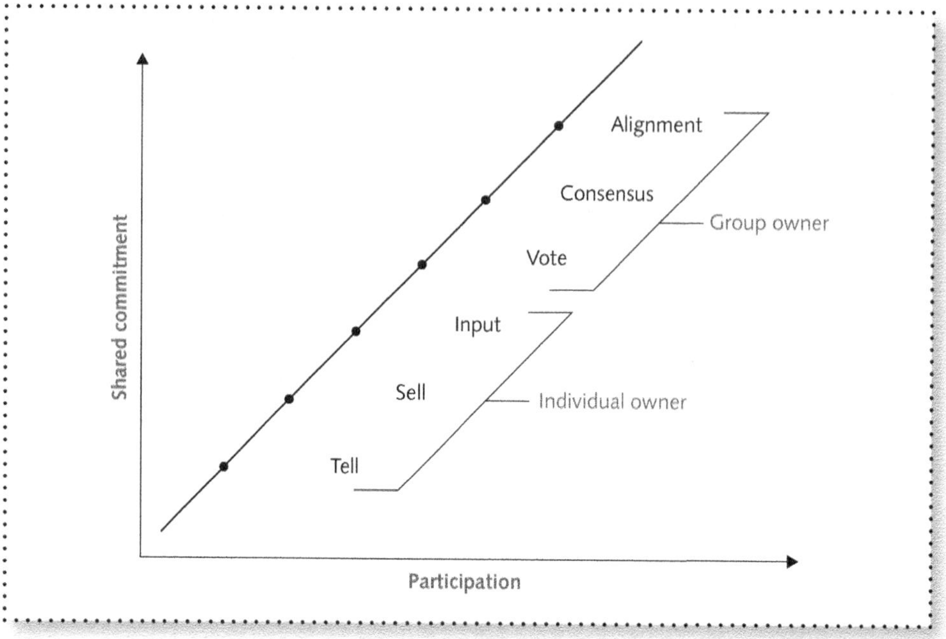

GROUP OWNER

▶ **Vote:** We take a group vote, and a designated percentage wins.

▶ **Consensus:** We all agree about how to proceed, even though some of us think a different decision might be better.

▶ **Alignment:** We all agree this is the very best decision.

Task I.E.4: Determine Required Initiatives and How to Unify Them

There are two parts to this task: identifying your initiatives, and unifying all that you can under one transformational umbrella. Your change strategy must spell out all of the change efforts that are in scope and clarify how all of the initiatives link with and support one another and your overall objectives. A unified effort streamlines the process dynamics of transformation and provides the workforce greater motivation and understanding than would separate or competing initiatives.

Your case for change, drivers of change, initial impact analysis, and leverage points for change should clarify your individual initiatives. If your organization's culture will be impacted by the change, make sure to include it as a legitimate initiative in your scope. When culture is a formal part of your overall change, you must look at how all of the other initiatives within your scope either affect the culture or are affected by a change in it. They, too, must include culture in their scope. When developing your unified theme for the overall change, consider the importance of the new culture as a theme running through all of the initiatives.

To create a unified effort, clarify the highest level outcome—the big picture within which all—or most—of the various content, culture, and people (e.g., mindset and behavior) initiatives fit. For example, you may have a number of individual initiatives occurring in the organization, such as restructuring, reengineering your supply chain, revamping your information technology, and redesigning your HR systems. Why is each of these change initiatives occurring? Perhaps you are attempting to operate over the Web, or are transforming from a national to a global company, or from distinct operating units to one integrated system. Employees must understand your highest level intent. We suggest that you use the rollout of your case for change and initial desired outcomes to tell employees the story of how everything fits together and what you are striving to create. If you have a major culture change underway, proactively drive your story line with the specific ways that your culture must change. Make sure that the theme of culture permeates every initiative you have within scope.

Task I.E.5: Determine Fit and Priority of Change Effort

The purpose of this task is to scan your organization for existing change efforts to assess where this one fits and how important it is in light of everything else that is going on. The leaders may discover that this transformation is more important than much of what is underway and thereby afford it priority status. Certainly, if this is an enterprise-wide effort, it will receive top priority. Leaders can use this clarity to reduce the organization's confusion about so much change by clarifying the position and priority this transformation has among all other efforts. Knowing this helps people put everything in perspective and focus their energy on the outcomes your changes are intending to produce.

In the previous task, you looked at the initiatives within your overall transformation, taking a "down and in" perspective. In this task, you will take an "up and across" view, first looking "up" at other major initiatives that yours may be a part of, and then looking "across" at those that may be running in parallel to yours. Use this information to ensure that your effort gets the attention and resources it rightfully requires, and also to inform your project integration strategy, which is the subject of the next task.

Task I.E.6: Create Multiple Project Integration Strategy

All initiatives, no matter how critical, must work together to support your overarching business strategy and goals for change. Therefore, all initiatives that are in any way interdependent require careful coordination, integration, pacing, and oversight. We frequently call this "Air Traffic Control." You have already done the work to identify the sub-initiatives within your overall effort, and to clarify the other efforts running in parallel or over and above yours. Each of these may require—and benefit from—tailored integration strategies.

This approach is designed to minimize cost, chaos, redundancy of effort, competition for time and resources, and negative political dynamics. It is one of your more powerful ways to demonstrate the importance of your organization's overarching Big Win from change. Your integration strategy can increase speed, action, and resource-sharing across all initiatives. Designing and securing the right level of engagement in lateral integration may require some mindset and culture work among leaders who still operate within a vertical "silo" worldview.

This task creates your strategy and structure for handling project integration. You may need two distinct strategies, one that handles the sub-initiatives within your change effort and one that handles the interdependencies of the up-and-across initiatives. Set up teams to manage the interdependencies and coordinate resources and schedules. Your teams must include the process leaders from your interdependent key initiatives. Each integration team will require a thoughtful launch to ensure that it is set up for success.

Formal team meetings can be used to identify opportunities for coordination and resolve collisions between initiatives. However, many issues requiring integration decisions do not wait for formal meetings to show up. So much is emergent and dynamic that you cannot rely on handling integration issues only at face-to-face meetings. Design your strategy so that the appropriate people can get together or conference to resolve issues when they surface as opposed to waiting for the entire team to meet. When we say "the appropriate people," we are referring to those who have information, expertise, and decision authority to handle the particular issue that has arisen. This requires flexibility and conscious awareness throughout the change effort. It is therefore important to stay on top of integration needs and decisions on a daily basis.

The leaders of a large research laboratory asked us to assist them in creating a change infrastructure to coordinate the thirty-one change initiatives they had going on in their organization. Things had already gotten out of control, with the sponsors of the key initiatives vigorously competing for resources, staff, and attention. We asked the executives to identify the most important initiatives underway in the organization. They selected eight and were able to cluster many of the smaller projects under these eight. We called a meeting of the top two people from each of the eight initiatives to obtain progress reports and address coordination issues. Our invitation was met with little enthusiasm. "We're busy enough! Why do we have to attend yet another meeting?" they queried.

We informed the invitees, with the CEO's blessing, that the meeting was designed to scan all of the initiatives and determine the best allocation of resources and schedules for key change activities. If the change leaders chose not to attend, decisions would be made for them affecting their plans. Of course, they all showed up!

We began the meeting with an overview of goals:

- To inform each change leader about the content and status of all of the projects underway in the organization
- To surface opportunities to cross-reference, fortify, and communicate a cohesive change message to the organization in word and action
- To discover and resolve issues, redundancies, confusions, and competition among the projects

To begin the work, we gave each pair of leaders a different colored pad of stick-on papers on which they were to write the key events in their project plans. They were to post the notes on a blank month-by-month calendar that stretched across one whole wall of the meeting room. When each of the teams had completed the task, everyone stood back and assessed the data. Without a word, everyone could see that the current lack of coordination among the eight initiatives would create immeasurable chaos in the organization over the next few months. Four of the eight project teams were independently planning organization-wide surveys in the month of February. Three of them

(continued)

were planning mandated training in the month of April. Three of them were competing for the same personnel to perform design studies. The impact of all this uncoordinated work would be to make the executive team look completely out of control and out of touch with the realities of the workforce. Nothing more was needed to convince these leaders of the importance of integrating their efforts. They agreed to meet weekly during their early planning phases and then monthly throughout the rest of the transformation. Note how the information they generated produced the right action. The CEO did not have to say a word, and we were granted full permission to design the integration strategy with no further resistance.

Many additional benefits of the multiple project integration strategy were also reaped. The leaders redesigned the reward system that was currently motivating them to compete with each other for their individual projects' success, creating shared rewards. They created a common story among all of the initiatives so the workforce could experience the one integrated transformation they were all serving. They modeled their desired culture of pursuing shared goals and acting as one enterprise, and overtly demonstrated new standards for quality and learning, which were the focus of two of the initiatives.

Major political battles were nipped in the bud because the team members agreed to act on behalf of what served the larger organization. Resources were reallocated to places of highest leverage and greatest need. The leaders felt enormous relief when they realigned the timetable of the various changes to better serve the readiness and capacity of the organization. Most importantly, by making the progress and course corrections of the team public, the change leaders became powerful models of the collaboration, synergy, and effective process management that were core to the organization's new culture.

Task I.E.7: Identify Bold Actions

Change leaders have two start-up challenges: (1) How to get the organization's attention to take the transformation seriously, and (2) how to mobilize the most powerful strategy to accomplish it. Getting a change effort off and running requires the leaders to overcome inertia, especially if their history was fraught with "flavor of the month" leadership. People must recognize that a transformation is underway, that it is real and big, and that significant action is required of them to make it happen.

In this task, the change leaders first determine the best way to get people's attention about the importance of the transformation. This action goes beyond sharing your case for change; it must alert or stun people into realizing that their world is changing in drastic ways. People's mindsets must be changed for them to get the true picture of what you are trying to do. In situations in which the organization has performed well for years and has become complacent about its success, or when leaders have too long ignored the wake-up calls for change, getting the attention of the organization to mobilize for change is a crucial part of change strategy.

To get people's attention, change leaders determine what we call "bold actions." Bold actions are highly visible, "outside the norm" moves that dramatically demonstrate that "things are very different around here" or, as we like to say in the United States, "Toto, we're not in Kansas anymore!" Bold actions are emphatic signals that send unequivocal messages about the new direction, like replacing resistant leaders or closing an obsolete plant. They need to confront the existing culture and people's assumptions about their current reality. They must alert people to a change in culture and ways of operating. Think through what effect you want your bold actions to have on mindset and culture in advance, and design accordingly.

Be sensitive that your bold actions do not negate the past but rather honor it without prolonging it. They must attend to both content and people changes. Consider these examples:

- Divest a major line of business or operations center
- Retire an existing product line
- Hold a funeral for the old way of operating
- Have all executives take a cut in pay to fund the retention of needed staff
- Design and apply rewards to specifically support your transformation
- Remove a complete layer of the organization's hierarchy
- Significantly alter the allocation of resources, for instance, to fund a new venture that symbolizes the future direction

Task I.E.8: Clarify Engagement Strategy

One of the most important design requirements for conscious transformation is wide-scale engagement by the organization in creating its desired future. When you force change on an organization, you generate greater resistance to change than if you engage people in creating it. Change that is heavy-handed triggers feelings in the workforce of being "done to" or taken advantage of. People need some way to influence their new reality, both in the process of how it is created and in the actual new state they are to implement. Engagement accomplishes this, giving people a focus for their energy and a way to make a positive contribution.

Beyond these beneficial outcomes, engagement is required to create a critical mass of commitment to the transformation, which is a key element of your change strategy. A premise of transformation is that, until a critical mass of people break through to the new mindset and behave in new ways, the transformation will never succeed. Engagement helps facilitate the breakthrough in mindset and behavior, as well as gives your people an avenue to contribute their good thinking to the design and implementation of the desired future. In this task, you will clarify how to create critical mass and what kinds of engagement to use to accomplish it.

This task may require some education or discussion about leaders' beliefs about high engagement. The subject of participation has been in the management literature for a long time. Yet many leaders are still uncomfortable or unfamiliar with how to determine and customize an engagement strategy. Many still fear it, falsely believing that if they ask for input, they must act on everything their people request or further resistance will result.

Leaders must better understand the direct relationship between influence and commitment. Generally speaking, the higher the influence people have, the higher their commitment to the change. Change education (Activity I.D) can address these perceptions and insights.

Different types of engagement have different degrees of influence. If people are invited only to stick their toe into the transformational water, they will have a toe-level experience of influence and commitment. If they are invited to dive in head first, they will be immersed in the transformational experience. There is a range of engagement strategies, each with a different amount of influence. Any of them can be used effectively as long as the leaders make the boundaries clear before requesting input. Figure 3.3 depicts a range of six types of engagement and the degree of influence each has.

Tailor your engagement plans to the different tasks in the CLR. For instance, you can use engagement to identify design requirements, create future state scenarios, or perform your impact analysis. When determining your engagement strategies for each task, consider the ideal level of participation, whom to ask for input, and how to engage. Also, think about obtaining input from sources outside of the organization, such

Figure 3.3. Types of Engagement

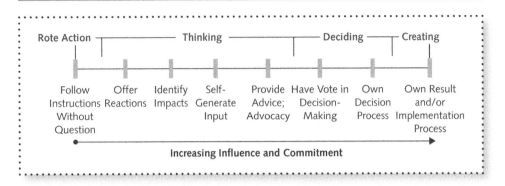

Table 3.1. Range of Audiences and Engagement Vehicles

Audience	Vehicles for Engagement
Individuals	Face-to-face, written, electronic or Web-based
Intact functional or business process groups	Focus groups, task forces with mandated or voluntary membership; blogs
Organization-wide, cross-functional, or cross-process large groups	World Café, Future Search Model, Conference Model, Real Time Strategic Change Model, Open Space, focus groups with selected or voluntary membership; blogs or Web-based discussion boards; social media vehicles
System-wide networks or communication vehicles	Ambassadors, representatives, advocates, change agents, advisory councils, newsletter with a response form, blogs or Web-based discussion boards; social media vehicles, World Café

as customers, suppliers, or government officials. Consider using a high-participation strategy as a bold action, such as large group visioning or design conferences, blogs or Web-based social media, a World Café gathering, or an Appreciative Inquiry conference to identify compelling recommendations for the future.

Table 3.1 offers a range of audiences to consider for inviting input as well as types of engagement vehicles. Use this list to trigger your discussion.

Task I.E.9: Design Overall Communication Plan

Communication is the life force of the organization, especially in times of change. In these early days of your change effort, as soon as people catch wind that a change is coming, their needs for information and attention escalate significantly. They want to know what will happen to them and whether their job is secure. In the worst cases, leaders, enmeshed in figuring out what has to be changed, keep people in the dark or only inform them when decisions are finally made, without giving people any opportunity for input, influence, or response—just when people's need for these is the greatest. Change often causes people to react emotionally, especially when it is first communicated. People's reactions, no matter what they are, must be considered when designing how to communicate your change.

One of the most common mistakes leaders make is to assume that when their corporate communications department has sent out the announcement, they can check the box of communication. Not so! Informing people about the change is only the first step in true communication and is a long way from checking the box. Even if the change leaders give an initial face-to-face briefing, the stress of the announcement can severely limit people's ability to retain and understand the information the leaders have communicated. People need to be able to ask questions, discuss the information they think they heard with their trusted peers, think about how it impacts them, and then react and be heard. If they don't have this opportunity, their anxiety grows. A memo or a briefing may inform them, but it is sorely inadequate to engage or enroll them. How are leaders going to address these very real human dynamics?

Leaders must attend to these dynamics by consciously designing a competent change communication plan and by developing understanding and skill in how best to communicate with people during change. This goes far beyond their initial announcement. (See Premium Content: Six Faulty Assumptions about Change Communications, www.pfeiffer.com/go/anderson.)

Exhibit 3.1 shows a matrix of the Five Levels of Communication, all of which are required to accomplish competent communications during change. Applying this model has profound impact on communication planning. The model begins where most people end their communication efforts—sharing information. It goes on to four subsequent levels in the communication process: building understanding, identifying implications, gaining commitment, and altering behavior. All five levels denote that change communications is a process of engagement, not an event.

Note the reliance on engagement vehicles as the preferred way to achieve each level of communication. This is a key reason to have the people most knowledgeable about engagement be the ones to co-design your change communication plan. Your communication plan should be developed in close partnership with your

Exhibit 3.1. Five Levels of Communication

Level and Outcome	Style	Media, Vehicles	Reaction when Achieved
1. Information-Sharing	Telling; one way	Lecture, presentation, memo, video	"Thank you for telling me this information."
2. Building Understanding	Dialogue; two-way; exploring and answering listener-generated questions	Small group meeting; breakouts to develop questions; facilitated Q&A; blogs	"Having explored my concerns and tested this, now I understand the focus of the change and why it is needed."
3. Identifying Implications	Introspection; discussing with co-workers what this means to you and the organization; multi-directional	Group interactive discussions ranging from multi-level, large or small groups to individual team discussions; most relevant exploration done with work team and immediate supervisor; open Web-based discussion boards	"I get it! This change means X for my department and Z for me and my job."
4. Gaining Commitment	Sorting out inner feelings and choices; may require time and multiple returns to the discussion; both internal and external commitment focused	Alone time for personal introspection or "talk time" with trusted colleagues, opportunity to re-address issues with co-workers, direct supervisor and/or sponsor of the change	"I personally want this change to succeed, and I am willing to ensure that it does. I see that my boss and our organizational leaders feel the same way."
5. Altering Behavior	Demonstrating new behavior; may require training, feedback mechanisms, and coaching over time to ensure that the behaviors stick	Training, coaching relationships; opportunities for practice and learning	"I am learning the new behaviors and skills required for this change to succeed, and I'm open to receiving your feedback and coaching to keep improving."

engagement strategy because the goals of each are interdependent. More and more, the partnership between engagement and communications is being recognized as critical, so much so that some organizations have created a new function responsible for both—the Internal Communications and Engagement department.

Each of the five levels of communication describes its own outcome. The culmination of all five outcomes defines excellent communication—behavior change or behavior reinforcement. In scanning the model, notice that each level requires a different style and medium to achieve its outcome. You may need only some of the levels of communication at any point in time. Again, your knowledge of all of the levels will assist you in choosing how and when to use them and their strategies. Keep in mind that if you want true commitment and behavioral change, you must use strategies that produce both. Information-sharing strategies will not produce behavior change.

This task builds your communication plan and your kickoff communication strategy. It also clarifies the best communication role for your change leaders. Your leaders must be visible spokespeople, prepare messages, make presentations, and respond to employee feedback and input. They need to quell rumors, overtly model the new mindset and behavior, and be candid about their personal experiences and challenges in making the transformation successful. The authenticity of communication, its timeliness, and leader credibility go hand-in-hand at this stage. When change is in the air, employees tend to be extra sensitive to tone, candor, and concern.

Once designed, support your communication plan with the appropriate resources, meeting planning, facilitators, logistics, and follow-up.

Planning Your Kickoff Communication

The second requirement of this task is planning how you will communicate the initiation of the transformation. Your kickoff communication may include any of the following content:

- Who is leading the change and in what capacity; who the sponsors are
- Your case for change, including the story of all seven drivers of the change
- Your overall change strategy, summarized for general consumption
- Scope of the change and why it is transformational, including the mindset and cultural imperatives for change
- Conditions for success
- Expectations for people's engagement and commitment
- Other decisions to be made in the remaining Phase I tasks, such as temporary policies and technology; the organization-wide visioning plan; resources; measurements; and rewards

It is very important that the style and tone of your kickoff communication be carefully planned. This communication will be the first time the change leaders will be "officially" communicating with the stakeholders of the change, and the impression the leaders make here will affect your entire start-up. Keep in mind that in change communications, one size does not fit all. Tailor your communication plan to the needs of various stakeholder groups whom you need to enroll in the change. We will have more to say about this when we discuss Phase II, when the plan is carried out.

Task I.E.10: Determine Change Acceleration Strategies

The speed of change is an important factor in most major change efforts. Faster is typically assumed to be better, as long as you still achieve a quality outcome. Your change strategy needs to address how you will accelerate the achievement of your change results.

When considering your options, it is important to be aware of the change leaders' mindsets about what speeds up or slows down change. In these economic times, leaders are making plans for change with great urgency, attempting to press the pace by cutting corners, skipping steps, or just demanding longer hours and more output from their people. While these strategies may initially make it look like the change is happening more quickly, they risk creating serious burnout, resentment, or poor quality, and actually slowing down the change in the long run.

This task is a great opportunity for change leaders to change their mindsets and approaches to speed up change. There are far more creative, energizing, and sustainable ways to accomplish change more quickly. The more you set up conditions for success, the more likelihood you create for that to happen. The more you build in the strategies that produce breakthrough results, the better and faster your change will go. Consider using large group meetings as acceleration strategies for any of the activities in the CLR. While they take time to plan, they can engage and enroll large numbers of people in co-creating the change. Put simply, the more upfront work you do to set up your change effort for success, the faster it will go. "You can pay me now, or you can pay me later!" The more you engage your stakeholders in creating their desired future, the more they will commit to make it happen. Chapter Fourteen includes a discussion of change acceleration strategies that is worth reviewing as you consider this task.

Task I.E.11: Secure Commitment for Resources

Key questions leaders ask before committing to making a change include "How much will this cost us?" and "Will it be worth it?" These are fair questions. We make the assumption in this task that the leaders are already committed to making this change, given their investment in building their case for change and progressing through the appropriate tasks in Phase I up to this point. Until now, resource questions were a bit premature because not enough information was available about the change effort's true demands. Now leaders can make fairly sound estimates about resource requirements.

In these challenging times, leaders want to accomplish the most they can with the least resources. However, candidly, they need to assess whether the resources they do allocate will generate the results they seek. If this is your situation, create a dialogue with your change leaders concerning their assumptions about resources and what the change requires. The leaders will need to commit to securing an *adequate* resource base for the transformation if they truly want it to succeed. They may have to confront their tendency to have greater expectations for the end result and its speed than their resource allocation will support. Initiate a frank, "get real" conversation about this.

As noted in Task I.C.1, when you address capacity issues, you also address resources. Be sure that you discuss the whole picture with the leaders—resources needed for both change and operations. Even at this point in your change, the leaders will not have accurate numbers about how many resources the effort will require. If your change is transformational, they will never have guaranteed numbers given how unpredictable and emergent the process is. However, they will have to make realistic guesses about the resources they do require to make a go/no go decision, and they must commit to providing *sufficient* resources through the entire life cycle of the change. Allocating ample resources is a telltale sign to the organization that the effort is a true priority, rather than just being given lip service.

Another surprise for many leaders is the variety of resources that must be provided. The typical assumption is that they need only money and people. They may also need space, technology, training, consulting support, Web support, and so on. Make sure to cover your bases.

Change consultants may need to coach change leaders to keep their commitment for providing sufficient resources throughout the entire change process and to be creative in generating additional resources as necessary. Keep your change leaders conscious of the real implications that their resource decisions have on people's ability to deliver what the organization needs within the expected timetable.

Task I.E.12: Identify Milestones and Timeline, and Compile Change Strategy

In this task, you will complete the two remaining change strategy elements—milestone events and general timeline—and compile all of your I.E work into your integrated change strategy. The change strategy is the culmination of the leaders' assumptions and decisions from Phase I for how they would *like* the organization's transformation to unfold. Exhibit 3.2 shows a template of the key elements of change strategy, including a list of the critical inputs from your early Phase I work. Use it as a worksheet for your own change strategy.

Your proposed milestone events of Phases II through IX allows the change leaders to make an *informed guess* about the general timeline for the transformation, which is a key element of change strategy. This estimated timeline cannot be used as a rigid measure of the transformation because it will undoubtedly have to be altered.

Exhibit 3.3 shows some brief highlights of a change strategy from an organization preparing itself for e-commerce through the realignment of its product groupings, the upgrade of its IT systems, and expansion of its ability to cross-sell products among its dispersed business units.

After the change leaders have compiled their change strategy, they must support it with conditions and infrastructures required to execute it successfully. This work takes place next, in Activity I.F, and completes the leaders' Phase I work. Some of the I.F support work will influence their strategy and how they will communicate and use it. Complete this work before finalizing how best to communicate your strategy to the organization.

Ideally, the change strategy is communicated at the same time as your case for change in your Phase II launch. This tells people the complete picture of why you must change, what will be changing, and how you will lead the change. However, the change leaders may decide that they want to communicate the case for change to enroll people in the need for change long before they have completed their change strategy, which also works. Do not proceed with your actual communication until you review the tasks of Activity I.F and determine which of them will help you launch your change in the most positive way.

The leaders began planning their kickoff communication strategy in Task I.E.9. Now, with more information known, they can fine-tune their communication plan and roll it out to begin Phase II of their change process.

Exhibit 3.2. Template for Building Your Change Strategy

INPUTS FROM PHASE I

- Case for change, including the following:
  - Drivers of change
  - Type of change
  - Leverage points for transformation
  - Target groups
  - Scope of the change
  - Degree of urgency
- Initial desired outcomes for the transformation
- Project community
- Organizational readiness assessment results
- Change capacity assessment
- Change capability assessment
- Conditions for success

ELEMENTS OF CHANGE STRATEGY

- Values and guiding principles
- Change governance: Roles, structure, decision making, and interface with ongoing operations
- Initiatives and how to unify them
- Fit and priority of this effort
- Multiple project integration strategy
- Bold actions
- Engagement strategy
- Change communication plan
- Acceleration strategies
- Resources
- Milestone events and general timeline

Exhibit 3.3. **Highlights of a Sample Change Strategy**

This case example illustrates some highlights of a change strategy from an organization preparing itself for e-commerce through the realignment of its product groupings, the upgrade of its information management systems, and the expansion of its ability to cross-sell products between its dispersed companies.

OVERALL OUTCOME

To become a preeminent e-business that sells customized families of XYZ products.

Values and Guiding Principles

- Immediate quality service
- Listening to our customers and understanding their needs
- Integrity and the highest of ethics
- Partnership in every cross-boundary relationship
- Continuous learning and rapid course correction of the change process
- Team atmosphere (all in this together, and everyone is needed)

Governance

- Senior executive change sponsor
- All business unit presidents on change leadership team
- World-wide change process leader skilled in IT, process design, and people's needs
- All business units appoint top-level change process leaders, linked to world-wide change process leader
- Multiple Project Integration Team of all initiative leaders
- Senior-level change consultants, with consulting support staff in every business unit, addressing content, people issues, and change plans; all coordinated through the corporate change process leader
- Open-door network of change advocates for design, impact analysis, and implementation planning
- World-wide, interactive communication and engagement infrastructure

Change Initiatives—All Top Priority

- Incorporate e-commerce strategies into every business.
- Consolidate interdependent products and services.
- Upgrade world-wide IT product and sales systems to enable cross-selling.
- Reposition brand in the marketplace as a one-stop shop.
- Reorganize customer point of contact for ease and expansion of sales.
- Replace all of Europe's IT systems.

(continued)

Exhibit 3.3.   Highlights of a Sample Change Strategy (continued)

- Hold executive level breakthrough training process for top 2,000 leaders to address obsolete mindset, leadership style, behavior, and working relationships.
- Create culture change to embed co-creative practices for all cross-boundary relationships and support.

Bold Actions

- Conduct large group employee meetings (100–1,000 people) in every market world-wide to generate input to the case for change and vision.
- Realign executive incentive program to motivate e-commerce support and lavishly reward cross-company collaboration and sales.
- Create new positions in every business unit: Product Super Stars responsible for training, co-creating integrated sales solutions, team liaison to all other Super Stars.
- Create a high-powered video that dramatizes the vision of world-wide inter-company selling over the Internet.
- Retire Product X.

Engagement and Communication Strategies

- Global change leadership intranet site
- Large group employee meetings, starting in sales
- Executive road trip to communicate and ask for input/questions
- World-wide e-conference to accomplish IT design concept; rolling World Café conferences
- Cross-company task forces to represent and share sales strategies
- International best practices study tour
- Change advocates identified from every product and service line
- Customer Advisory Council

Acceleration Strategies

- Create capacity for making this change for key change leaders.
- Visibly reward rapid course corrections.
- Use Leadership Breakthrough process to catalyze new vision and commitments.
- Conduct large group employee meetings (100–1,000 people) in every market world-wide to generate input to case for change and vision.
- Realign executive incentive program.
- Provide adequate resources from the beginning.

(continued)

Milestone Events

- **January, Year 1:** Launch with interactive video; large group meetings world-wide
- **January–March, Year 1:** Team-based communications about case for change, vision, and change strategy world-wide; initiate rollout of Leadership Breakthrough process; executive road trip; perform benchmark research
- **March–June, Year 1:** IT compatibility assessment; change readiness assessment in every business unit; cross-product sales education process
- **September, Year 1:** Retire Product X; initiate design process
- **January, Year 2:** Turnkey date for Europe's new information management systems; world-wide impact analysis
- **February, Year 2:** Develop implementation master plan for pilot test in Asia
- **March, Year 2:** Pilot inter-company electronic selling in Asia with Products A, B, and C; begin new public branding promotion
- **September, Year 2:** Evaluate pilot and integrate learnings into IT and sales structure design and organization-wide implementation plans
- **December, Year 2:** World-wide promotion of e-commerce availability and benefits
- **January, Year 3:** World-wide rollout

Timeline

- **Year 1:** Assessment and design
- **Year 2:** Pilot, design refinement, and begin implementation; rebranding effort
- **Years 2/3/4:** Marketing of the e-commerce brand and rollout of the new business model

SUMMARY

The development of your change strategy is the leaders' primary deliverable from Phase I. Leaders will complete their preparations for setting up the change for success in Activity I.F. At this point in the process, you should have clear leadership roles and working relationships, a compelling case for change, initial desired outcomes, an accurate scope of initiatives, and an integrated change strategy for navigating the transformation. Ideally, all of this is led by your change process leader.

Phase I represents a sizable and significant investment of time and attention. Often work begins in all six activities of Phase I concurrently, so the more familiar you are with them all, the better able you will be to accelerate and coordinate your start-up decisions and streamline the work required. How much can be accomplished quickly depends on the resources, time, and conditions that your leaders allot to setting up the change to be successful. A key part of doing this is attending to the many decisions that enable the organization to carry out the transformation effectively. The next chapter helps leaders identify and build the organizational infrastructure and conditions to support their change effort.

CONSULTING QUESTIONS FOR ACTIVITY I.E: CLARIFY OVERALL CHANGE STRATEGY

Task I.E.1: Design Process for Building Change Strategy

▶ Do the change leaders fully understand the importance of building a change strategy and using it to drive the change?

▶ How will you develop your change strategy? Will the change process leader guide this work? Who else will be involved and in what elements?

▶ What elements will you include in your change strategy, and how will you format it?

Task I.E.2: Define Values and Guiding Principles

▶ Does your organization have existing values and cultural principles that you can use to drive this change?

▶ What values and guiding principles will you use to shape how you lead the change?

▶ How can you use your leadership of the change to drive your desired culture?

Task I.E.3: Clarify Governance and Decision-Making

▶ What roles do you need to lead this change? Who will fill them?

▶ How will you organize all of the people leading or supporting the change so that they understand who is responsible for what and how to work together?

▶ What decision-making roles need to be specified? What style and process of decision making will you use to make good change decisions and further reinforce your desired culture?

- How will you ensure that those leading the change will work well with those running the ongoing business? How will you deal with predictable pinch points between the change and operations?

Task I.E.4: Determine Required Initiatives and How to Unify Them

- Does your roster of initiatives include both organization/technical efforts and human/cultural changes?
- If culture change is a major part of your overall effort, is culture identified as a legitimate initiative within your scope? Is it legitimately represented in the scope of each other content initiative?
- Is the transformation currently designed as one unified effort or as a collection of separate initiatives?
- How can the "the change" best be described? What is the best strategy for integrating all of these change efforts into one change? Can you use your culture changes to unify the overall transformation?

Task I.E.5: Determine Fit and Priority of Change Effort

- What other change efforts or major events are currently underway in the organization that may have an impact on your change effort?
- Where does this effort fit among all of the organization's change initiatives? What is its level of priority?
- Do any of the other change efforts fit within this transformation? Can you reposition them?
- Given the organization's capacity and readiness level for making more change, is your initiative positioned to get the resources and support it needs?

Task I.E.6: Create Multiple Project Integration Strategy

- How will you determine the interdependent or relevant initiatives within your overall effort that need an integration strategy?
- How will you structure your integration strategy and process? Who will participate?

- Will you need more than one integration team and process?

- How will you handle emergent integration issues that show up and cannot wait for a team meeting?

- What level of authority will the leaders give to the members of the Integration Team so that they can expedite course corrections and rapid action on the change?

Task I.E.7: Identify Bold Actions

- How will you determine bold actions for making this transformation happen in the organization, for both the content changes and people changes?

- What bold actions will be used to wake up the organization to the necessity for this transformation?

- What bold actions are needed to communicate that the old way of operating is now an honored part of the past?

- How can you use bold actions to affect your desired changes in mindset and culture?

Task I.E.8: Clarify Engagement Strategy

- What are the current norms about using stakeholder engagement in the organization?

- What key tasks in your change process are prime opportunities for stakeholder engagement? Which stakeholder groups will you engage in them, and how?

- How can you use engagement to gain a critical mass of commitment for the transformation?

- Who will oversee your engagement strategies?

- How will you integrate your engagement strategies with your change communication plan? Who will oversee this work?

Task I.E.9: Design Overall Communication Plan

- Who will lead the development of your change communication strategy? How can you use your corporate communications staff to help?

- What roles will the change leaders play in communications during the transformation?

- How will you ensure that your communications reflect and fulfill all five levels of communication?

- How will you ensure your kickoff communication plan enrolls your stakeholders, engages them optimally, and responds to their questions and needs?

- Do any rumors need to be dispelled? How will you handle informal communication dynamics like the rumor mill?

Task I.E.10: Determine Change Acceleration Strategies

- How will you set up your change effort to ensure optimal speed without cutting risky corners?

- How will you use your change capacity assessment data to inform your acceleration strategies?

Task I.E.11: Secure Commitment for Resources

- What types of resources will your change effort need?

- Without having detailed estimates for resources at this time, how can you ensure executive commitment to *adequate* resources throughout the entire change effort?

- If sufficient resources are not available, what will you do to address this issue with the change leaders?

- How will you align the change leaders' expectations for the transformation with the actual resources they provide to support it?

Task I.E.12: Identify Milestones and Timeline, and Compile Change Strategy

- How will you identify critical milestones for your entire change process?

- Who will be a part of this determination?

- How will you graphically portray critical milestones so that the organization understands the process it is now engaged in?

- How will you establish the general timeline for your transformation? On what data will you base it?

- How will you ensure that the leaders understand that this timeline is an educated guess that will be adjusted later in the change process when more information relevant to the timeline is known?

- How will you use your change capacity assessment data to inform your pace of change?

- How will you summarize your change strategy so that you can effectively communicate it to the organization?

CHAPTER

4

PHASE I
Prepare to Lead the Change: Build the Infrastructure and Conditions to Support Your Change Effort

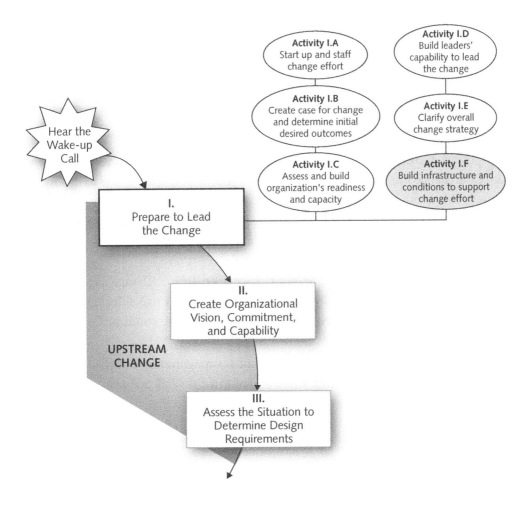

Hear the Wake-up Call

Activity I.A
Start up and staff change effort

Activity I.B
Create case for change and determine initial desired outcomes

Activity I.C
Assess and build organization's readiness and capacity

Activity I.D
Build leaders' capability to lead the change

Activity I.E
Clarify overall change strategy

Activity I.F
Build infrastructure and conditions to support change effort

I.
Prepare to Lead the Change

II.
Create Organizational Vision, Commitment, and Capability

III.
Assess the Situation to Determine Design Requirements

UPSTREAM CHANGE

ACTIVITY I.F: TASK DELIVERABLES

I.F.1: The political dynamics within the change effort and among the change leaders have been identified, and strategies for dealing with them have been established.

I.F.2: Conditions for success have been identified, committed to, and initiated.

I.F.3: Your strategy to create shared vision in the organization has been developed.

I.F.4: Formal strategies for generating and using new information have been developed. Mechanisms for managing and tracking existing information have been created.

I.F.5: A course correction strategy and system have been designed to ensure that the change process remains on the best possible track.

I.F.6: Current change plans have been assessed for their likely impact on people, and a strategy to address people's reactions to these impacts has been developed.

I.F7: Temporary change support structures, systems, policies, and technologies have been designed and initiated.

I.F.8: Measurements for the change process and outcome have been determined, and the strategy for how these measurements will be obtained and used is clear.

I.F.9: Temporary rewards for supporting the change process have been designed and are aligned with the organization's existing rewards.

I.F.10: The Phase II through V roadmap has been determined.

Now that you have developed your change strategy, it is time to complete the change infrastructure that will support its implementation. You have built some key elements of your change infrastructure in the prior activities in Phase I, and the majority of them are created in this activity. We will reference each as we go.

There are four main components of a change infrastructure:

▶ **Change Leadership Roles:** Sponsor, Executive Team, Change Leadership Team, Change Process Leader, Initiative Lead, Change Project Team, Change Consultant. You determined these in Task I.A.2 and confirmed them in Task I.E.3.

▶ **Governance Structure:** All change roles and teams with clearly defined authority, decision making, meeting rhythms, information management, initiative integration, and interfaces with each other and the ongoing business. You designed this in Task I.E.3.

- **Conditions for Success:** Factors or states that must be in place and sustained to ensure the success of your change from the beginning. You will generate and establish these in this activity.
- **Support Mechanisms:** Ways to facilitate and enable your change process. You will generate these in this activity.

Transformation requires both a strong infrastructure and consciously created conditions that support its start-up and ongoing process. This activity discusses ten key support mechanisms that, like spokes of a wheel, are essential to the smooth rollout of the transformation. If one or more spokes are weak or missing, the wheel will not turn smoothly, or for very long, before shattering under the weight of the transformational "load."

The spokes are the tasks in this activity. They address specific vehicles to make both the change process and the people dynamics go more smoothly and effectively. Each task is included because it has been shown to have a significant impact on the success of change. If addressed well, the tasks collectively add viability, speed, and energy for the entire transformational journey. They also provide a tangible opportunity to design your change effort in ways that model its intended mindset, culture, and outcomes.

The needs of the transformation and the state of your organization will help you determine which of the ten tasks are critical to your particular effort. Remember, the CLR is intended to be a thinking discipline, not a mandatory checklist. You will not need to attend to every task, at least not with the same level of thoroughness. Consider them all before determining which you will address and which you can afford to skip or touch on superficially. Time, resources, and a quick assessment of each task's costs and benefits should be considered in your decisions at the outset of every change you lead.

It is important to continuously monitor and adjust the elements of your infrastructure to ensure that it serves the needs of your change effort as things unfold. Be careful not to over-bureaucratize your infrastructure. It should make the effort easier, not be a burden. In Phase IX, you will dismantle the temporary aspects of your infrastructure that no longer serve your change or your ongoing operation.

ACTIVITY I.F: BUILD INFRASTRUCTURE AND CONDITIONS TO SUPPORT CHANGE EFFORT

Task I.F.1: Initiate Strategies for Dealing with Political Dynamics

Some of the most powerful forces occurring in change are the political dynamics created by the introduction of a new direction. People naturally want things to go their own way, to be viewed as "winners" in the change, and therefore act to benefit their own interests. However, political maneuvering is rarely focused on what is good for the larger organization. Long before a major change is announced, personally motivated political behavior escalates. Individuals and factions exert influence over others for their own agendas. Uncertainty, risk, and opportunity for power suddenly increase, especially when decision making and authority may not be clear. In some cases, both covert and explicit power dynamics mushroom, leading to chaos, competition, and even malicious behavior. All of this reflects an unconscious mindset.

Political behavior is far more obvious than its perpetrators would like to believe. Most people assume their efforts to influence others are invisible, with most political maneuvering occurring behind closed doors. Yet in reality, people see it clearly, discuss it actively, and can even predict it. As long as people collude with the unconscious norm of never discussing negative political realities overtly with the players involved, they allow its consequences to run rampant, which does not support the organization or the transformation to be led in a conscious way.

Depending on the organization's culture and the breadth of the transformation, politics can have a damaging effect on your success. It is our bias that political dynamics be addressed and dealt with openly, *consciously*. Unless they are worked out through open dialogue, they can derail even the best of changes. As uncomfortable as it may be to unravel political behavior, leaders need to deal with their own power struggles and the negative impact they have on the transformation, the project community, and across the organization. Therefore, staying on top of the political terrain is critical to shaping a sound and conscious change strategy.

It is essential to create a positive climate within the change leadership team for addressing difficult political realities. The relationship, team, and personal development work initiated in Activity I.D is invaluable in supporting the constructive resolution of potentially damaging politics and for preventing further political disruptions. In particular, building commitment and alignment to the larger business outcomes of the transformation and creating a solid case for change and shared vision help immensely. Much of this work can also be initiated and supported through the Leadership Breakthrough process because it creates a safe space for historical issues to be named and healed, and for consciously preventing future political dynamics from occurring.

This task ensures that you create specific ground rules for how to deal with negative political behavior when it arises, which it will. At this early stage of the change process, it is helpful to scan existing political dynamics to identify the patterns currently at play, assess their impact on the transformation, and then devise positive strategies for how to deal with them.

Another powerful influence strategy is to create a "critical mass of support" for the change by identifying top executives, special experts, opinion leaders, important customers, and grass-roots representatives throughout the organization and mobilizing their advocacy for the new direction. Project community members can serve as the basis for your critical mass network. They can be tasked with influencing others, including resisters and "fence-sitters," to back the effort and spread the word. Eventually, when enough people support the transformation, the point of critical mass will actually be attained, and the change will take on a life of its own. When this occurs, leaders can guide the process toward their desired outcomes and let go of any notion of forcing it through political manipulation.

Task I.F.2: Create Conditions for Success

It is safe to assume that all change leaders *want* their transformations to be successful. However, to increase the probability of success, they must establish practices, circumstances, and resources that will enable it to flourish. This task identifies the factors and conditions that change leaders believe are required for their particular transformations to succeed. We call these factors *conditions for success.*

Conditions for success are requirements essential to the achievement of your desired outcomes from a content, people, and process standpoint. Examples include adequate resources, sufficient time to do a quality job, or communications and engagement that both inform and enroll stakeholders. Conditions for success may also refer to particular states of being that enable the transformation to occur more smoothly, such as the leaders taking a conscious approach, the executives staying fully aligned, and people realizing that their needs are actually being considered as the transformation is planned and implemented.

Conditions for success can also support the personal transformation work required by the change, such as creating a safe environment for truth-telling, supporting personal breakthrough, and encouraging cross-boundary conflict resolution, communication, and collaboration.

Imagine your conditions for success as gas pedals for accelerating your change. They set the stage for an expedient journey and a positive outcome from the beginning. Once agreed to, they influence leadership, management, and employee behavior to support the entire transformational process. An added advantage is to use them periodically as a template to measure how the transformation is going and whether the change leaders are walking their talk. This review can trigger immediate course corrections when the conditions are not being lived up to. Conditions for success are also great inputs to Task I.F.8, *Determine Measurements of Change*.

To generate your conditions, each change leader should reflect on their own experience and the situation they face, and identify their unique list. Then collectively, they must determine the specific conditions they will create as a team and commit to support. They must agree on how to establish each condition in the organization, identify who will oversee and monitor them (likely the change process leader), and determine how the conditions will be used to have the greatest impact on the transformational experience. It is important that your conditions be supported by leadership. Generating a list and only giving it "lip service" will damage the change leaders' credibility and hinder your success.

The following sidebar provides a sample list of conditions for success. Notice that the statements are written in the present tense. This is intentional, to model the conscious transformational principle, "Lead as if the future is now." We have found that doing this with conditions for success, as well as with vision statements, helps people experience the future they want to create as an existing reality, thereby accelerating its actual creation.

Task I.F.3: Identify Process for Creating Shared Vision

This task is based on two assumptions we make about leading change: (1) Transformation has more vitality and meaning when it is inspired by a compelling future state—a vision—that mobilizes action throughout the organization, and (2) the vision for the change is most powerful when co-created by a large number of stakeholders rather than handed down by executives. When people participate in

- Total organization (management and workforce) shares a common vision for the desired outcome.
- Leadership presents a unified front in support of producing breakthrough results.
- A learning-oriented, feedback-seeking climate is encouraged.
- A collaborative relationship exists between those who run the ongoing business and those who are changing it.
- Sufficient time and resources are allocated to the change effort.
- The reward system directly reinforces support for the change process and the desired state.
- People impacted by the change have timely input to the design, impact analysis, and course corrections affecting them.
- Communication is frequent, accurate, and candid.
- Leaders consistently and visibly support efforts to achieve the future state. They are models of the mindset and behavioral changes required by our new culture.
- Mindset and behavior change are supported and expected from all stakeholders in the transformation.

the formation of a shared vision—something they choose—they are far more likely to achieve it. This is especially true if you are changing the organization's culture. Because culture change requires mindset change, when people engage in reshaping how they want to work in and lead the organization, they accelerate the shift in their mindsets exponentially. Now, we must also say that we have seen examples where a vision, created only by the top leaders or executive team, produced sufficient energy and motivation to catalyze an organization-wide transformation. These particular leaders were well-respected and charismatic in their own right. While either strategy can work, we prefer a collective visioning strategy because we believe it has a higher probability of building shared commitment, responsibility for success, and breakthrough results.

This task reflects our assumptions. It is one of the most important for addressing all quadrants, all levels, and the process in the Conscious Change Leader

Accountability Model. The change leaders may have already explored their own requirements for a new business or cultural future in Task I.B.8. They can use that input in the process they design for creating a shared vision for the overall organization, its culture, and/or the transformation itself. They may choose to develop the vision themselves and then devise a compelling rollout strategy, or they can create a more engaging approach. If you are changing the organization's culture, strive to make the design of your visioning process an obvious reflection of the culture you want to create. You will then carry out the visioning strategy in Phase II in sync with the leaders communicating to the organization the case for change and change strategy.

Designing an engaging visioning process is an important exercise for leaders. It tests their commitment to employee involvement, their change leadership style, and their process design skills. There are many options for creating shared vision. The process chosen by the change leaders will be a function of their mindset, style, and comfort zone. Conscious change leadership teams typically decide to involve all or a significant part of their project community stakeholders in the visioning process. Options for high-engagement visioning processes include the following:

- A cross-organizational visioning committee of stakeholder representatives that produces the vision statement
- An iterative cascade of a draft of the vision, inviting input and improvement
- The tailoring of the vision for and by each segment of the organization
- Large group visioning sessions during which participants collectively work on different aspects of the vision in unison, and then put it all together into a future that excites them all

Some organizations use large group meeting approaches such as World Café (Brown and Isaacs, 2005) Future Search (Weisbord and Janoff, 1995), Real Time Strategic Change (Jacobs, 1994), Visioning Conferences (Axelrod, 1992), or Appreciative Inquiry Design Conferences (Watkins and Mohr, 2001). These innovative processes are well worth the effort because this type of engagement can save months, if not years, of implementation time after people are on board with the change. They are powerful strategies for generating a critical mass of commitment to the outcome of the transformation because they engage people's internal realities and motivation. Ideally, the visioning process leaves people chomping at the bit for making the transformation they envision a reality.

Task I.F.4: Design Information Generation and Management Strategies

Transformational change is emergent, dynamic, and complex. Therefore, staying on top of information that informs you both about your potential future state and what is happening in the process is absolutely critical. There are two essential requirements concerning information in change. The first is the generation of *new* information needed to shape the creation of your desired outcomes and the best process to achieve it. The second is the effective management of *existing* project information throughout the full lifecycle of the effort. This task addresses these two needs and ensures that change leaders are clear about their requirements and methods for doing both.

Information Generation

Information generation is critical to conscious change leadership. You must constantly pursue new information about what is needed for your transformation process to succeed, and use it to guide continuous adjustments to where you are going and how to get there. The challenge is to sort out what information is actually relevant. This is the purpose of having an information generation strategy, or at least awareness to treat new data with conscious intention.

What is new information and information generation? Old information is what you already know. New information is what you are currently discovering or learning—outside-the-box—that has the potential to alter your understanding or perception of reality, or, in this case, the outcomes or process of your transformation. Information generation is proactively seeking new information to help drive decisions about the change, which might come from any of the four quadrants, levels, or processes from the Conscious Change Leader Accountability Model.

You never know where and when new information will surface. Being open to new information enabled 3M's discovery of its wildly successful Post-it™ Notes. Google's discovery of the potential of social networking launched exponential growth.

Although uncovering new information may prove disruptive or disconcerting to some leaders, it is an essential condition for success for both breakthrough results and long-term transformation. Task I.F.7 describes an information generation network as a potential element of your formal change infrastructure. To create it, you would identify your potential types and sources of new information and methods for its discovery. For sources of information, consider people both internal and external to the organization, your project community, your customers or vendors, other organizations inside and outside of your industry, and other disciplines or bodies of knowledge. Consider how you might use social media technology to encourage, generate, and capture new information.

Information Management

Most leaders assume information management to be an obvious requirement. We intentionally highlight it because of the special attention it deserves given the complex amount and types of information surfacing within transformational change efforts. It is imperative that you clarify responsibilities and methods for how you will gather, track, store, share, and update project data for every phase of your effort.

Fortunately, sophisticated software exists to handle this work. You will need to determine which software programs you will use, who will oversee their use, and who has access and input to them. Also, you will need to clarify the non-electronic means you will use to gather and share information. Refer back to your role and relationship agreements in your change governance structure, and clarify who needs to keep who informed on various topics throughout the change.

Task I.F.5: Initiate Course Correction Strategy and System

Transformational change is fraught with the unknown. Even the best of plans will never unfold the way they look on screen. You are constantly seeking to discover what your future state needs to be, and how and when to take action to move in the right direction. Leaders depend on good plans built from their best thinking, and then must have the openness and discipline to consciously engage in the process of learning and course correcting as they go. Learning and course correcting go hand-in-hand with information generation. Leaders must stay alert, take action based on their best thinking or intuition, and then rapidly realign their expectations, outcomes, or plans based on what they discover. This is the core of conscious transformational leadership, and mastering its change process competency.

The notion of course correction is one of the most valuable, powerful, and underused ideas in organizations today. Fortunately, many organizations have already initiated continuous improvement and learning practices in their cultures. We encourage you to build off of this momentum and apply the learning and course correction strategy to the leadership of change, especially transformation. Figure 4.1 shows the Course Correction Model.

Different from evaluation, measurement, and audit, which are based on the assumption that a preconceived *right* answer or standard exists, the process of course correction consists of the following:

- Setting a direction based on your best intelligence
- Commencing action to reach your vision
- Pursuing feedback, wake-up calls, and new information in the environment, your stakeholders, and organization for whether you are on or off course

Figure 4.1. Course Correction Model

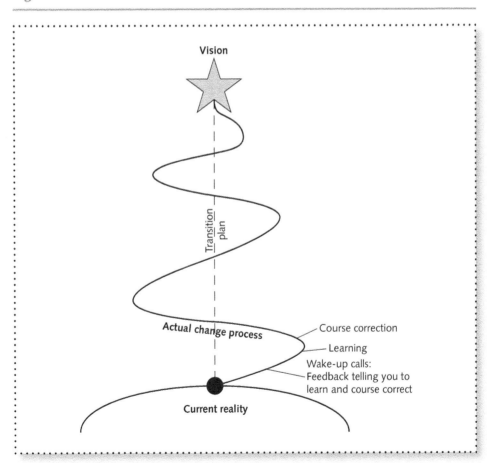

- Consciously reflecting on the feedback and new information for what they mean about your desired outcomes, mindset, knowledge, skills, behavior, culture, and change plan
- Testing new insights for further learning about what to do differently
- Altering both the process and/or the outcome of the transformation based on your latest intelligence

The notion of course correction requires education, not only of leaders but of employees as well. Employees, like leaders, typically want security and predictability. Traditionally, employees want their leaders to have the right answers and show them the way. However, if leaders have not made course correction explicit in how the transformation needs to be led, and then make frequent course corrections, employees will likely feel that their leaders are lost, adrift in a rudderless boat. That dynamic can be very disconcerting—a good excuse for employees to criticize leadership and resist the change.

Change leaders must communicate clearly—right from the start—that information generation and course correction are critical aspects of their change strategy and process. They must be prepared to overtly model course correction, in their organizational decisions, interactions, and behavior. Then, as they course correct, they can openly communicate that the alteration is the result of their course correction strategy working well, rather than a failure of their initial plans. Leaders must consciously demonstrate the importance of getting smarter by the day, as quickly as possible.

Information generation and course correction are also critical engagement strategies. The more people that you enroll in generating new information for course correction, the better. High engagement generates more complete information and simultaneously builds commitment and ownership for the change strategy it informs.

Designing and using a widespread course correction system can also have a potent effect on shifting fear-based cultural norms in the organization (e.g., "Kill the messenger who brings bad news!") to ones that are based on learning and innovation (e.g., "Go ahead. Make me smarter!"). If an organization is eager to embrace learning, it has to be willing to shatter the myths that "The leader has all of the answers" and "Having a plan is a guarantee for success." Valuing rapid course correction keeps people attentive and engaged in pushing the envelope of innovation and breakthrough. Exhibit 4.1 offers a checklist of elements for building your course correction system.

Exhibit 4.1. **Checklist of Elements for Building Your Course Correction System**

- A philosophy statement linking this approach with your desired leadership style, new mindsets, and culture
- Target areas of assessment or inquiry
- Stakeholders representing all levels of the organization, target groups, users, and customers identified and tasked to seek feedback and input on how things are going or what is needed
- Communication and engagement vehicles and training to ensure that these stakeholders know the intended outcomes of the change, the process for achieving them, and any subsequent adjustments to the change process or outcome
- Means for gathering outside-the-box data and feedback (use your information generation strategies and social media)
- A place, person, Web site, or group to bring aberrant data or wake-up calls for consideration
- A process for dealing with and deciding how to use feedback and data
- A process for communicating the impact of feedback and data, whether or not it was used
- Reinforcement or reward for generating useful data
- Resources to support all of the above
- Training to support all of the above, if necessary

Task I.F.6: Initiate Strategies for Supporting People Through Emotional Reactions and Resistance

In these early stages of change, the rumor mill in your organization is likely in full gear. People who are aware that a change is imminent may be flip-flopping between excitement and anger, fear and hope. Performance may be affected, and your e-mail system is probably flooded with time-consuming commentary about what is going to happen and who is going to get "the boot." Perhaps some of the top leaders are at their wits' end about how to stop the growing wave of concern, and a few are likely ready to erupt emotionally themselves. How do you deal with all of this when you haven't actually changed anything yet?

People will have a full array of natural reactions to both what is being changed and your change process. Because an organization cannot transform without affecting people, a critical condition for success for your change strategy is that it *proactively minimize the negative impacts of the change on people and maximize people's commitment.* It must also position the leaders to respond effectively to people's reactions throughout the change. Our discussion of the human dynamics of change in *Beyond Change Management* delves into much of what leaders need to be aware of to do this effectively. This content and guidance is essential reading in preparation for doing this work well. This task develops strategy, mechanisms, and resources to consciously minimize and handle people's reactions in your change, including turning their resistance into commitment.

Resistance is inevitable. It is a person's behavioral expression of either not feeling aligned with the new direction the organization is taking or thinking it is not what is best for him or her personally. Rather than be reactive to your people's resistance when it shows up, actively seek to understand what is causing it and what value that information might bring to the change. Our advice is simply to set up a safe environment in which to explore people's resistance and then listen, listen, listen. People need to have their concerns heard and legitimized. True listening is the most powerful and direct way to defuse resistance. People's issues might even surface a different perspective for more effectively making the change.

Your change communications and engagement strategies are prime opportunities to listen to people and give them the chance to feel heard and valued for their point of view. Again, you do not need to do what they request, but through genuine consideration of their ideas, people will be more likely to go along with the change. This will increase the possibility for turning their resistance into support and alignment.

It is important to note that this task is designed for the change leaders to clarify how to support the workforce through their emotional reactions. Keep in mind that the leaders *themselves* also need this support. Although traditionally it may not be considered acceptable for leaders to be overt about their emotional reactions or needs, in a conscious approach, the leaders' humanness is as important as anyone's. If your leaders are upset, hurt, or out of balance, they will undoubtedly miss important signals about what the transformation requires. Be sure to address how to provide emotional support for the leaders when doing executive and change leadership team development and executive coaching.

How People React to Change

In recent years, many leaders have come to recognize that people naturally react to change and that leaders must deal differently with the people affected by change. There are a number of valuable models used to educate leaders about how people react to change and how to respond to people's reactions. William Bridges'

Transition Model (2003) is particularly useful, as is John Adams' Stages of Personal Adjustment to Transition Model (2002). The Adams model is shown in Figure 4.2.

The core message of Adams' model is straightforward: People have a series of natural reactions to change. They will lose focus, deny, and react strongly, all being seen as forms of resistance. They will enter the "pit" (anger, withdrawal, confusion, victimization, blame) before letting go of their old reality, and then proceed to find ways to deal effectively with their new reality, committing to make it a success. Leaders throughout the organization must support and facilitate people through the *entire* cycle, even people's descent into the pit. Trying to avoid or rush the pit phase actually lengthens its duration because people need to acknowledge being in acute reaction before they can let it go and move on.

Almost everything leaders do in change triggers diverse reactions in people. In today's economic climate, rash actions that hurt people abound. Abusive examples include telling people that they no longer have jobs by putting the infamous "pink slip" in with their final paychecks, or bosses calling people in to their offices and telling them they have the remainder of the day to exit the building and leave

Figure 4.2.   Stages of Personal Adjustment to Transition Model

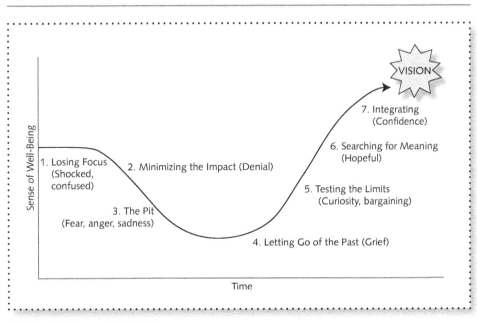

© John D. Adams, 1976, 1990

their key and files behind. These are inhumane strategies and have a negative effect on the people who get to stay as they do to those asked to leave.

Perhaps the leaders who have used insensitive approaches deny the personal trauma they cause because they do not understand how people respond to change, or perhaps it is because they do not want to take responsibility for the pain or anger their decisions have created in their workers. In either case, it is far more powerful to understand how people naturally react to change, to address people's concerns overtly and compassionately, and to plan the change process to minimize known negative impacts on people. A conscious approach also calls for leaders to acknowledge the truth of their own feelings about the pain their actions may cause others. This task is an opportunity for leaders to model a conscious shift in cultural expectations and leadership.

Conscious approaches to reducing people's trauma include Appreciative Inquiry approaches (see Watkins and Mohr, 2001), dialogue, personalized communications, employee assistance programs, "letting go" rituals, celebrations, stress management programs, large group engagement strategies, training, outplacement, listening and support groups, and leadership modeling.

Review your recent and current change strategies to assess their potential for causing emotional upheaval. Redesign them with people's emotional needs in mind. Completing this task does not mean that people won't have bad reactions; they likely will, even in the best of circumstances. The intent, however, is to minimize unnecessary negative reactions and maximize strategies that will engage people in enlivening, constructive ways.

Task I.F.7: Initiate Temporary Change Support Mechanisms

Your organization is about to face a unique set of circumstances in which it must continue to operate while undergoing its transformation. This stage is temporary and requires temporary supports to enable and accelerate the transformational process. Consequently, temporary structures, systems, policies, and technology must be designed to handle the interim needs of the change and to balance its demands with ongoing operations. This task completes your change infrastructure, although you will continue to adjust it over time.

Temporary supports are designed to promote efficiency, streamline decision making, and remove bureaucratic constraints that would otherwise inhibit action on the change. Having referred to these supports as temporary, it is important to note that many organizations recognize so much benefit from them that they incorporate them into their "normal" operations. This helps address the sluggishness when the established bureaucracy fails to act quickly enough as new priorities emerge. This trend reflects the move toward greater resiliency and designing organizations to respond to emergent needs, rather than have the rigidity of the organization squash them.

This task introduces various options for designing temporary structures, systems, policies, and technologies and develops those needed to support your transformation. Some of these strategies will be used immediately, some will be implemented later, and some will be adapted throughout the process. You will dismantle all of them or redefine them as "permanent" at the conclusion of Phase IX of the change process. We will describe this task in two sections: (1) temporary change structures and (2) temporary management systems, policies, and technologies.

Temporary Change Structures

Your change effort may benefit from additional structures in your change infrastructure. Remember, you already have temporary change leadership roles, a governance structure, and a multiple project integration structure. In addition, consider these options:

- Special project teams
- Culture scanning group or network
- Change navigation center
- Information generation network
- Barrier buster teams

Each is described next:

Special project teams: The number and types of personnel needed to support transformation will vary with the organization and complexity of the effort. You may need special teams for any number of change activities, such as to conduct benchmarking, organize your visioning process or large communication events, evaluate new software solutions, engage in design, research new products or analyze sets of data, and so forth. To staff these teams, consider both internal and external people who have functional expertise, planning skills, and ability to facilitate and model the change. These people may work full-time or part-time, face-to-face or electronically, throughout the transformation or until their team's task is completed. Be certain to start up each team with a clear charter and accelerated team-building.

Culture scanning group or network: Transformational changes are culture-dependent and require a focused effort to study the organization's current culture and design its desired culture. In addition to the classic components of culture (i.e., values, norms, language, stories, etc.), this includes assessing and shaping the mindset of the organization—its assumptions and beliefs, ways of being and relating, and mental models about its reality. Assessment of the organization's current culture might precede the creation of this group or be led by it. They might use an online culture assessment such as those offered by Human Synergistics International, or focus groups of representatives from all levels, areas, business units, and types of employees in your project community. This group, which might function like a network, might also facilitate the design of the organization's desired culture, or if it has already been created, this group can monitor the organization's daily operations for examples of the old culture that need to change, as well as examples of the new culture that can be promoted and celebrated. Any aspect of culture, mindset, style, and behavior may come under this group's attention.

This network is a great opportunity for engagement, especially for people who are enthusiastic about advocating conscious attention to the human dynamics in the organization. Ideally, these people have a direct line of communication to the change process leader and change leadership team to raise issues and make recommendations on behalf of the new culture and mindset.

Change navigation center: Transformational changes can be supported with a "nerve center," often called the navigation center. This is a meeting place where change leaders make decisions, share information, and shape plans. The navigation center notion contributes to the valued sense of strong change leadership.

Navigation centers can be actual locations, virtual locations, or both. As an actual location, the navigation center is often an office or conference room converted into a headquarters for change activity. As a virtual location, it can be designed in numerous ways. It can serve as an intranet site "discussion board" for change leaders, or be open to the entire organization. It can be a communication vehicle, posting announcements or reporting status, or be part of the information generation system. Often, the change process leader and change teams meet both in the actual navigation center and virtually on their intranet site—for planning and design meetings.

Information generation network: As described in Task I.F.4, information is the "fuel" that drives all types of change. New information can come from anywhere. However, its discovery can be assisted through an information generation network. This network is made up of internal and external people who actively seek outside-the-box information. The types of information they seek, the sources of that information, and the methods for obtaining it will depend on each change. A system is required for inputting, considering, and acting on the information generated to support this function. The project community at large can play a vital role in this network. Consider using social media to support this effort.

Barrier buster teams: Organizations committed to dismantling bureaucratic cultures, practices, and structures during their transformations can form "barrier buster" teams. These teams, often in each business line, seek out, assess, and recommend the removal of unnecessary red tape, bottlenecks, convoluted processes, and "busy work"—all barriers to efficient and resilient organizations. Barrier buster teams help identify anything that might prevent desired outcomes. They have a direct line into the change leadership team. We have seen several organizations have a lot of fun unleashing and celebrating the success of these teams!

Temporary Management Systems, Policies, and Technology

At times, temporary management systems, policies, and technologies are necessary to enhance critical steps, communications, or functions during the change process. Without them, the organization's normal systems and practices might become overloaded bottlenecks when trying to handle the magnitude of activity and urgent pace. Temporary systems and policies can be used to override or accelerate normal procedures. Technology can expedite the generation of information, communications, engagement, and problem solving.

For example, during a major structural change, temporary selection procedures have to be created to expedite the matching of large pools of candidates with all of the open positions. Standard job posting systems, often taking months to fill a position, will overload and "blow the fuse" of the change process. So a temporary accelerated selection process is required and can be expedited through the use of technology and virtual meetings.

SAMPLE TEMPORARY MANAGEMENT SYSTEMS

▶ Staffing system

▶ Job design and evaluation system

▶ Outplacement: selection and support packages

▶ Relocation process

▶ Information management and communication systems

▶ Team-building processes or new department start-up procedures

▶ Accelerated decision-making processes

▶ Rewards for contributing to the transformation

▶ Approval levels and system

▶ Performance reviews

▶ Intensive technical or people skills and knowledge training; retraining; cross-training

▶ Interim supply, distribution, and materials management systems or policies

▶ Interim operations tracking or scheduling procedures

▶ Counseling and employee assistance services

▶ Logistics and space allocation/facilities management systems

Temporary policies may also be needed. For example, if you are able to announce *at the beginning* of a change that everyone will actually maintain employment or retain his or her current salary and health insurance benefits, employees will breathe a sigh of relief and receive the news of the transformation in a more positive light. These policies can greatly assist you with some of the predictable human dynamics.

SAMPLE TEMPORARY POLICIES

▶ Hiring freeze

▶ Job reclassification

▶ Job security/guarantee

▶ Salary protection

▶ Mandated training or voluntary cross-training

▶ Labor/management agreements

▶ Performance review delays

- Across the board salary adjustments
- Health insurance coverage extensions
- Relocation or termination packages

Temporary technologies can expedite two-way communications, engagement, and action among your stakeholders, no matter where in the world they reside. However, a word of caution is needed. Technology can make your change effort impersonal and divert people's attention from the real human-to-human contact necessary. Definitely leverage technology to your advantage, but be careful not to over-extend its application into "human contact" arenas where it is insufficient.

Technology can be blended with other methods and used effectively in five distinct areas, which are listed next, along with specific examples of application. Select and tailor the appropriate uses for your transformation.

COMMUNICATIONS AND ENGAGEMENT

- Intranet or internet site
- Interactive conferences for virtual team working sessions
- Webinars
- Social media vehicles for engagement, such as visioning, design, and impact analysis
- Video announcements
- Teleconferences

INFORMATION MANAGEMENT

- Information generation vehicles
- Sorting information
- Tracking decisions, issues, and activities
- Dissemination channels
- Archiving

PROJECT MANAGEMENT

- Project planning and reporting
- Forecasting timelines and resources
- Cost management

- Scheduling
- Project integration

EDUCATION

- Change leadership development
- Support of many types of training
- Vehicles for offering expert resources
- Making change tools and articles available online

ASSESSMENTS

- Readiness and capacity assessments
- Change history assessments
- Organization assessments
- Design requirements
- Culture assessments
- Change project audits
- Change leadership style assessments
- Impact analysis
- Customer requirements

Be sure to dismantle your temporary management systems, policies, and technologies publicly when they no longer serve your needs.

Task I.F.8: Determine Measurements of Change

When executives think about transforming their organizations, one of the most predictable concerns is how to measure progress and results. Logically, leaders want to know how well the change is proceeding and whether the outcome will produce the return they expect. The desire for accurate and regular measurement is one reason that classic project management methods are attractive for leading change. These approaches provide good quantifiable measurement and, with it, some semblance of comfort and control over the action.

This is appropriate when changes are predictable and controllable. However, as we have stated, transformational change is neither. Because transformation requires significant personal and cultural change, many aspects of it are not predictable, controllable, nor easily evaluated. This makes complete objective measurement of it challenging. In addition, because leaders have historically used measurement to control the organization and induce specific behavior and action, you may need to address people's historical intimidation by measurement so as not to impede the kind of breakthrough and innovation you want from your transformation.

We have already made the case that successful transformation requires the organization to respond to emerging, spontaneously occurring dynamics that could not be predicted earlier. Rigid adherence to measures can stifle these critical course corrections. Having explicit, preconceived outcomes is not bad; they just need to be balanced with ensuring that metrics are adjusted to required course corrections. This is a subtle but very powerful mindset shift for leaders. Measurement can assist, but it should not drive transformation or be used as a control strategy.

This task designs your measurement strategy. Consider both objective and subjective measures. The change leaders must discuss and determine the following:

- Their need and purpose for having measurements
- The impacts, both positive and negative, that measurement might have on a predictably dynamic change process
- What will be measured both objectively and subjectively (e.g., timeliness, goal achievement, responsiveness, units of production, savings, speed, quality of product or service, effectiveness of working relationships and communication, demonstrated skill and knowledge, actual and projected costs, customer satisfaction, employee satisfaction)
- Standards of measurement (frequency, speed, number of occurrences, improvements, learnings)
- Methods (interviews, surveys, checklists, group input)

Change leaders must do this for both the outcomes of the change and the change process itself so that measurement can support the ongoing course correction of both.

Task I.F.9: Initiate Temporary Rewards

People will do what they are rewarded for. When making major change, especially transformational change, the organization's old reward system frequently

In one Fortune 500 company, we brought the executives together to launch their change process and define their role as change leaders. After a briefing on change strategy and The Change Leader's Roadmap methodology, the senior vice president, to whom they all reported, told the leaders that, beyond their accountability for the outcomes of the change, they would also be held accountable for their influence on the *change process* and that 20 percent of their annual executive incentive would be attached to their change leadership performance. To make their accountability as change leaders tangible and observable, we gave the executives the task of collectively identifying their own performance standards for excellent change leadership, in specific actionable terms.

After a few minutes of predictable shock, they saw and accepted the inherent challenge and proceeded to take the information they had just learned about the CLR and their role, and create a set of realistic change leadership standards for themselves. Their list included the following:

▶ Achievement of specific activities in the process
▶ Effectiveness of their communications to the workforce for creating behavior supportive of the change, including engagement for real benefit to the change
▶ Visibility as a model of the new culture
▶ Knowledge about the status of the transformation
▶ Creation of an effective change infrastructure and conditions for success
▶ Timely execution of change decisions
▶ Support for essential course corrections
▶ Ability to find adequate resources to support their part of the overall change

The senior vice president used the list as his guide for evaluating their performance and in fact, kept his word on tying it to their annual bonus. In hindsight, the executives clearly recognized the power of determining their own requirements for change leadership, which deepened their understanding of the value of taking responsibility for their own performance standards.

motivates behavior that is contrary to your desired state. You will need to identify and address discrepancies.

This task develops, communicates, and initiates new (often temporary) rewards that purposely influence people's behavior to support your change. These rewards motivate people to make the transformation a reality—personally, behaviorally, and operationally. Then, as part of the new state that you will design in Phase IV, you can revise the full-scale reward system to support behavior required in the new state.

Please note that fully redesigning the organization's reward system at this point will cause upset and chaos, and *should not be done!* Employees are still assimilating the case for change and what impacts the change *might* have on them. Changing operating rewards too early can create tremendous resistance and confusion. Focus here on choosing rewards that motivate people to support the *process* of the transformation.

Task I.F.10: Determine Phase II Through V Roadmap

In Task I.A.5, you created your Phase I roadmap to bring you to this very point in your change. Now it is time to create your Phase II through V roadmap to carry you up to the creation of your Implementation Master Plan. Scan the tasks of Phases II through V. Select only those you require to achieve your deliverables.

Use your roadmap to guide your change leaders in their plans going forward. You can also use it to communicate to your key stakeholder groups your expected path. And use it to assess the time, resources, and capacity the change will require given your current understanding. Remember, you will likely need to adjust your roadmap as you proceed.

SUMMARY

You have now determined and identified the most appropriate infrastructures for your change effort, including the creation of your conditions for success. This work, led by the change process leader, paves the way for a well-supported change effort. Add this work to your change strategy, and determine how best to communicate it and establish your support mechanisms.

CONSULTING QUESTIONS FOR ACTIVITY I.F: BUILD INFRASTRUCTURE AND CONDITIONS TO SUPPORT CHANGE EFFORT

Task I.F.1: Initiate Strategies for Dealing with Political Dynamics

▶ What are the current political dynamics among the change leaders and in the organization that may have a direct or negative impact on the success of your transformation?

▶ How can you encourage the leaders to be willing to address political issues on behalf of the results they collectively need from the change effort?

▶ What is the best way to resolve or improve these dynamics among the leaders?

▶ What ground rules are needed among the change leaders for dealing constructively with political dynamics that arise as the transformation unfolds? How will you establish and monitor these ground rules?

Task I.F.2: Create Conditions for Success

▶ Do the change leaders understand conditions for success as direct ways to obtain the outcomes of their transformation?

▶ How will the leaders determine their conditions for success?

▶ How will you secure their agreement to commit to the actual creation of these conditions in the organization?

▶ How will you use these conditions to help manage, measure, and course-correct the transformation as it rolls out?

Task I.F.3: Identify Process for Creating Shared Vision

▶ What work have the change leaders already done to create a vision for this transformation?

▶ How willing are the change leaders to engage the organization in the creation of a shared vision beyond what they have done themselves?

- Who is responsible for designing and facilitating the visioning work?

- What methods will you use to engage stakeholders, managers, and employees in shaping the vision? Will you use any large group interventions? Social media?

- If you are changing the culture of the organization, how can you design the visioning process to reflect what you are moving to?

- After a vision statement has been created, how will you communicate and roll it out in the organization?

- How will you publicly sustain the link between the vision and your change effort's progress toward it over time?

Task I.F.4: Design Information Generation and Management Strategies

- Do the change leaders and the organization understand what "new information" is and the role it plays in transformational change?

- How will you establish the expectation in the organization for generating new information related to the transformation? Will you create a new information network?

- What will be done with new information when it is surfaced? How will you screen it for relevancy? Who will do this?

- What information management mechanisms will you use to help run an effective change effort? How will you establish and oversee them?

Task I.F.5: Initiate Course Correction Strategy and System

- Do the change leaders understand the notion of course correction?

- Do current cultural norms support giving feedback upward, downward, and across boundaries? Do they support learning from mistakes? If they don't, how will you address this?

- How will you design your system for surfacing feedback and course-correcting the change process and desired outcomes?

- How will you establish the expectation for course correction and your course correction system in the organization?

How will the change leaders communicate course corrections they have made in the change process or outcomes?

Task I.F.6: Initiate Strategies for Supporting People Through Emotional Reactions and Resistance

- Has the leadership of past changes caused significant trauma for people in the organization?
- What are the potential negative impacts on people in your current change strategy and plan? How can these be minimized?
- To what degree do the change leaders understand people's cycle of emotional reactions during change?
- What strategies can the change leaders initiate to help people manage their emotional reactions during the change process and transform their resistance into commitment?
- What resources already exist in the organization for employee assistance?
- Does the culture of the organization support people to take advantage of these resources?
- What strategies will you use to help the change leaders deal with their personal emotional reactions to the transformation?

Task I.F.7: Initiate Temporary Support Mechanisms

- To what degree do the executives and change leaders understand the function of temporary change structures, systems, policies, and technology?
- How will you introduce these options?
- Which of these mechanisms would benefit the transformation?
- How will you design, approve, and establish each?

Task I.F.8: Determine Measurements of Change

- How has measurement been used in the past?
- Is this traditional approach aligned with the outcomes, mindset, and desired culture for this transformation?
- What do the change leaders want to measure in this change process?

- What is their purpose for measuring these things?

- What measurement standards will you use?

- Are all of the target areas for measurement quantifiable? If not, how will you devise appropriate subjective measures?

- How will you communicate your metrics for the change to the people who will be measured by them?

Task I.F.9: Initiate Temporary Rewards

- Does the existing reward system reinforce leaders' and employees' support for the transformation? If not, what in it is contrary?

- How will you undo existing rewards that may hinder leaders' or employees' support of the change process or outcome?

- What rewards are needed to encourage the cultural, behavioral, and mindset changes required for the transformation?

- How will you define and establish these in the organization?

- Who will oversee their use?

Task I.F.10: Determine Phase II Through V Roadmap

- What are the most important tasks to attend to in your Phase II through V roadmap?

- How will you use your roadmap? How will you adjust it over time?

- Who needs to know about and use this roadmap to orchestrate their work on the transformation?

CHAPTER

5

PHASE II
Create Organizational Vision, Commitment, and Capability

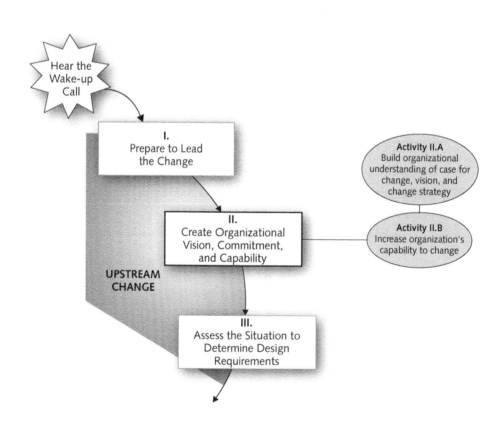

PHASE II: TASK DELIVERABLES

II.A.1: Your case for change and change strategy has been communicated, and a critical mass of the organization supports them.

II.A.2: Your organization understands the vision for the transformation and is committed to creating it.

II.A.3: The majority of the workforce understands that the old way of operating is gone and accepts the future direction.

II.B.1: Your organization has the required change knowledge and skills to achieve the outcomes of this transformation.

II.B.2: The preferred mindset and behaviors are clear and being adopted by a critical mass of stakeholders.

Phase II shifts your focus from preparing the leaders to succeed in the transformation to engaging the organization in the initiation of the change. The purpose of Phase II is to build organization-wide commitment, momentum, and capability for supporting and engaging in the transformation. It brings people up to speed about the real challenges the organization faces and why this transformation is important to the organization's future. It engages stakeholders in clarifying what is possible to create here—their vision of the future—and draws them into the change experience through robust conversations. This is where you demonstrate how the change is specifically relevant to business success and strive to make it personally meaningful to people.

Phase II has two primary goals, each addressed in its two activities. First is to create *collective intention* for producing transformational results. The broader the shared intention for succeeding in the transformation, the easier the process will be. What do we mean by "collective intention"? This term refers to a critical mass of people joining in a concerted effort, with clear purpose and resolve, to create new outcomes for the organization. All of the levels of the organization are access points for creating collective intention. How do you establish it? There is no set formula, yet there are many options:

- Wide-scale engagement in building the case for change and vision for the future

- Interactive dialogue that deepens people's understanding and builds their excitement

- Planned experiences that impact people's mindsets and emotions, such as Leadership Breakthrough training or rites of passage from the old to the new

- Employee input on key change issues that demonstrably influences leaders' thinking

- Making the distinction overt between the limitations of old ways of operating and the value of new ways

- Sharing responsibility for critical action and authority with *all levels* of the organization

The second primary goal of Phase II is to build the change capability that you need to succeed. This requires developing the mindsets, behavior, knowledge, and skills of change leadership in your key stakeholder groups. The more you can increase your organization's change competency, the faster your change efforts will go.

You will know you have been successful with these two goals when a critical mass of people in your project community is moving forward toward the organization's desired future—ready, emotionally aligned, and capable of taking on the work to make the transformation a reality. This phase is an opportunity for bold action. You will want to design it to wake up and mobilize the organization, while minimizing resistance and emotional attachment to the past. When people see you are committed to their being successful in the future, they will be much more likely to be full players in the change.

ACTIVITY II.A: BUILD ORGANIZATIONAL UNDERSTANDING OF CASE FOR CHANGE, VISION, AND CHANGE STRATEGY

Task II.A.1: Communicate Case for Change and Change Strategy

In this task, the change leaders and change team members inform the organization about the change through their kickoff communication strategy from Phase I. We assume that the size of your change effort will dictate the depth and design of your kickoff strategy. What is described here fits large-scale transformation.

The kickoff communication process is your change leaders' formal declaration to the organization that a transformation is underway. Its content, tone, and delivery have a significant impact on how people respond to the impending challenge. It sets the stage for how the executives will be perceived as leaders of this transformation, how much commitment to change exists within the organization, and whether employees believe in your overall change strategy. Make no mistake, this initial communication about the case for change, vision, and change strategy is a critical process for aligning the organization, the leaders, and the conditions required to make this transformation successful. It is one of the most important opportunities you have to mobilize the organization and its collective intention to change through open dialogue and exchange. *It is an opportunity not to be missed!*

Typically, people have already heard about the change, and stories and reactions are probably rampant. It is rare that some information has not already leaked into the organization and is triggering rumors. Therefore, you may want to design your communication to *refocus* people to what the effort is actually about and how it is going to be led. If necessary, use this task to course-correct people's perceptions of the change. You want people to be talking about what is possible, not how bad it is. Your Phase I project briefing and the assessment of people's capacity for change are good sources of input for this course correction.

This task must be designed as a process rather than as an event. Remember the Five Levels of Communication Model described in Task I.E.9. It suggests that your communication process must include multiple opportunities for employees to hear your message, talk and think about it, formulate their questions, and have their concerns addressed. The intervals between conversations will enable employees to discuss their concerns with their coworkers, which, in turn, will generate more questions to be asked. Eventually, the process will generate greater understanding and acceptance. Honoring the "process" nature of effective communications will help ensure a successful kickoff to your transformation and build the required critical mass of commitment and intention.

You may also be rolling out a shared visioning process, which is the focus of the next task. This series of interactions with employees may also be the prime opportunity to engage them in envisioning a future they are excited to create. You might blend your communications kickoff strategy with your visioning process.

People's initial reactions to the transformation may be colored by three dynamics: (1) their concern for what the change means to them personally; (2) their attachment to the status quo; and (3) the emotions they still have about past changes in which they were adversely affected. If they are having strong reactions, you will definitely have to communicate the same information about the transformation on several different occasions in different ways.

Furthermore, "selling" the future in words doesn't suffice; leaders will have to create a way in which people can *experience* the value of the future for themselves during this series of communications. If the leaders are communicating that this transformation will be very different from past changes, they will have to allow people time to observe whether the leaders' behavior matches their words. People will be watching like hawks to see whether the leaders' intentions to lead this transformation differently are authentic. This is particularly true if you are changing the organization's culture. Putting your desired culture into words will sound like a "good idea" until people actually feel its benefits in real time and recognize that the new norms and behaviors will sustain over time.

Here is one recommended scenario for the design of this kickoff communication process. It attends to many of the common forces at play in the organization at the start of a change and includes a variety of communication vehicles and methods. Imagine yourself in this story as you read, tailoring it to fit the challenges you face today.

An Effective Communications Rollout Scenario

The sponsors, key change leaders, and select representatives from management and employee stakeholder groups deliver the initial communication—in person, through numerous large group meetings, by teleconference or video. More than one person speaks to enliven the delivery, including representatives of the various stakeholder groups. They share the case for change and change strategy, and request input to the vision for the future. This is followed by a series of town hall meetings—or Web discussions or blogs—that cascade throughout the organization and your project community, all of which are led by the executives as well as the managers and employees who worked on the case for change. A short time is provided between sessions or events to allow employees to talk about and post what they heard, which they will do unprompted.

In the town hall meetings and/or Web-based discussion boards or blogs, the change sponsors openly discuss what was said in their initial communication, reiterating the facts and their perceptions, hopes, and fears. The managers and employees also offer their perspectives, and the audience asks questions and voices concerns. The leaders listen carefully to the audience's questions and issues, responding to all of them as best they can. They share their intentions and plans, identify issues that do not yet have answers, and commit to bring the issues back to the planning process for consideration. Through this interchange, the leaders openly gather impacts about the transformation that they may not have originally seen. Doing this with public acknowledgement deepens people's engagement.

Next comes facilitated breakout conversations about general reactions or key issues (or online blogs), which allows for active involvement by all participants. Major messages from the breakout groups are brought back to the large group (or main online conference) for presentation to and response by the leaders. The leaders conclude each meeting (or the interactive conference) with a request for volunteers to staff an informal network of change advocates who will be asked for input on the vision of the future and to represent their functions' interests as the transformation is planned and implemented.

Over the next two weeks, team leaders facilitate discussions in their work teams or using blogs about the transformation and its implications for the team and the individual members. The teams are tasked with identifying what they already have going for them, likely barriers to the effort, and necessary conditions for success. They may also request design requirements for the best future state.

The next step is a mass communication vehicle that provides a current status report of the transformation effort and highlights actions taken and outcomes produced as a direct result of employees' previous input. The leaders share stories about how various stakeholders have had insights or breakthroughs or have mobilized action central to the transformation's success.

What to Communicate and How to Position the Transformation

The content of your initial round of communications is as critical as the process and methods for delivering it. Often, the content is only delivered by the most senior leaders. We suggest that select managers and employees—also change leaders—take an active role in this delivery as well. Their participation makes the content more credible and demonstrates that change is already occurring. Here is one scenario for what change leaders might deliver.

Imagine the change leaders being genuine, energized, and inviting in their tone. They begin by explaining what has led to this transformation and what has been happening so far. They point out the historical achievements and events they are very proud of and describe how each has contributed to the success of the organization. The leaders are candid about where their own focus has been, sharing how their thinking has recently been impacted by new information and how they themselves have finally heard the wake-up call for this transformation. The sponsors, managers, and employees each speak for their part of the organization. They describe the case for change in powerful terms, linking all seven drivers, speaking directly to the challenges the organization faces. They emphasize the importance of the changes in culture, behavior, and mindset.

The change leaders report how the effort will be led and staffed, especially if their approach will be radically different from the past. The sponsors introduce the change process leader and his or her role and authority. They communicate that everyone in position to add value to this effort is considered a change leader, irrespective of his or her position or level in the organization. Every leadership contribution will be needed. The change leaders highlight the key elements of their change strategy, featuring the key initiatives and changes to the culture. They announce their bold actions (only if doing so will not steal any thunder when they actually take place) and other relevant decisions about infrastructure and conditions for success.

The change leaders model the new norm of course correction, admitting that some of the organization's historical change practices must be altered immediately based on new insights. They tell how this transformation fits into the big picture of other organizational events and lay out the required pace of activity and their rationale for it. They convey their genuine understanding of the additional burden this pace may place on the workforce and describe how they will do their best to provide adequate resources and free up capacity to enable people to succeed in making their contribution to this transformation while maintaining their well-being and current performance.

The change leaders personalize the transformation by sharing what is needed from them as its strategic leaders and as representatives of each level of the organization. They describe how their mindsets and perceptions are changing to enable this effort and reinforce that mindset change is also needed throughout the organization. They share how people will be invited to participate, making a compelling case for everyone to pull together and make his or her best contribution. The change leaders tell how this effort will benefit various employee and management groups and speak truthfully about certain groups that will be adversely affected but treated fairly and humanely.

If appropriate, the change leaders also model new language and behavior, perhaps by emphasizing that they do not have all of the answers about the future and, therefore, want everyone to stay alert for new information and learning, which is different from their normal way of doing things. They describe the transformation as a journey that everyone must undertake together. That journey will include a combination of expertise and discovery. They describe the need for culture change and declare it essential to success. If the organizations' current culture has inhibited risk-taking and changes to plan, they publicly acknowledge the need to lead this transformation differently. The leaders lay out the upcoming opportunities where people will be asked to provide input, including the organization-wide visioning process. If they have committed to build the organization's change leadership capability, they reinforce this as one of their goals for succeeding at this transformation and note that they are holding themselves accountable for becoming more conscious as leaders of change.

They reiterate that the transformation is a courageous undertaking and that everyone's full commitment is required for the organization's collective success. They again honor where the organization has been and how this next chapter in its life is the most important and challenging yet. The change leaders conclude with their personal commitment to do whatever is necessary to create this new reality in a way that benefits the organization, its stockholders (or patients or constituents), and its people.

Task II.A.2: Roll Out Process to Create Shared Vision and Commitment

There is no greater accelerator of change than people who have a vision they are collectively committed to creating. In Task I.F.3, *Identify Process for Creating Shared Vision*, you designed your strategy for engaging the organization in the visioning process. Sometimes, the leaders will create the vision of the transformation themselves and announce it. Our recommendation is that your stakeholders be involved in building the vision of their future, along with executive guidance. This is especially true if you are changing the culture of the organization. Whatever your strategy, you implement it here. Keep in mind that you may be integrating the visioning process into your initial communication events when introducing your change.

There are three parts to visioning. The first is obtaining agreement about the content of the vision—the actual direction and outcomes of the transformation. The second part is crafting the vision statement in words that capture the compelling possibilities for what you will create. The third part is ensuring that the entire organization understands the vision and commits to making it real. The outcome of this third piece is creating *collective intention* for the success of the transformation. People must figure out where they personally fit in, what their role in the transformation is, and what action is required of them. If people do this to their satisfaction, they will be on-board with the change.

Leaders can choose to do the first two parts of visioning—developing the content and the wording of the vision—or they can use stakeholder engagement to do it. It takes about the same amount of time to accomplish all three parts of visioning, whether the leaders develop the content and wording of the vision themselves or use engagement. When leaders develop the content and wording themselves, creating collective intention takes much longer. It can be a slow process to determine the content and wording en masse, yet collective intention is created at the same time.

Determining the Content of Your Vision

What is the ideal outcome for the transformation? Exhibit 5.1, Worksheet: Questions for Visioning, provides several questions to assist you in building the most powerful vision for your effort. Each question creates a different conversation about the same thing: the outcomes you want the transformation to create. You may not have to use all of the information these questions generate, but their answers will embellish and enliven the conversation about the vision.

Writing a Vision Statement

Vision statements are written in words that are compelling and meaningful to people. They should act like a fuel injector for people's excitement. Nice words, safe words, do not jazz people. Vision statements must be bold and challenging. "We want to be the best" doesn't differentiate you from anyone else who is thinking about his or her vision. However, "Every family vehicle capable of 75 miles per gallon" or "clean water for every human being" are examples that have some energy to them! Use words that viscerally energize people.

Rather than writing your vision statement in future tense, which describes something yet to be created, it is more powerful to write it in *present* tense, describing your vision *as if it were your current reality*. This causes people to act as if the vision is already true. It alters people's mindsets about the possibility and mobilizes positive momentum for action.

Building Collective Ownership for Your Vision

Prior to or in parallel with creating the vision statement, design a process to build ownership for creating the vision throughout the organization. This dissemination does not just mean publishing the words. Many leaders believe that announcing the vision will suffice for its execution. In fact, they are confusing announcement with the emotional commitment and mental integration required

Exhibit 5.1.   **Questions for Visioning**

WORKSHEET

- What is the ideal outcome for the transformation?

- Beyond creating greater profitability, what is your purpose in making this change?

- What difference will it make in the lives of your customers?

- What difference will it make in the lives of the people in the organization?

- How will it add value to each of your stakeholders?

- How will this transformation help the organization better meet the demands of its marketplace?

- What excites you the most about making this change?

- What strengths does the organization have now which support the future?

- What would happen if the organization did not complete this transformation successfully? What would be lost? What is at risk?

- How would the organization ideally operate to achieve this reality?

- What are the ideal structural, technological, and financial conditions for supporting this outcome?

- What is the ideal culture for the organization to produce this outcome?

- What are the ideal mindsets, behaviors, and values of the leaders and employees to support this transformation?

for implementation. Again, remember the Five Levels of Communication Model. Address at least the first four levels in your vision rollout strategy. People must not only understand and commit to the vision, but they have to talk about it to know how it changes their work and lives so they can decide what level of commitment they have to make it real. If you do not share your vision statement in meaningful ways, and enable people to discuss and think about it, you will lose a great opportunity for building momentum. Go back and review the previous task on the process for communicating your case for change, and check for where and how your vision rollout might occur.

Remember that after the vision is shared, each segment of the organization will have to explore the implications it has on its operations and culture. The dissemination process you design should include this tailoring and many opportunities

CASE-IN-POINT

In one large telephone company, a very creative strategy was employed to disseminate its new values-based vision. The Values Group, after completing their statement and the story behind it, designed a piece of jewelry—a pin—to symbolize the core values of their vision. They initiated their vision dissemination process by having each group member "pin" two other people out in the organization who were demonstrating the new values by their behavior. Each person being pinned was told the story of the values and given the pin and a card with an oath to be true to the values. The group member then asked that each of those people go through the same ritual while pinning two more people in the organization and telling the values story. Each person was given two pins and cards and the charge to continue the ritual until a critical mass of people had been pinned and had communicated the new vision to others.

The organic nature of the ceremony embedded the values and the vision faster and more sincerely than any formal announcement could have. A large granite version of the pin's design was placed in the lobby of the headquarters building to represent the importance of its message to the whole organization. Every company building erected a "Values Wall" in its lobby to exhibit photographs of people living the values. These displays were changed quarterly to keep the values momentum alive.

for conversation. Keep in mind that in Phase III, you will design the future state in concrete terms that you believe will bring you closer to achieving your vision. Then, in Phase V, you will officially perform an in-depth impact analysis on the design, involving studying the impact on the various operating practices and norms currently at play. For now, just know that people will be thinking and talking about the impact that the vision will have on their work.

Task II.A.3: Demonstrate That Old Way of Operating Is Gone

In every change, there is a dynamic at play called inertia—people being attached to the old ways and not moving ahead. This phenomenon is very real in organizations that have become accustomed to their normal way of operating or invested in their current level of success. To overcome inertia, people must recognize that the future promised by the transformation is better and more essential than the past or the present. They must understand the relevance and meaning of what you are asking them to create. This is especially true if you are changing the organization's culture. Otherwise, they will not be willing to change.

Depending on the magnitude of the transformation, people may feel sad or angry about leaving behind the work or ways of operating they have been devoted to. This is to be expected. However, *until people let go of the reality they are living in, they will not be able to embrace something new.* No amount of pleading, selling, or coercion will force them to let go. So you must make sure they feel honored and respected for what they have been doing up until the moment you tell them it is no longer going to be the way. Keep this in mind as you plan your culture change and people strategies.

There are two basic approaches to the task of getting people's attention—abrupt and gradual. We have already discussed bold actions in Chapter Three. You can create bold action activities that are stunning, graphic wake-up calls that the old is now dead, as in the two following cases, or you can gradually deliver this message over time through more subtle actions. Our preference is to use both approaches. Be sure to use your bold actions to demonstrate that the existing way of doing things has served its purpose, and the future will be very different. Again, be very conscious of your messages for changing old cultural norms, as they have a tendency to come back or stick around. You might need to use a series of bold actions to demonstrate your intent to change the culture.

A steel company's leaders gathered the members of one of its poorly perform-ing plant management team together very early one morning. They wanted the managers to read the town's newspaper headlines for that day all at once, in person. Unbeknownst to the managers, the corporate leaders had printed a special "in-house" edition of the newspaper, just for this meeting. Their goal was to give the managers a very loud wake-up call.

The newspaper headline read, "Steel Plant to Close for Lack of Performance. Town Goes Belly Up!" It took several seconds for the impact of the headline to register with the managers. The leaders silently let the weight of the trumped-up news sink in. Then they revealed that the newspaper was a prop, and the discussion about the impending change began.

A manufacturing company's leaders wanted to signal to their organization that their old successful product line was going to be replaced by more technologically advanced versions. Not wanting to tarnish the respect and fame that the old line had produced, the leaders unveiled a museum in their corporate headquarters lobby. Under glass, in the most revered display, were prime samples of the long line of products that had been previously retired, *including the most current versions.* The products were honored, and the message was clear that each was now a "thing of the past."

This task is a tricky one in cases in which the current reality must continue but in a lesser or different way. In the electric utility industry, for example, regu-lated businesses continue. Rather than being the only show in town, though, they also share the stage with more entrepreneurial businesses. In manufacturing, there are still standard products made and sold, but customization of unique solutions must also be embraced. The challenge remains for how to maintain relevant current operations while still clearly signaling the need to take on a new reality.

ACTIVITY II.B: INCREASE ORGANIZATION'S CAPABILITY TO CHANGE

Although all organizations have experienced major change, few have done it consistently well, and most have struggled. Not very many leaders have taken the time to learn from their experience and integrate their learnings into how they plan and run their required changes going forward. Building people's *ongoing* ability to change is a major investment in the organization's future.

In the Introduction to this book, we presented our assumptions that change is now the norm in organizations and that leaders increasingly recognize the strategic advantage of establishing change leadership capability and formal disciplines for change in-house. It is also our assumption that change leadership does not just live at the top of the organization. Change leaders are needed in all levels; anyone affected by change can directly support creating the future.

The first step in developing greater change capability in the organization is assessing the need for it. You did this for the change leaders in Task I.C.1. Here you will determine who in the organization needs greater change capability, and build it.

There are two types of development required to build people's change capability—change knowledge and skills, and realigning their mindsets and behavior. The decision to develop people in the first is easier to take on because it relates to their intellect and competencies, both familiar territories. Commitment to change mindset and behavior, however, is an overt statement by leaders that people must transform along with the organization's structures and systems. Allocating resources and time to personal change communicates how important people are to the future success of the organization. We often feel that it is a breakthrough in leadership's thinking to recognize and fund this work. However, we realize that managers and employees are not always receptive to this type of training, especially in harsh economic times.

Like the executives, workers may not recognize the need to change themselves personally to support a transformation. They may feel threatened, manipulated, or fearful of engaging in something they consider too "personal." Many people will not want to participate unless they first see the executives modeling this work and experience the value it brings.

Special consideration must be given to how you position this type of development so that you make it compelling for people. Make all development relevant to the needs of the transformation and not about people's behavior outside of the work environment. People must come to recognize that the change imperatives demand new ways of thinking, behaving, and relating that are of direct importance to their performance. In this context, the personal development work has practical relevance and benefit to those who must change. Again, the leaders must go first. If you have not already read *Beyond Change Management*, do so to better understand what this work requires. It is a central theme of that book.

Task II.B.1: Build Organization's Change Knowledge and Skills

Most leaders have invested in the formal discipline of project management as their sole vehicle for leading all change. Some have added change management practices to help deal with communications, training, or resistance issues. As we described in *Beyond Change Management*, neither is adequate to leading transformational change, or most other large-scale changes. In most organizations, little training is provided to change leaders about the unique people and process dynamics of transformation. Often, no attention or resources are devoted to building change skills, embedding a common process methodology, or deploying best change practices. When your organization is undergoing a major transformation, this is a prime opportunity to develop capability while you produce results. The upcoming Case-in-Point describes one such strategy.

This Phase II task formalizes the awareness, skills, and knowledge various people or groups in the organization require to best support the transformation, and then initiates this development. We recommend education about known best practices for change, The Change Leader's Roadmap methodology and its resources, conscious process design, rapid course correction, and other change leadership competencies. We also recommend providing this training using your actual change as the basis for application and discovery. Beyond training, other development vehicles may include coaching, mentoring, consulting, or various communication mechanisms. You might post a range of recommended change tools on a change leadership intranet site for common usage. In organizations that have five or more change consultants, we also recommend the creation of a Change Leadership Community of Practice or Center of Excellence to support and accelerate conscious learning and consulting success.

Whom do you target for development? Consider the individuals and groups in your project community. You already have a process in place for the core change leaders (Task I.D.4). Now consider upper and middle management, first-line supervisors, project managers, staff groups involved in the change, in-house change agents and consultants, union leadership, and other groups. If there are external consulting firms helping you with this change, ensure that each has an understanding of The Change Leader's Roadmap and how it impacts their work for you and with each other. You might also involve customers and suppliers if they must participate in your change process in an informed way.

We recommend that you work closely with your human resources and training departments to integrate your development plans with the organization's general executive, management, and employee development strategies. Some organizations have included the development of change leadership capability as a feature of their talent development processes. Make sure to engage your organization development function to leverage their work with internal clients to promote greater change capability.

Task II.B.2: Promote Required Mindset and Behavior Change

All transformational changes require new ways of thinking and behaving in a critical mass of the organization. Many transitional changes do as well. In fact, these changes will not happen unless people change their mindsets and ways of relating. What mindsets are needed? That depends on your change. New worldviews about leadership style, power and control, engagement, shared responsibility across boundaries, being of service, quality and safety, and the need to nurture long-term relationships are some of the more critical mindset shifts required. Behavior changes might pertain to sharing information across functions and levels, authentic communication, taking risks, collaboration, innovation, interpersonal relationships, and customer service. To determine what mindsets and behaviors your particular transformation demands, you must understand its human and cultural requirements. Your work in Activity I.B, where your scoped your change, can inform this. Then you can develop a plan to promote your required shifts in mindset and behavior in your key stakeholder groups.

The purpose of this task is to help you create these plans. However, even with the importance of this work, it is our experience that leaders rarely focus sufficient attention on the need for new mindsets and behaviors, for all of the reasons we have been discussing. Our experience with some of the most advanced, creative high-tech giants has shown their reluctance to deal with anything "personal." It has been

A six-region, seven-hospital healthcare system was facing a major transformation to integrate its systems and processes and streamline its care delivery approach and procedures to ensure greater patient safety, quality care, and reduced costs. The internal director of change management decided to use The Change Leader's Roadmap methodology as the one approach to both build change leadership capability and provide consistent support to all of the changes required over the transformation's seven-year roadmap.

Initially, the organization's change consultants and key change stakeholders were introduced to the CLR in a working session that applied it to a familiar change effort. This group included a few physician leaders who understood the need to lead their changes more effectively. The working group recognized the value and fit of the CLR with their approach and culture, and agreed to have the senior executives—all of whom were to be sponsors of upcoming transformational initiatives—briefed in the model.

After the first set of transformational initiatives was identified and announced, a series of CLR trainings was scheduled for their initiative leaders, project managers, project coordinators, and change teams. All of the trainings were directly applied to the launch or continuation of the initiatives. Where appropriate, external consultants who brought a specific content expertise to projects were also trained in the use of the CLR. Their effective use of it, however, required a good deal of coaching from the internal change consultants.

The internal change consultants partnered closely with Being First consultants and continued to master the CLR through live application and direct coaching. Periodically, the change consultants and Being First consultants met with various project teams to evaluate their progress, provide coaching on their plans and use of CLR resources, and identify needs for course correction. This helped keep everything on track and made the development process overt and relevant to their projects.

Progress reports were provided to the transformation's System Change Leadership Team, made up mostly of the organizations' executives. These sessions also provided the opportunity for the Being First consultant to observe and coach the senior leaders to walk the talk of the transformation, address enterprise issues strategically, and shift their mindsets, behavior, and culture. As various initiatives ended or new people joined the teams or formed new teams, the organization continued to offer one or two trainings a year on the use of the CLR to the leads and project teams.

This change capability approach led to much better results from various initiatives, early detection of major course corrections, required changes in project leadership, and the establishment of common change practices and capability to drive all future change. Above all, it made the leadership of change an organizational priority and gave the executives the strategic oversight of the vast number of changes required for their transformation to succeed.

very interesting for us to observe the difficulties a number of these organizations are facing, which we attribute in part to their over-focus on external results and neglect of internal human development aligned to their change outcomes.

In this methodology, executives, managers, and the workforce are encouraged to actively participate in personal transformation that is directly relevant to creating their new business outcomes. To start, you might hold discussions about prevailing mindsets that these groups observe and the impact they have on the changes underway. You might invite brainstormed ideas of the new mindsets and behaviors required for the change to succeed. Often, if you invite anonymous suggestions and examples of what is needed and what has to change for that to happen, for example, in a blog, you will get very honest and very insightful recommendations to consider. Where possible, tie these new ways to your performance management and reward systems and make them real.

In more in-depth cases, you might initiate a "breakthrough process"—a series of events designed to raise people's self-awareness and define the personal changes they must make. You would establish the purpose for the process when communicating your case for change. You would likely carry it out and reinforce these changes over the course of your entire transformation. This work needs to be integrated with the Leadership Breakthrough process begun in Activity I.D.

Some of the breakthrough work can be done in existing work groups, while some can be accomplished in training settings or large group meetings where a shared experience and greater momentum is more easily created, such as that described in the Leadership Breakthrough process of DTE Energy in Task I.D.2 in Chapter Two.

SUMMARY

You have now begun to build momentum for your transformation. The organization understands the case for change and your change strategy and has participated in creating a shared vision of the future it will create. You have initiated strategies throughout the organization to increase the level of knowledge and skill for succeeding in the transformation, including mindset and behavioral change for the workforce.

CONSULTING QUESTIONS FOR ACTIVITY II.A: BUILD ORGANIZATIONAL UNDERSTANDING OF CASE FOR CHANGE, VISION, AND CHANGE STRATEGY

Task II.A.1: Communicate Case for Change and Change Strategy

▶ How will you communicate the case for change and your change strategy? How will you ensure that they are understood and supported by your stakeholders?

▶ How will you ensure that people have a safe and positive way to dialogue about what they are hearing and what it means to them?

▶ How will you handle people's resistance and upset about what the organization is planning to do?

▶ How do the change leaders want to be perceived in this communication? How will you support them to achieve this intention?

Task II.A.2: Roll Out Process to Create Shared Vision and Commitment

▶ How will you engage the organization in either building or understanding the vision for the transformation?

▶ How will you build commitment for the vision and what it requires?

▶ How will you ensure that all segments of the organization understand their part in creating the vision?

Task II.A.3: Demonstrate That Old Way of Operating Is Gone

▶ How will you demonstrate that the old ways of operating are gone?

▶ How will you pay respect to the past?

▶ How will you reinforce that the past is the past should people start to slip back into old habits?

CONSULTING QUESTIONS FOR ACTIVITY II.B: INCREASE YOUR ORGANIZATION'S CAPABILITY TO CHANGE

Task II.B.1: Build Your Organization's Change Knowledge and Skills

▶ What stakeholder groups will you target for developing change knowledge and skills?

▶ Which people working on specific change initiatives need more change leadership capability to succeed?

▶ What specific change knowledge areas and skills will you develop?

▶ How will you build the required change knowledge and skills to directly support the work of change projects?

▶ How will you embed best change practices and tools from The Change Leader's Roadmap?

Task II.B.2: Promote Required Mindset and Behavior Change

▶ How will you position this personal change work in the organization so that it is acceptable and relevant to people?

▶ Will you use external expertise to facilitate this work? What criteria will you use to select a vendor?

▶ How can you use your change leaders to be models of this process? How can they assist it while furthering their own mindset and behavior change?

▶ If you use breakthrough trainings for the workforce, how will you integrate the outcomes of these sessions with the leaders' own breakthrough process?

▶ How will you reinforce new mindsets and behaviors throughout the life of the transformation?

CHAPTER

6

PHASE III
Assess the Situation to Determine Design Requirements

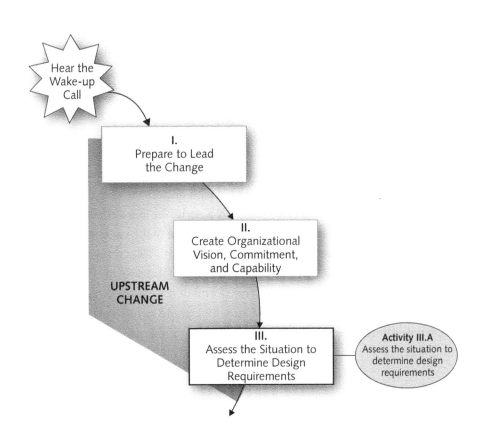

Hear the
Wake-up
Call

I.
Prepare to Lead
the Change

II.
Create Organizational
Vision, Commitment,
and Capability

UPSTREAM
CHANGE

III.
Assess the Situation to
Determine Design
Requirements

Activity III.A
Assess the situation to
determine design
requirements

PHASE III: TASK DELIVERABLES

III.A.1: Assessment of relevant aspects of the organization's current reality is complete. Aspects that must stay in place, be dismantled, or be created have been identified.

III.A.2: Relevant best practices from other organizations have been identified.

III.A.3: Customer requirements are clear.

III.A.4: The statement of design requirements is complete.

Phase III is the last phase in the upstream stage of change. You have set your foundations for success, have a clear vision of your desired future, and are increasing momentum for the transformation throughout the organization. It is now time to get specific about what the future state actually needs to look like and how it has to operate to meet the expectations of your vision, and the needs of your end users. To do this consciously, you must generate accurate and adequate information to guide the design process coming up in the next phase. How will you know which road to take? How will you know what currently exists in the organization that you will carry forward? How will you know which of your possible design scenarios will best serve the needs of your customers and users? Have the leaders declared any boundary conditions that the future state design must respect?

People are generally all too eager to jump headlong into designing various future state scenarios based on their opinions or political positions, rather than on relevant parameters. Phase III surfaces information that defines what success means in specific terms and what the organization already has in place that supports this success. This information is formulated into tangible *design requirements*. You will use these requirements to shape your future state so that it satisfies your transformational imperatives, including the needs of the people who must make the change a reality.

This information is generated through a series of assessments—of the current state of your organization, of other organizations that have engaged in similar changes, and of your customers' or end users' needs. Your design requirements are the culmination of the four tasks of this phase. You will use them to design your future state in Phase IV. If your transformation focuses on culture, you will assess the current or "old" culture and use this data to help shape what you need the desired culture to be, and what already exists in the organization that supports that future.

There are valuable benefits from clarifying design requirements:

- They articulate clear expectations for success, which includes meeting customer and user needs.
- They ensure that the leaders are aligned about what the design of the future needs to produce.
- They influence the creation of various design scenarios.
- They can be used to evaluate design options.
- They can trigger needed course corrections during implementation.
- They can be a part of your evaluation of the desired state after implementation is complete.
- They can further clarify what in your current organization supports the future state, what must change, and what must be left behind.

ACTIVITY III.A: ASSESS THE SITUATION TO DETERMINE DESIGN REQUIREMENTS

Task III.A.1: Assess Relevant Aspects of Your Organization

Your vision of the future is by definition different from the current reality in the organization. To know just how different the two are, you need to design and perform an assessment to compare them. This assessment focuses on the requirement the vision has in both business/operational aspects and human/cultural aspects of the organization. If your change is transformational, make sure that this assessment studies all relevant aspects of your current culture. It is important to know the following:

- What already exists in the organization that supports your vision in each of these areas
- What you will have to change or dismantle
- What you must create from scratch

This information is essential to shaping your design requirements. Seek information from your project community, especially people who are deeply involved in the transformation, are the end users of the new state, are impacted by it, or have a stake in it. Customers and others outside your organization can be a valuable source of insight. If the leaders have provided clear boundary conditions from their Phase I work, use those to influence the requirements your assessment generates.

Change assessment studies are different from generic survey research assessments performed in traditional organization development practices. Generic organizational studies are typically open-ended and general, searching out anything that is not working well in the organization. Change assessments are purposely designed to provide *specific* information necessary to create a realistic future state. For instance, if your transformation is about establishing an e-commerce business platform, your assessment would ask about products and services that could be sold over the Internet and how selling such products might best be handled. You would not want to hear about other matters occurring in the organization that do not specifically relate to your e-commerce vision.

You can use change assessments to raise people's expectations and investment in the transformation. For instance, you might ask people-in-the-know their opinions about the three most important features required for the new organization or culture to succeed, or what they believe to be the three greatest hurdles to that success. You might ask what the managers or workers see that they think the executives may be overlooking as they plan for the future. Clearly, you would ask about the types of design requirements they think are essential.

Exhibit 6.1, Determining Your Design Requirements, lists several types of design requirements and gives examples of each. You may find that other types of requirements are essential to your design as well. Be sure to clarify the types of design requirements you are researching before conducting your assessment. You can use this list as a worksheet to assist with your own determination of design requirements or customize your own worksheet based on the types of design requirements you are seeking.

The assessment methods you choose—be they individual or group interviews, large group interventions, or an online survey—will influence the level of receptivity people have for the change. Inviting engagement in a study fuels positive momentum. People then anticipate some result to occur and will expect to hear back from you. Be sure to inform your assessment participants about the results of the study and how you will use these results to influence your design. Consider communicating about your assessment results to the general organization to keep people abreast of progress.

Exhibit 6.1. Types of Design Requirements

ORGANIZATIONAL CONSTRAINTS, BOUNDARY CONDITIONS, OR "MUST HAVES"

What factors must absolutely be included in the design? What is considered "in game" or "out of game"? Categories might include financial parameters, customer or user requirements, equipment, people involved, management processes, time-to-market, and so on.
   Examples: Maximum staff size; required use of existing technology

MISSION, VISION, AND BUSINESS IMPERATIVES

Examples: Enables e-business marketing and sales; allows an integrated product sales approach; promotes patient-centric service or optimizes ambulatory care

ASSESSMENT ISSUES

Any concern or benefit raised in the assessment study
   Examples: Enables a ten-day or faster production time; enables on-time delivery; ensures accurate and timely input of data or sharing of data across organizational boundaries

JOB REQUIREMENTS/TASKS

Any requirement for workflow or content of jobs or functions
   Examples: Centralizes scheduling function; approves all financial decisions; enables immediate access to patient records

ORGANIZATIONAL MINDSET AND BEHAVIOR

Any requirements for modeling and demonstrating the organization's desired mindset and behavior
   Examples: Values and ensures early customer input to new product designs and upgrades (market-driven mindset); enables teamwork, shared responsibility, cross-boundary communication; allows for high engagement and innovation and less top-down control and risk aversion

POLITICAL IMPLICATIONS

Any relationship or circumstance that involves political influence, turf, reputation, or power
   Examples: Retains strategy-level decision making in the office of the chief executive; titles reflect contribution, not hierarchical power

CULTURAL IMPERATIVES/VALUES TO MODEL

Examples: Ensures and rewards cross-boundary sharing of information; promotes a service culture; puts patient safety first

(continued)

Exhibit 6.1. Types of Design Requirements (continued)

TECHNOLOGICAL NEEDS

Examples: Uses existing plant equipment; enables bedside input of patient data; enables smooth assimilation of software upgrades

PEOPLE REQUIREMENTS

Examples: Maintains existing complement levels; enhances on-the-job development opportunities and cross-training; brands us as a "best place to work" organization

You may also generate design requirements by having your respondents answer the following:

- "We want an organization (or system, culture, process, or technological solution) that is able to. . . ."
- "This organization (or system, etc.) will be successful if it. . . ."
- "To meet customer requirements, we must have an organization (or culture, etc.) that. . . ."

Task III.A.2: Benchmark Other Organizations for Best Practices

Since the quality movement began, benchmarking has become common practice. Fortunately, it is seen as an honor to be perceived publicly as a "benchmark organization." Because benchmark organizations are open to sharing their "secrets" with the world, learning from them can be very valuable at this point in your process. Their relevant best practices can be strategically used to help define your design requirements.

The first step in this task is to uncover organizations that are "top-in-class" in the specific content areas of your change (e.g., customer service, culture, EHR [electronic health record] usage, manufacturing processes, IT). Set a clear scope for your search before beginning. Your process might include site visits, telephone interviews, literature searches, Web searches, or any other form of research that will surface recommended design requirements.

Task III.A.3: Clarify Customer Requirements

This task is one of the most important to determine what your future state needs to achieve. It provides a way to engage your customers in clarifying how your organization must change to serve them better. We continue to be surprised at the number of change efforts that are run by content experts who do not think to ask the people whose needs their solution is meant to serve what they need from it. Recently, we became aware of a multi-billion dollar U.S. government change effort initiated by then President G. W. Bush for the Homeland Security Administration. The effort is to create a "virtual fence" to monitor and protect the U.S. border with Mexico, stretching over 2,000 miles. In 2006, the contract to produce a visual surveillance system for the Border Patrol was granted to the Boeing Corporation, which promised a fast, economical, and secure solution by 2009. Three years later, they had installed a beta prototype for the first 28 miles of the U.S.-Mexico border that was providing slight help but failing to produce the promised outcomes.

The Director of Homeland Security for the Government Accountability Office was asked to investigate what was happening, and what value was coming from the $1 billion dollars already spent. He discovered that in the government's and Boeing's zeal to act, they had neglected to ask the Border Patrol—the end users—what their needs were and what conditions had to be taken into account for the technology to work. The Border Patrol identified that the beta prototype was ineffective in the desert weather, heat, over the distances requiring patrol, and in vehicles driving over very uneven ground. The beta system is now being recalled, and a new system is being designed for the same 28 miles—a system that will now take these design requirements into account. However, the absence of customer design requirements cost the U.S. government three years and more than a billion dollars.

Your customers' needs are key drivers of your future state solution and will define your success. Your customers may be your external customers, clients, or patients. Or they may be the people in the organization whose needs your change effort is meeting—your end users, or target groups for the change. These may be doctors, operational groups, front-line supervisors, sales teams, employee groups, researchers, and so on. How you go about contacting, interviewing, and relating to your external and your internal customers can pave the way for long-lasting and mutually satisfying relationships. The more you create partnerships with them, the better your chances of learning about their evolving needs and serving them over time. When you assessed the drivers of your change in Task I.B.2, you identified marketplace requirements and customers' needs. Be sure to build on this work.

Which customers are your best sources of guidance? How will you use this inquiry to strengthen your relationship with them? Consider creating a customer or stakeholder council to advise you throughout your transformation. Be aware of the mindset shifts that you are making and whether your customers are thinking outside of their own boxes when they give you guidance. You may have to create a mindset-shifting strategy for your customers so that together, you can push the envelope of change to create a much improved reality for them.

This is one area where an integrated effort is critical. Be sure to ask all your change initiative leaders which customers they will be speaking to. You do not want to alienate your customers with multiple requests.

Task III.A.4: Write Statement of Design Requirements

The output of Phase III is your statement of design requirements. Create this list using a compilation of your organization's assessment results, boundary conditions, best practices from other organizations, and your customers' and target groups' requirements. Review these inputs in light of your vision, and note any gaps. This review will reveal the high-leverage requirements for the design of your desired state.

SUMMARY

You have now completed the upstream stage of change. Take a moment to glance back at the ground you have covered. You have staffed your effort, developed its leaders to lead it collectively, and motivated the workforce to make your transformation a reality. Your reason for transforming is clear and compelling. Your change strategy provides the level of guidance necessary for an integrated and realistic rollout. Your change infrastructure provides the resources and support for handling the transformation in the midst of everyday pressures. And you have prepared yourself and the organization to design its future. We now proceed to Section Two, the *midstream stage* of the change process.

CONSULTING QUESTIONS FOR ACTIVITY III.A: ASSESS THE SITUATION TO DETERMINE DESIGN REQUIREMENTS

Task III.A.1: Assess Relevant Aspects of Your Organization

▶ What aspects of your current organization will you assess to determine the gap between what you have and what your vision demands?

▶ How will you assess the organization in light of any boundary conditions you have been given by the senior leaders?

- If your effort is transformational, how will you assess the organization's current culture against what it needs to be?
- What assessment methods will you use?
- Which people or groups will you engage in your assessment?
- How will you position this work to continue to generate momentum for your transformation?

Task III.A.2: Benchmark Other Organizations for Best Practices

- What benchmark information are you looking to gather?
- How will you identify benchmark organizations?
- How will you carry out this research, and who will do it?

Task III.A.3: Clarify Customer Requirements

- Who are your customers, your end users or target groups for this change?
- How will you determine your customers' requirements?
- What kind of a process will you use to keep your customers involved in shaping the outcomes of your transformation?
- Who are your best customer contacts for this work?
- Do you need to coordinate this effort among your various initiatives?

Task III.A.4: Write Statement of Design Requirements

- How will you compile your design requirements from all of the data you have collected?
- Who must approve these requirements?
- How will you ensure that your design requirements drive the creation of your design scenarios and respect any boundary conditions?

Midstream Change

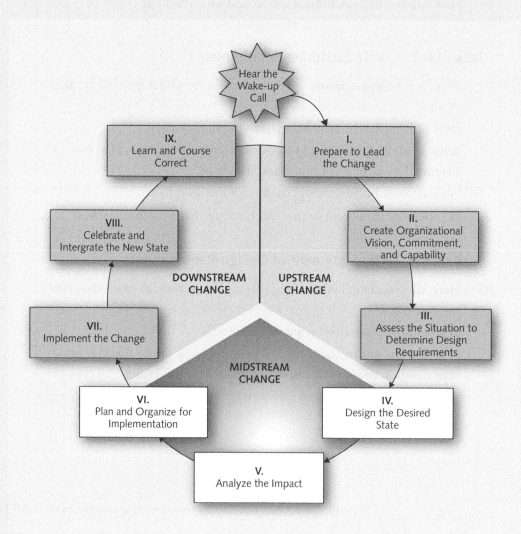

Hear the Wake-up Call

IX.
Learn and Course Correct

I.
Prepare to Lead the Change

VIII.
Celebrate and Intergrate the New State

II.
Create Organizational Vision, Commitment, and Capability

DOWNSTREAM CHANGE

UPSTREAM CHANGE

VII.
Implement the Change

III.
Assess the Situation to Determine Design Requirements

MIDSTREAM CHANGE

VI.
Plan and Organize for Implementation

IV.
Design the Desired State

V.
Analyze the Impact

PHASE IV

PHASE V

PHASE VI

CHAPTER

PHASE IV
Design the Desired State

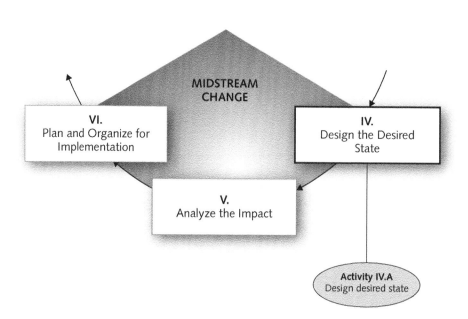

PHASE IV: TASK DELIVERABLES

IV.A.1: The process for designing your desired state has been defined, staffed, and mobilized.

IV.A.2: Your preferred desired state scenario has been created and approved.

IV.A.3: Your desired state has been tested in preparation for planning its implementation.

IV.A.4: Your desired state has been effectively communicated to the organization.

The midstream stage of change focuses on designing your desired state solution, determining the magnitude of work, resources, and time required to implement it successfully, and preparing the organization for implementation. The upstream preparation you have done will make this stage go more smoothly and expeditiously.

The purpose of Phase IV is to design the specific organizational and cultural solutions that will enable your organization to achieve its vision. We must clarify the difference between the *vision of the transformation*, which you have already articulated, and the *design of the future state*.

The vision of the transformation creates a compelling picture of the organization's reality when the transformation has been successfully implemented. It is, by definition, a quest, a dramatic stretch that energizes and motivates the organization to pursue this very different and exciting outcome. Metaphorically, the vision is the picture of the future from the 30,000-foot level. The vision is directional and inspirational, not necessarily tangible.

The design of the desired state is the view of the future from the 5,000-foot vantage point. It is the organization's best guess at what *specific* changes you require to accomplish to progress toward your vision and produce the results your business strategy needs. The design is much more tangible and addresses your scope of change, perhaps including changes to structure, systems, processes, technology, work practices, jobs, mindset, relationships, and cultural norms. It is still a picture of the future, but much more concrete.

To balance both the organizational and human requirements for success, make sure that your desired state design serves the people who must make it work, not just the results it is designed to produce. You must create the culture, relationships, rewards, and technology interfaces to support your people as well as operations, sales, and outcomes.

The activities of this phase use the design requirements you created in Phase III to develop the best future state scenarios, test them, and determine which one is the most likely to create an organization that will be successful. You will also be considering the aspects of your current organization that already serve your future state, so be sure to bring them into this process. From this point on in the change, the transformation is driven by your design of the desired state.

ACTIVITY IV.A: DESIGN DESIRED STATE

Task IV.A.1: Create Process and Structure to Design Desired State

There is a wide range of strategies for determining your desired state. Your process will vary depending on the type and scope of the change, mindset and style of the change leaders, and degree of in-house expertise needed to design the desired state. The process you use will impact not only your resulting design scenario but also the organization's understanding and commitment to make it happen. In the best of cases, the process to design your desired state is crafted by the change process leader, whose job is to ensure the right use of content experts to create an optimal design solution. This task should *not* be handed off to your content experts as, we will discuss shortly.

Your design process should enable you to specify, reinforce, and help drive the culture you are trying to create, even if the change effort is about structure or technology. The design process should model the desired values, guiding principles, mindset, and cultural norms you identified in Phase I. For instance, if culturally you are moving toward a more engaged workforce, you must design your future state in an engaging way. Your IT or structure content experts may not understand this perspective, yet it is a key success factor in transformational changes.

There are a number of political considerations to keep in mind in how you design your desired state. For instance, who gives input, what design features are given priority, and which design is selected will all have political implications. Keep these factors in mind as you proceed with this phase.

If you are using in-house resources to create your design, consider forming a design team of expert personnel or representatives from a cross-section of the organization impacted by the change or hosting a Future Search Conference, World Café, or other large group intervention. Remember, if your transformation includes a focus on culture, you must include people who are skilled at defining the details of culture.

Exhibit 7.1. How to Develop Your Desired State Design

- Who will oversee the design of this process?
- Who will you engage to create your various desired state scenarios?
- Will you use external content expertise, do the work in-house, or both?
- If you use external consultants as well as in-house resources, how will you ensure that the two groups work effectively together?
- If your transformation includes a focus on culture, who are the best people to define the details of the desired culture?
- Who will lead the design work from within the organization? If this person is known as a key content expert, how will you ensure that he or she uses the most appropriate process that reflects your desired culture and accounts for the many human dynamics at play?
- What role will the change leaders and the executives play in design? Have they approved your design requirements?
- What training or professional support does your in-house design team require?
- How will the actual desired state scenarios be generated? How will you use your design requirements and boundary conditions to guide this work?
- How will you handle the political dynamics that arise during the process?
- How will the various design scenarios be evaluated?
- What is the timetable for this entire phase?
- How will the effort be supported and given resources?
- How will the decision about the best desired state scenario be made?

Exhibit 7.1, How to Develop Your Desired State Design, offers several questions to guide your thinking for this task.

Use of External Consulting Services

When the magnitude of the transformation and the need for specialized expertise are great, many organizations turn their design effort over to external consulting firms. This can be a very effective approach—if these expert consultants are integrated into the overall process and style of the transformation. Problems arise, however, when the organization's executives make two serious mistakes: The first is when leaders believe change happens through only two stages, design and implementation (midstream and downstream stages). With this mindset, it seems reasonable to think that consultants could come in, determine the best design, and then leave the organization to its own devices to implement the solution. If no upstream preparation has been done, you can expect increased resistance from your internal experts and users, poor communications, more political jockeying, and a greater likelihood of a messy implementation.

The second major mistake happens when leaders think only about changing "content"—the formal aspects of their organizations, such as structure, IT, or business processes. You might commonly hear, "Oh, this is only an IT implementation." Caution! Remember the three elements of a comprehensive change strategy—content, people, and process. The narrow focus on content can inadvertently cause upheaval for your stakeholders, and for the change process. We have seen far too many organizations retain consulting firms that, under the promise of providing design help and efficiency, come in, take over, alienate key internal stakeholders, neglect the human dimensions, and behave in ways that are counter to the mindset and culture in the existing or desired state. This usually does more harm than good, creating major impediments to your change.

These problems arise because so many content consulting firms have a limited view of the people and process requirements of transformation. They rarely understand the importance of employee engagement, readiness, or how to handle people's reactions. They do not address mindset, culture, and behavior change. They are not trained or experienced in these areas and often prefer to stick to their technical specialties. Unfortunately, they are not exempt from negatively impacting the change process or the culture and human dynamics that surface strongly during the design phase, especially if the change is transformational. If left on their own, they can seriously complicate the political and emotional dynamics of your change effort. Because the consultants cannot be isolated from the organization's operating style and culture, they must at least take these factors consciously into account as they work to model *your* culture.

Having said this, we do support the use of expert consulting firms when leaders need their content expertise in the design phase of their overall transformation. However, leaders must be purposeful about how these consultants are used. Always ensure that your content consultants gather data from a full range of stakeholders and target groups about what they think will work best in your organization—especially from your direct users. Be sure they do *not* attempt to sell you on a standardized design just because it worked somewhere else.

In the absence of a skilled and legitimized change process leader to oversee a major change, many organizations are beginning to form partnerships between content consultants (internal and external) and organization development (OD) or change management (CM) practitioners (internal or external) to take advantage of the important process and people expertise OD and CM bring. This is a relatively new approach and requires emotional maturity from everyone to succeed. Decision-making authority, spans of control, roles, and professional contributions must be clearly differentiated, and the means for monitoring and course-correcting the interactions among all parties must be firmly in place from the onset. It is essential that change leaders set very clear ground rules for how they expect the different consulting groups to work together because these relationships can get very messy if left without accountability or coordination. Done well, this strategy can leverage the unique value each consulting firm brings, plus streamline the number and types of consultants being used.

Most of the major expert consulting firms have recognized the problem of having inadequate people and process expertise and have been building in-house capability to incorporate this expertise into their content design services and their marketing materials. Where many firms still separate people and process from content, some are attempting to integrate the three. They are also attempting to provide implementation services to support their design deliverables. From our observations, however, even if the words look good on paper, no one firm has yet mastered either of these integrations throughout the ranks of consultants who do the actual work in their client organizations. Where the requirements for these integrations may be clear with their practice leaders, the onsite delivery staffs usually have much to learn. Our recommendation is to use an internal change process leader who can create a design process to optimize your content expertise and take into consideration the organization's people and process dynamics.

Integrating Design Efforts Across the Organization

Most organizations have many interdependent change initiatives underway that may be in their design phase at the same time. Tasks I.E5 and I.E6 recommended that you perform an organization-wide scan of all change initiatives that may impact your current transformation. This scan should be able to tell you which initiatives are currently in design and, of those, which should be integrated into your transformation's design work, which have to be coordinated in parallel with it, and which are totally separate. This information should be reflected in your integration strategy and your design requirements for the organization's overall transformation. This is especially important if you are changing the organization's culture and have several content initiatives underway that will each affect that culture. Make sure to address culture consistently in all of them!

Task IV.A.2: Design Desired State

After the people you selected to develop the desired state are on board, knowledgeable about their task, and clear about their roles and the process, they proceed with the important work of designing the actual future state solution. Make sure that they use the design requirements you developed in Phase III to craft various scenarios for consideration.

Review the executives' roles in the design process and decision making before you begin. Frequently, executives want to stay close to the design process, usually to ensure that things are going the way they want. This can be advantageous as long as roles and decision making remain consistent with your previous start-up agreements or are *overtly* altered and agreed to by everyone engaged in design. Having people in power inappropriately step in and exert control at this juncture can do tremendous damage to the people's confidence about generating a sound design and outcome.

The scope of the transformation and any boundary conditions will indicate what the design work has to cover. Design may be needed for any relevant aspect of the organization—product or service development, business process development, organization and/or work redesign, culture, technology, information systems, or software design. Each area may require its own unique design process. Be sure to seek out expertise for the best designs for each of the featured content areas of your scope of change. And make sure that all of the pieces designed fit together into one integrated picture that will actually work on the ground.

There is a logical process to follow to create a design that will match your needs and function well in reality. Build your scenarios to fulfill the requirements of four sequential levels of design: vision, strategic, managerial, and operational. The first—vision—is the most conceptual. The next—strategic level—provides more direction of what is needed. The third then—managerial—shows how the overall design will function, and the fourth—operational—is the most concrete and definitive. Note that each of the words, "vision," "strategic," "managerial," and "operational" refers to a level of design; none of them refer, in this case, to the organization's vision, its strategy, its management, or its operations. Figure 7.1 illustrates the levels and gives some general examples of what is typically included in each level. Exhibit 7.2 applies the levels of design to the specific example of a reorganization. The example given is in prose, and a complete design for a reorganization would also include drawings of the actual new structure.

To complete your design scenario, you will work through all four levels, starting with vision and ending with operational. If you skip one of the higher levels, your managerial and operational designs may not function the way you intend, or they may actually compete with your desired outcomes. It is useful to check which levels of design reflect the various design requirements you are to meet.

It is essential for the people doing the design to be clear about what level they are designing and what information exists about the levels above their current focus. Nothing is more frustrating than working diligently on an operational design and

Figure 7.1. **Levels of Design Model**

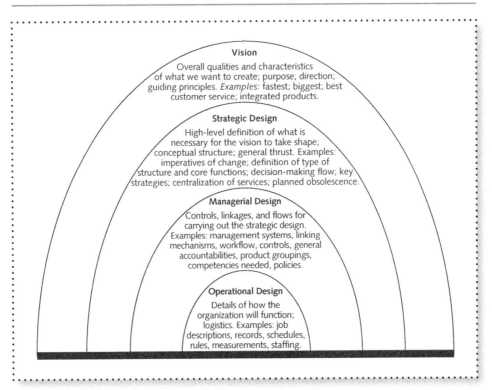

Vision
Overall qualities and characteristics of what we want to create; purpose; direction; guiding principles. *Examples:* fastest; biggest; best customer service; integrated products.

Strategic Design
High-level definition of what is necessary for the vision to take shape; conceptual structure; general thrust. Examples: imperatives of change; definition of type of structure and core functions; decision-making flow; key strategies; centralization of services; planned obsolescence.

Managerial Design
Controls, linkages, and flows for carrying out the strategic design. Examples: management systems, linking mechanisms, workflow, controls, general accountabilities, product groupings, competencies needed, policies.

Operational Design
Details of how the organization will function; logistics. Examples: job descriptions, records, schedules, rules, measurements, staffing.

Exhibit 7.2. Levels of Design Example Applied to Reorganization

- **Vision level:** Integrated system, efficient and adaptive, close to the customer
- **Strategy level:** Consolidate functions A, B, and C; move to strategic business units; create single point of customer contact within each business; create shared services; one CRM system for all
- **Managerial level:** Executive committee composed of all strategic business unit presidents; cross-business councils; shared services and one platform for all affected functions; business planning expertise in each business unit; interdependent and integrated customer service system
- **Operational level:** Twenty customer service centers staffed by fifty customer service representatives; "xyz" CRM system; customer satisfaction measurements; standardized information processing procedures; job descriptions; shared rewards

---

discovering that the strategic design is either not clear or emphasizes a different direction. Too often, leaders delegate the task of operational design without having thought about or reached consensus on the strategic or managerial levels, causing costly political and emotional battles. A very helpful design practice is to complete one level of design and have it approved before fine-tuning the next more tangible level. The approval process typically surfaces boundary conditions that were not previously known or obvious to the leaders. Better to find this out now than to have to make more costly course corrections after the design is thought to be complete.

It is common to complete the vision, strategy, and most of the managerial levels of design during this phase. Frequently, operational design must wait for more information to be available or for the people who will actually be leading the new business functions to be positioned to do this work to suit their needs. Keep in mind that some design work will also be accomplished during Phase VI, *Plan and Organize for Implementation*, when the impacts of the desired state are resolved and translated into specific actions for implementation.

Task IV.A.3: Pilot Test

Sometimes your desired state design is radically different from your old ways of operating or so complicated, costly, or risky that you may decide to test the design before proceeding with full-scale implementation. This task guides your planning and execution of a pilot test, learning from it, and refining your design, if necessary, before you proceed to gain full approval of it.

In one organization we worked with, the change process leader, a very conscious and creative man, decided that the organization needed to run a pilot program. Concerned about resistance, he announced to the organization that a pilot test would be run on the desired state scenario and that two sites would have the opportunity to contribute to the organization's future by testing the desired state, as well as be a year ahead of the game if they were successful in their efforts. He invited any site that was interested in pioneering the future to tell him why they should be selected and how they would proceed. Much to our surprise, more than half of the thirty potential sites submitted proposals. At the time, the desired state scenario was defined through the managerial level of design, requiring the chosen test sites to complete their own operational-level design as they figured out how to implement. Two sites were chosen; the test period was to be one year.

The two sites represented two very different leadership styles and cultures within the organization. One was more controlling, conservative, and pressured; the other was more engaging, open, and risk-taking. The conservative site rolled out its implementation with no consulting help, little margin for error, and minimal foundation-setting. The innovative site used the internal organization development consultants, selected its own change team to design the change strategy, spent considerable effort to identify and create conditions for success, and involved the front-line teams that were most impacted by the design.

Upon completion of the pilots, both sites reported important findings about the desired state, the change strategy used for their rollout, and the receptivity of the various target audiences in their organizations. The results of the pilots revealed predictable outcomes—the more innovative site that took a proactive and engaging approach proved to be the more positive. The conservative site was also considered "successful," although the culture, morale, and performance of the innovative site had observably more vitality, commitment, and buy-in. It was clearly the preferred wave of the future.

When designing a pilot, determine your strategy, the scope of your test, the outcomes you are after, the political implications of the site or areas you select for the test, and what criteria you will use to evaluate your results. Some leaders attempt to run pilot tests strictly to validate their design decision as-is. This imposed pressure can limit objective results. Some organizations attempt to run pilots as if in a "pure" laboratory environment, just setting them up in standard form and letting them unfold as they will. Others set the pilot up using their conditions for success and vision of the future, giving the test the greatest likelihood of demonstrating what they hope to achieve with their transformation. While any of the approaches are valid, the latter moves the process along with greater conscious intention.

Task IV.A.4: Communicate Desired State

After you have determined your preferred desired state, you will communicate it to your target groups, the organization, and all stakeholders. If your change is transformational, it carries no guarantees, and you must communicate your future state with a caveat: "This desired state is the organization's current best guess about what will bring us success. As the transformation toward this new state proceeds, everybody has to be on the lookout for emergent information or feedback that something better or different may still be required. Full commitment to this future state is critical, along with the understanding that the organization is in a learning process and that the future will continue to evolve until we figure out the specifics of how to achieve our vision."

This caveat is extremely important for transformational change to be successful. It reinforces the very nature of transformation and can help you to further dismantle the mindset that the leaders always have the right answers or that after a plan is put in motion, it must be completed with minimal change orders. This communication is a central part of waking up the organization's members to being full players in its *conscious* transformational process. Everybody has to be willing to provide feedback for course correction without being afraid of attack or becoming disheartened when further adjustments are needed. You want to prevent the common reaction that "the organization didn't get it right the first time." Instead, you want to instill the idea that course correction is the essence of transformation, and everyone has a part in it.

SUMMARY

You now have a desired state scenario that meets your design requirements. It is your best estimation of what will generate your transformational outcomes. The organization now understands what its future looks like and can proceed with the next step in making it a reality. The desired state is, by definition, different from the current reality in the organization. This fact brings us to the next critical phase in the change process, *Analyze the Impact*.

CONSULTING QUESTIONS FOR ACTIVITY IV.A: DESIGN DESIRED STATE

Task IV.A.1: Create Process and Structure to Design Desired State

▶ See Exhibit 7.1 for consulting questions on this task.

Task IV.A.2: Design Desired State

▶ How will you handle all four levels of design?

▶ Who has to approve each level of design for each major aspect of the desired state scenario?

▶ How will you integrate all of the pieces of your design for a complete picture of the future you will create?

▶ If your transformation focuses on culture change, how will you ensure that the organization's desired culture is designed and aligned with each of the other content change efforts underway?

Task IV.A.3: Pilot Test

▶ If a pilot test is required, how will you determine the best site(s) for the test?

▶ Will you set up your pilot test intentionally with conditions for success or allow it to unfold in the organization naturally?

▶ How will you measure the effectiveness of your pilot test(s)?

How will you deal with data that surface in your pilot(s) indicating the need to course correct your desired state design? To handle redesign, will you involve everyone from the original design process or select a few for fine-tuning?

What is your timeline for the pilot(s)? Does this timeline allow for an adequate test?

Task IV.4: Communicate Desired State

How will you communicate the desired state to your entire organization?

If your change is transformational, how will you position it with the "caveat" to encourage stakeholders to look out for its continuous evolution?

How will you communicate where you are in the overall change process and what the organization can expect next?

PHASE V
Analyze the Impact

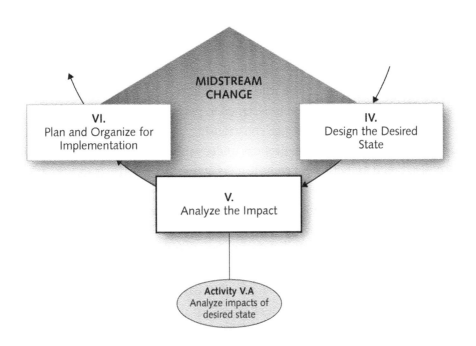

PHASE V: TASK DELIVERABLES

V.A.1: Your impact analysis process has been designed, communicated, and initiated.

V.A.2: The impacts of the change effort have been identified, grouped, and assigned for resolution.

V.A.3: The magnitude of individual and collective impacts has been assessed and prioritized.

V.A.4: The desired state has been refined.

Too often, executives announce their desired state and then proceed head-first into implementation before having a realistic picture of how disruptive making this change will be on operations and their people, and how best to handle its complexity. They assume that people will deal with whatever is required of them to make the change on their own. By diving into implementation without understanding the true magnitude of its impact, they force their organizations into reaction, not acknowledging what they are really dealing with nor caring about how burdensome the change will be for those who must make it happen. These are costly and stressful mistakes, and this phase is designed to prevent them. It is one of the most important phases for leading change consciously.

The impact analysis process deepens understanding of the transformation and your desired state for both the change leaders and the workforce. It secures greater buy-in from those who have had a chance to give input—resisters and supporters alike—and drives a more realistic change plan. Handled well, it is the turning point in the process from imagining the transformation to acting on it.

Phase V accomplishes six important functions: (1) it determines what in the current state can be brought forward to support the desired state, thus minimizing some of the disruption of change; (2) it reveals the true magnitude of work required to implement the desired state; (3) it enables clear decision making about capacity requirements to make the change in your given timeframe; (4) it surfaces show-stopper issues that will impede the achievement of your vision; (5) it gives your resisters an opportunity to input to the change process in a constructive way; and (6) it ensures that the desired state will function effectively as an integrated system.

To handle the first two functions, Phase V assesses the impacts of the desired state on the current organization and its culture and people. In essence, this function is a detailed gap analysis, determining the differences between the old state and your desired state—what already works and can stay in place, what directly blocks the future state and must be dismantled, and what must be created anew to have the new state work. Impact analysis surfaces the issues that remain before you can devise a clear and realistic implementation plan.

Accomplishing this work in a conscious way addresses functions 3 through 6 just mentioned. Registering just how much work is required to implement effectively brings to light the actual capacity and pacing requirements. You must ensure that you have this capacity to execute implementation. Your investigation into the realities of how the desired state must operate may identify things that will absolutely not work in the desired state—show stoppers—and you may have to refine your design. Perhaps these issues are too radical or too costly. It is better to uncover them here than be surprised by them during implementation.

This is a perfect place to engage your "nay-sayers" in the organization. It is a time when you *want* to hear what your most oppositional people think because they likely see things that you don't want to about what is required for the change to work. And lastly, thinking through how your desired state needs to work for its optimal performance demands that you recognize all of the factors in the existing organization that must be aligned to support it.

All of this work happens between this phase and Phase VI. Your analysis and identification of magnitude of change happens here, and the actual issue resolution and planning for an optimal implementation occurs in Phase VI. A good deal of work to think things through occurs between these two phases. Figure 8.1, Impact Analysis and Implementation Planning Process, shows the work of these two phases in a flow chart, culminating in your actual Implementation Master Plan.

Your Phase V impact analysis differs from the initial impact analysis you performed when building your case for change in Phase I. The initial impact analysis is designed to assess the general magnitude of your transformation so you can determine its accurate scope. Now that you have a more precise picture of what your new state will entail, you can perform a more comprehensive analysis of the full scope with which to plan implementation. The Conscious Change Leader Accountability Model is the backdrop for looking consciously at all quadrants, all levels, and the process to determine the work to successfully implement your future state.

It is important to note that the work of impact analysis is "located" in this particular phase. However, many people make the faulty assumption that after they complete impact analysis here, they can check the box and be done with it.

Figure 8.1. Impact Analysis and Implementation Planning Process

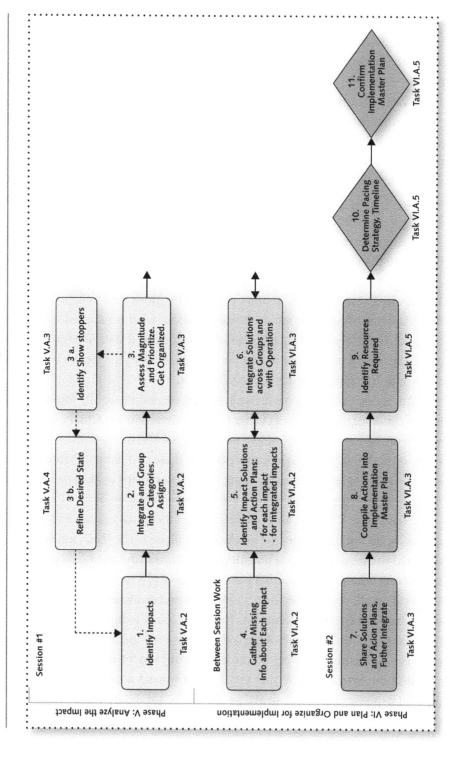

In reality, you always need to be aware of impacts—from the moment you determine your scope of change in Phase I, all the way through the realization of your results in Phase IX. It is ongoing. Any time you alter scope or make a course correction, review for impacts and add them to this phase or resolve them as you go.

ACTIVITY V.A: ANALYZE IMPACTS OF DESIRED STATE

To design your impact analysis process, you will need to hone the types of impacts you are looking for. There are three areas of focus for generating impact issues: (1) the formal organization, including structures, management systems, business processes, skills, numbers of people, technology, functions or departments, customers, and work practices; (2) the human and cultural aspects of the organization, including mindset, behavior, relationships, and all elements of culture; and (3) interactions between any of the factors on either list.

You can apply the tool you used to perform your initial impact analysis (see Chapter One, Task I.B.5, Exhibit 1.3) to identify impacts from the first two parts of this assessment. It covers both the formal elements and the human elements of the organization. Scan it again with your desired state scenario in mind, adding any additional items requiring attention in this detailed assessment. Interactive impacts can be identified through open dialogue among change leaders and/or the stakeholders you engage in the impact analysis process.

Here is a sample list of types of impacts you may discover. Note they are phrased in actionable terms so that you are clear about the work required to resolve them:

- Study the organizational structure for how to reduce it by one layer of management.
- Research how to consolidate products X and Y for ease of joint sale and delivery to customers.
- Study mindset, behavior, and protocols in surgery to improve patient safety and reduce adverse events.
- Redesign the resource allocation process to match new operating priorities.
- Assess cultural norms in sales to identify how to build stronger and more sustainable customer relationships.
- Study how to broaden the "abc" family of products (e.g., acquisition or in-house start-up?).

- Figure out how to overcome the attitude of entitlement in the R&D department.
- Redesign the reward system to motivate greater team performance and reduce "rugged individualism."

Task V.A.1: Design Process for Conducting Impact Analysis

There are many ways to go about analyzing the impacts of your desired state and many areas to study. The impact analysis process looks different for every change effort. In some cases, you may design a formal study; in others, you may use an intuitive scan. Design your study to involve all levels and parts of the organization affected. Include representatives of all groups who have a stake in the transformation, especially those who will be most impacted by it. They are primary sources of impact issues and information. Who knows the impact of a future scenario better than those who will be directly affected by it?

Impact analysis is a particularly valuable activity in which to use stakeholder engagement, especially from resisters. Your goal is to discover all that stands in the way of the transformation happening successfully. The identification of obstacles, issues, and conflicts is welcome information to you at this point, and when you listen to and validate the perceptions of the people opposed to the change, you will likely surface unforeseen good ideas, reduce these people's resistance, and enroll them more in the transformation. Their input may even change the face of the effort!

This first task creates the process for conducting the impact analysis. Read over the remaining tasks before designing your study process. Because the work of this phase moves seamlessly into the work of Phase VI, consider designing your process for these two phases simultaneously. Exhibit 8.1, Steps in the Impact Analysis and Implementation Planning Process, outlines the work for doing so. It matches and builds on the flow chart in Figure 8.1 in the introduction to this activity. The change process leader typically guides the design of this work.

Task V.A.2: Identify and Group Impacts

In most large-scale changes, a thorough impact analysis can generate hundreds of issues. This can cause the dynamic called "analysis paralysis" and thoroughly overwhelm people. Be aware of this tendency, especially in organizations with cultures that support detail and thoroughness. Your challenge is to obtain the

Exhibit 8.1. **Steps in the Impact Analysis (IA) and Implementation Planning Process**

1. Design your IA process and the vehicles you will use. Determine who will be involved in what activities. Select and list the topics you want people to assess, and be open to new topics that you may not yet have considered. You will be assessing both formal organizational/technical topics, as well as cultural and human impacts.

2. Select and gather the appropriate people to input to the impact analysis. Consider selecting people who have expertise in the areas being analyzed, people who will have to learn to use the new state solution on the ground, and people who understand the human impacts of making these kinds of changes. Ensure everyone is adequately familiar with the desired state design.

3. Conduct your impact analysis, comparing your current state with your desired state design. First, identify what already exists to support the desired state. You will need to sustain and reinforce these. Then identify impacts by considering the following:

   a. What directly blocks the desired state and must be dismantled

   b. What needs to be created anew to support the desired state

   c. Questions that need answers

   d. Issues that need resolution

4. Categorize impacts into thematic groups. Remove redundancies and consolidate into streamlined lists. Assign oversight of each grouping to an impact group leader.

5. Impact group leaders select and gather their team members and their roster of impact issues to resolve.

6. Impact groups prioritize impacts to assess the magnitude of change the impacts will have. Determine the terms by which you will assess magnitude. Rate each issue by Show Stopper, High, Medium, or Low rankings, where:

   ▸ **Show Stoppers** are radical impacts that require immediate attention by decision makers, as they will likely require a change in the desired state design. Leaders must review these impacts and confirm or alter the design as quickly as possible to minimize people doing impact resolution work that could be made irrelevant by a change of design.

   ▸ **High** impacts can go directly into implementation planning and have no redesign implications. High impacts are very significant and need immediate attention because of their sheer size, or because their resolution will have bearing on how other impacts might get resolved. Consequently, attend to them quickly to maximize efficiency.

   ▸ **Medium** impacts are critical to identify their solution now but do not have top priority. These impacts can often be resolved within an impact grouping team and usually do not have cross-group interdependencies.

   ▸ **Low** means impacts that you do not need to attend to right now or that may resolve as a part of operational activity as the change proceeds.

(continued)

7. Review your priority ratings. Immediately bring any show-stopper issues to the appropriate leaders' attention to decide if a redesign of the desired state is needed. Work with the sponsor to chart a course of action.

   If necessary, refine the desired state design. You will need to conduct another impact analysis process after you have a newly refined desired state design.

8. Impact group leaders agree on the issue resolution process they will all use to identify solutions and action plans.

9. Impact group teams identify impact solutions and actions, integrating interdependent solutions and actions, both within and between groups, and within and between groups and operations. They integrate individual and group action plans for resolution to make the best use of resources and to streamline activity during implementation.

10. Impact group leaders agree on how to compile and format the Implementation Master Plan.

11. Impact group leaders meet to share solutions and compile integrated action plans into the Implementation Master Plan format. They make actions as specific and manageable as possible.

12. Determine required resources based on the scope of work laid out in the Implementation Master Plan.

13. Determine appropriate pacing strategy and timeline based on an accurate assessment of work required to implement.

14. Complete the Implementation Master Plan and obtain approval.

15. Communicate the Implementation Master Plan to the appropriate stakeholders.

---

most accurate and realistic information to plan implementation and continue to engage the organization without bogging it down.

To address this dynamic and assist with managing the issues, you will group the impacts into categories of similar interdependent topics, such as human resource issues, cultural issues, structural issues, socio-technical issues, workstreams, or issues relating to a specific product or business process. The categories you use depend on the scope of the transformation and desired state design. Exhibit 8.2, Ways to Categorize Impact Issues, offers a list of typical categories.

After you have generated your lists of issues and grouped them, assign someone to be responsible for resolving each of the categories, which is work that occurs in the next phase. We call these people "impact group leaders." They must have direct access to the executives who own the ultimate design decisions because some of the issues may require some redesign of the desired state. The impact group leaders will "own" their issues, resolving, integrating, and presenting their solutions during the development of the Implementation Master Plan,

Exhibit 8.2. Ways to Categorize Impact Issues

- By customer requirement or business segment
- Within a function
- Across specific functions
- Within a business process
- Enterprise-wide
- Between specific levels of the organization
- Between stakeholder groups
- If a design issue (managerial or operational design)
- Culture-related
- By geography
- By specialty
- People-related or HR-related
- Technical training needs
- Mindset and behavioral training needs
- Management development training needs

CASE-IN-POINT: IMPACT ANALYSIS WORKSHOP

A global software company was reinventing its sales force in response to dramatically shifting trends in customer sophistication and buying patterns. The change was initially conceived of as "a large reorganization" to be designed behind closed doors and then announced by the executives and implemented within the annual planning window. However, the change process leader was convinced that the magnitude of the changes required a break from "business as usual" to be successful. He persuaded the change sponsor and his executive peers to recognize the magnitude of the change and pulled together a cross-functional, cross-level team to engage in a comprehensive Impact Analysis (IA) Workshop and subsequent implementation planning. This was a first for the organization.

The design of the one-day IA workshop challenged the existing mindset and culture. It broadened engagement by inviting key players into the process and by setting up equal participation by executives and managers; it called for candid dialogue versus debating organization charts and PowerPoint slides; and it created an active process versus sitting at a table listening to

(continued)

presentations. The leaders and teams for every workstream required to accomplish the reorganization were invited.

The workshop began with a level set where each workstream team reported on its progress, highlighting any concerns or issues, addressing questions, and requesting support. After a brief CLR introduction, the teams used the Initial Impact Analysis Audit tool and an individual dot voting process to begin prioritizing key impact categories, with everyone's voice equally considered. Based on the dot votes, the participants broke up into small groups to brainstorm and discuss all impacts related to their assigned impact categories.

Each impact was noted on a separate sticky note and added to posted flipchart category pages. The whole group then engaged in a Gallery Walk, during which everyone rotated through each impact category station, questioning, learning, and adding their perspectives and concerns to each category. The original teams then reviewed all inputs, clustered and prioritized impacts, and completed an initial magnitude assessment to surface any show-stopper issues.

Each category team then reported out to the full group, resulting in further dialogue, during which impact categories were assigned owners to drive resolution. Impact group leaders then were formed into a FastTrack Team charged with planning and executing an Implementation Planning Workshop and leading the impact resolution, implementation, and course correction process together.

The participants had entered the IA workshop feeling uninformed, with a siloed sense of their issues, and ready to defend their turf. They finished the day as a team, energized and inspired to take shared leadership in the longer-term transformation. All participants noted that they could clearly see why past change initiatives had not achieved their intended outcomes, and that they had gained a deeper appreciation for how to truly lead a change process. In particular, they noted that potentially serious human impacts had historically been overlooked. The IA process resulted in a more robust implementation plan, which led to a major reset in context: speaking about this initiative as "a multi-year journey for evolving the organization" rather than as "a reorganization." The team reconvened to capture key learnings so they could carry them into future change initiatives. Several of the core team members were tapped as experienced change leaders for future change projects.

which also occurs in the next phase. It is important to remind impact group leaders that their primary allegiance is to the overall success of the transformation, not just to their impact group. Group leaders must work well together for the good of the whole effort.

Task V.A.3: Assess Magnitude of Impacts and Prioritize

After the impacts are grouped, you must evaluate them for the magnitude of change they require and the cost or disruption of making that change. Some impacts will need to be evaluated individually, and many collectively, so that you maintain awareness of how things need to work as an integrated system. Assess costs and disruption in terms of dollars, time, legal risk, resources, expertise, culture shock, or morale. Consider the adequacy of your existing technology, management processes, risk to quality or safety, capacity to make the change, or impact on customers or vendors. Use this information to ensure the viability of your desired state design and to obtain a more accurate level of effort and emotional stamina that the transformation will require. Have the most informed people review your impact issues for this information, as well as for any additional red flags that can be obstacles to the effectiveness of your desired state. If you must resolve key issues before you can accurately assess them for magnitude, then do that work concurrently with this task.

Task V.A.4: Refine Desired State

If you discover impacts that are of a magnitude that require you to refine or alter your desired state, make those changes here. Revisit your design requirements and boundary conditions. Sometimes this refinement calls for only a minor adjustment to the design—other times a major overhaul. Making this critical course correction now is a worthy investment of time in creating the outcome you want.

After you have refined your desired state, you might need to perform another impact analysis on the latest iteration to ensure that it is now viable and capable of being implemented. Continue to gather impact analysis data as it shows up, incorporating it appropriately into your change plans.

SUMMARY

You now have a detailed assessment of the magnitude of work required to plan for implementation. You, and all of the people who contributed to the impact analysis, have a more thorough understanding of the workings and requirements of your desired state. Phase VI moves this understanding toward action, in preparation for implementation.

CONSULTING QUESTIONS FOR ACTIVITY V.A: ANALYZE IMPACTS OF DESIRED STATE

Task V.A.1: Design Process for Conducting Impact Analysis

▶ Who are the best people to perform this work? What criteria will you use to select them? Review your project community map. Will you engage known resisters?

▶ How will you organize to accomplish impact analysis? Consider study teams, large group interventions, or impact analysis round tables. Will you engage external expert consultants?

▶ What will be the scope of your study? What types of impacts will you study?

▶ What degree of detail do you want when identifying impact issues? Consider using the Levels of Design Model for consistency (i.e., vision, strategic guidance, managerial input, operational detail).

▶ How will you record and manage your lists of impact issues?

▶ What is your timetable for accomplishing this work?

▶ How will you monitor for political, emotional, and cultural dynamics triggered by issue identification?

▶ How will you ensure that the change leaders continue to assess for new impacts as the initiative proceeds?

Task V.A.2: Identify and Group Impacts

▶ How will you organize and group your impact issues?

▶ Who are the best people to lead your impact groups through to resolution?

Task V.A.3: Assess Magnitude of Impacts and Prioritize

▶ What criteria will you use to assess the magnitude of your impact issues?

▶ Who are the best people to assess the magnitude and implications of your impact issues?

▶ How will you identify show-stopper issues that require a refinement of your desired state design?

Task V.A.4: Refine Desired State

▶ What are the political implications of refining the desired state design at this point? How will you deal with them?

▶ What process will you use to refine your desired state design?

▶ Who will do this work, and who must approve the new design?

PHASE VI
Plan and Organize for Implementation

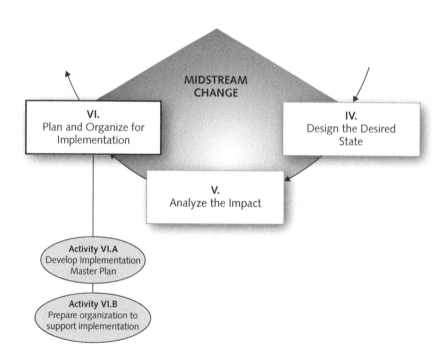

PHASE VI: TASK DELIVERABLES

VI.A.1: The process for developing the Implementation Master Plan has been created and approved.

VI.A.2: Solutions for individual and interdependent impact issues have been identified, and action plans created.

VI.A.3: Solutions and action plans have been integrated and compiled into the detailed Implementation Master Plan.

VI.A.4: Strategies to sustain the energy for the entire transformation have been designed and integrated into the Implementation Master Plan.

VI.A.5: Based on the magnitude of implementation work, resources, pacing strategy, and a realistic timeline have been determined. The Implementation Master Plan has been approved.

VI.B.1: The infrastructure and conditions to support implementation are in place.

VI.B.2: Strategies for supporting people to embrace the desired state and manage their reactions to the change have been identified and initiated.

VI.B.3: The target groups of the change, the organization, and all stakeholders understand the Implementation Master Plan.

Impact analysis always generates a lot of energy for the change effort. Now your challenge is to focus all of that energy and channel it into a viable, tangible plan of action—your Implementation Master Plan. At this point in the process, impact issues must be resolved and their solutions translated into implementation actions. You will integrate as many of the solutions and actions as you can so that your Implementation Master Plan is as streamlined as possible. This will give you the data you need to determine a realistic estimate of resources and timetable for completion.

Your Implementation Master Plan is your organization's guide for how the transformation will unfold. It is the detailed version of the critical milestones you identified in your Phase I change strategy, adjusted, of course, to fit your current knowledge and circumstances. The plan enumerates the what, who, where, and when of the implementation phase of your transformation. Its purpose is to facilitate and coordinate the multitude of activities necessary to create your future state in a way that reflects your desired culture and mindset.

A complete Implementation Master Plan would overwhelm and perhaps alienate any organization that was not prepared to receive and respond to it. Therefore, in the second activity of this phase, you will prepare the organization—and leadership—to support the plan. You will refine and establish the infrastructure and conditions required for successful implementation. The infrastructure includes mechanisms to coordinate, monitor, and course correct the work of implementation. Your conditions might include sufficient resources, a smooth interface with operations, and leaders knowing their role in overseeing and supporting the rollout of the change. They are key to being able and willing to remove barriers to a successful implementation and to minimize activities that may distract from it.

In addition, because your plan will take place over time, you will need to identify actions to keep everybody's energy for the change in "go mode." It is too easy for people's attention to drift after a while, or go back to focusing only on normal operations. You must think through how to keep your key target groups and stakeholders focused and engaged in making this change a reality, especially when they are likely so busy with their normal jobs. The speed and ease of implementation will be a direct result of this work.

ACTIVITY VI.A: DEVELOP IMPLEMENTATION MASTER PLAN

Task VI.A.1: Design Process to Develop Implementation Master Plan

The work of this task is critical to the success of the transformation. It translates the impact issues into design solutions for the transformation and then translates these solutions into specific implementation actions, both of which are required steps for developing a realistic Implementation Master Plan. The process you use in this task can make this complex activity either smooth or very cumbersome. You may have already designed your process for this work—including the next four tasks—when you designed the process for impact analysis in Task V.A.1. If so, carry it out as you proceed with this activity.

Your impact group leaders are responsible for the work of this phase. They will oversee issue resolution, integration of impacts and solutions, identification of the most streamlined actions to implement the desired state, and the compilation of this work into the Implementation Master Plan. Because this is one of the most intensive and complicated phases in the change process, it is essential for them to have clear procedures and aligned leadership.

Impact group leaders should choose the most knowledgeable, insightful, action-oriented people to participate in the resolution and integration process. They might create special study teams, hire external consultants, or give issue responsibility to the most consciously competent individuals in the organization.

Where appropriate, we strongly advise creating teams of diverse talents, including synthesizers, systems and process thinkers, detail-lovers, and complexity masters.

Task VI.A.2: Identify Impact Solutions and Action Plans

In this task, the impact group leaders facilitate the resolution process for each impact and between impacts within their group. They are responsible for ensuring that the solutions their teams recommend reflect the required transformational breakthroughs, design requirements, and new culture.

The people assigned to the issues identify the desired outcomes, actions, resources, and cultural norms required to implement their solutions, using what is best for the overall desired state as their guide. They may need to gather missing information to do this work, such as historical data, the scope of the issue, perceptions about the desired outcomes from stakeholders, impacts on operations, available resources, and certainly any design requirements or boundary conditions affecting their solution.

Issues in one area inevitably ripple out into other impacts. The leaders must proactively work with their teams to share information, integrate or combine related impacts to minimize redundancies, prevent negative system dynamics, and optimize the needs of the whole organization.

Exhibit 9.1 provides a generic impact resolution process.

Task VI.A.3: Integrate Solutions and Action Plans and Compile Implementation Master Plan

To ensure the most streamlined, cost-effective solutions for your collective impacts, impact group leaders must work together to integrate their solutions and action plans across impact groups. Your goal is two-fold: to combine solutions and actions so that implementation is accelerated and efficient, and to determine the most effective solutions so your desired state functions optimally. In silo-oriented organizations in which managers have historically focused only on their own functions, you may face resistance to the need for cross-functional integration and even sharing information. Often, serious political struggles surface. If this occurs, completing this task successfully could require a significant mindset and behavior shift. Strive to embed conscious awareness of what is best for the overall organization long term.

The second requirement of this task is to compile and sequence your myriad impact resolution plans into your detailed Implementation Master Plan.

Exhibit 9.1. Generic Impact Resolution Process

1. Clarify the questions or needs identified by the impact (or group of impacts) you will be resolving. Make sure you are working on the right questions or needs and have scoped each accurately.

2. Clarify the decision owner(s) and decision style they will use to make final decisions about impact solutions.

3. Review impacts and decision protocols with people involved in the change effort's original vision, desired outcomes, and design requirements to see how they may influence your solution. Identify parameters or boundary conditions that may shape your process, resources, or outcomes.

4. Openly explore all information currently known about the background, current state, or solution preferences. Explore any current political or cultural factors to consider as you proceed, for all levels of the organization involved.

5. Generate potential solutions to the impact(s). Provide enough detail to support making a decision. If your impact has cross-impact interdependency, be sure to collaborate with the other impact owners as you identify potential solutions.

6. Review the pros and cons of your various scenarios, and apply your design requirements and parameters to them.

7. Decide on the best impact solution.

8. As you identify solutions, constantly assess their impact on other aspects of the organization or the change effort, and whether any can be integrated to ease action planning, reduce resource needs, or accelerate implementation.

9. Identify the actions required to implement each impact solution, both standalone impacts and those that have interface issues or interdependencies.

10. Confirm your solutions and actions.

11. Get approval for your solutions and actions as needed.

Carefully coordinate this process. There are five major elements to include in your Implementation Master Plan:

- The sequenced actions required for implementation
- Who will accomplish these actions and who will be engaged in them
- When the actions will be initiated and completed
- Where in the organization the actions will occur
- The resources required for all of this to be completed effectively

Also include your communications work, training, and phase gates in the process if you are using them.

In one very large telephone company, the need for integration created a turning point in how the leaders thought about running their new integrated company. The leaders were redesigning their organization to improve functional efficiencies across several states. At this point in their change process, each state's change leader was asked to come to an organization-wide meeting to present his or her plans for resolving impacts. The leaders resisted attending the meeting, complaining that their functional plans were clear and that they were ready to implement. The change sponsor insisted, and all of the leaders—state and functional—attended.

During the reports about the critical events and actions required within each function, one leader announced the need to downsize a key function in his state by 150 people. The next functional leader then offered his report and announced a critical need to hire 50 new people to staff his function. It happened that these new people were needed in the same state in which the prior leader planned to downsize.

The two men looked at each other, "mental gears" turning, and agreed to meet to integrate their plans to support one another's outcomes without costing the organization or the affected people beyond what was necessary. Whereas the old culture had never required these leaders to communicate across the boundaries of their functions, the leaders immediately recognized that their own successes, as well as the effectiveness of the integrated organization, were suddenly dependent on this kind of cross-boundary communication and teamwork.

There is a range of style options for how to compose and format your plan. Detail-oriented organizations may dive into capturing the fine points with relish and create detailed electronic project plans. Fast-moving organizations, such as high-tech firms, may be far more conceptual in their plans and depend more on the implementers' real-time decisions to handle the details. Adapt your style and format to your organization's desired culture.

Task VI.A.4: Design Strategies to Sustain Energy for Change

Because most large-scale changes take a long time to complete, it is essential to determine strategies and actions that will help sustain people's momentum and intention for the change over time. Too often, complex implementation plans consist of a barrage of planned activity at the beginning and then dramatically drop off. This pattern often leads to the failure or "drifting" of the change effort, as there is no clear way to sustain it or to follow up consistently. This is a human dynamic that is manageable. Change leaders can prevent it by consciously planning to sustain people's energy for the change and identifying the actions required to see it through over the long term. This is an example of good process thinking. Build these momentum-sustaining plans into your Implementation Master Plan and continuously tailor them as new needs arise during the dynamic course of implementation.

The following sidebar offers several examples of strategies. Some are one-time events; others are ongoing.

ENERGY-SUSTAINING STRATEGIES

- Publicize and celebrate progress.
- Grant periodic surprise rewards, outside the norm.
- Periodically review conditions for success, and re-establish those that are faltering.
- Neutralize or remove blockages quickly.
- Tell the story of the organization's history, where this transformation fits in it, how you are living the values of the organization, and the next series of chapters yet to be "written."
- Create champions of the transformation.
- Remove major bureaucratic red tape and any barriers to information flow and engagement.
- Hold dynamic, engaging large group meetings with senior leader involvement and candor.
- Have managers who are further ahead become mentors and models for other managers and levels of the organization, participating in training and communication events as spokespeople.
- Introduce new symbols, mottos, or language.
- Create group rituals or rites of passage.
- Debunk rumors.
- Encourage naturally emerging forays into new state scenarios and creative possibilities.

- Hold a burial for the past.
- Hold a contest for solving some quandary in the transformation.
- Design a media blitz, internally or externally, especially if you are rebranding the organization.
- Conduct special luncheons for change team members or target groups.
- Expose and dismantle negative system dynamics.
- Model and celebrate learning opportunities and overt changes in mindset and culture.
- Secure newspaper and television coverage.

In addition to formally planning these strategies prior to implementation, also use them when you have made a course correction to your change process or outcome. People often need a psychological boost when asked to alter course repeatedly. Because course correction is so common in transformational change, energy-sustaining strategies are key throughout implementation.

Task VI.A.5: Determine Resources, Pacing Strategy, and Timeline

After you have compiled your Implementation Master Plan actions, you then need to assess the resources it will require and how much time the plan will take to accomplish. In Phase I, the change leaders developed their change strategy with an estimate of resources and a proposed timeline. Their estimates of both were based on strategic-level information and, in truth, either good guesswork or political pressure. Their "guesstimate" may prove to have no basis in reality. It is only now, after you have completed the actual planning for implementation, that you can more accurately determine the resources and your timeline. Both are essential to obtaining approval for the Implementation Master Plan, and both require true commitment and understanding by the executives.

The timeline and your estimate of resources may be interdependent. The data you generated in your impact analysis, plus the results of your Phase I assessment of the organization's capacity to take on the change, provide the basis for making a more realistic decision about resources and timeline. Keep your perceptions of people's readiness, capacity, and ability in mind for these decisions. Too often, we find competent people being emotionally burdened by unrealistic time pressures they cannot renegotiate because the change sponsors lack awareness or openness about their capacity and stamina. More resources might be necessary in these cases. Review the results and actions you generated from your capacity review if you performed one in Task I.C.1.

Beyond your start and end dates, there are a number of decisions to make about timing, wrapped up into what we call a pacing strategy. A *pacing strategy* consists of the speed of change, the scope of the organization that is changing at any one time, and the rollout sequence of actions. Speed is determined by the time actually required to complete the work of implementation. The *scope of the organization* refers to the parts of the organization to be involved in making the change at any one time, such as functions, levels, locations, business units, and so on. The *rollout sequence* involves the selection of one or more of the following strategies:

▶ All at once

▶ By phases that overlap

▶ Sequentially through independent steps where one step is completed before the next step begins

▶ Gradual, incremental, evolutionary change over a long period of time.

Keep in mind the requirements for the ongoing operation as you determine your pacing strategy.

When you have determined a realistic pacing strategy, compare it with the original timeline created by the executives in Phase I and renegotiate it, given the reality of the work required. As mentioned previously, unrealistic timetables are a leading factor in the failure of major change. If you think about it, a realistic

---

CASE-IN-POINT

A major oil company was undergoing a massive restructuring of its refining organization. The restructuring required eight months for implementation, based on the impact analysis. The change leaders designed a pacing strategy to be completed in three phases. The strategy prioritized the most critical organizations and functions that had to and could move first. It initiated these moves while preparing for its second-phase moves and then its third-phase moves. At one point, all these phases were in motion. By the time the third-phase moves were integrated into the new structure, the new state organization was largely functional, and disruption was minimized.

judgment about how long implementation will likely take can only occur after you have determined the impacts of the change and clarified solutions and actions for how to handle them during implementation.

There is another timing reality for you to consider. Changing culture, which is a critical part of transformational change, takes much longer than changing the structural, system, and technical aspects of your organization. The completion of culture change is hard to map on a timeline because dealing with the human factors of mindset, emotions, relationships, and behavior is not controllable or predictable. However, you *can* map key events and actions designed to impact culture and mindset in your Implementation Master Plan.

After you have an agreeable pacing strategy, apply it to the Implementation Master Plan, and proceed with securing approval for your plan.

ACTIVITY VI.B: PREPARE ORGANIZATION TO SUPPORT IMPLEMENTATION

Task VI.B.1: Establish Infrastructure and Conditions to Support Implementation

In Phase I, you created your change strategy, generated required capacity for making the change, and planned for the infrastructure and conditions that would ensure your success in this change effort. You created ways to support both the change process and people's needs. Now, with your Implementation Master Plan in hand, you can more accurately refine what you need to support implementation and the people who must make the change happen. Incorporate your plan for doing this into your Implementation Master Plan actions. Consider your relevant decisions from Phase I:

- Strategies for freeing up adequate capacity for change
- Stakeholder engagement strategies
- Change communication plans
- Resources
- Conditions for success
- Temporary change support structures, systems, policies, and technologies
- Strategies for generating new information and inputs for course correction
- Ways to help people through their emotional reactions to the change process

- Ways to engage your project community members
- Ways to model the desired mindset, behaviors, and new cultural values and norms
- Rewards to support your change process and outcomes
- Strategies for dealing with political dynamics during the transformation
- Trainings for managers to help their staff through the change, personally and professionally

Use this list to prompt your thinking about how to support an optimal implementation.

Task VI.B.2: Support People Through Implementation

This task provides a powerful opportunity to demonstrate the fundamental value that your people are important and deserve to be treated with respect and concern. As you proceed with implementation, people will no longer be able to deny the inevitable: this change is real. This is when their true feelings about making the change will emerge.

In Task I.F.6, *Initiate Strategies for Supporting People through Emotional Reactions and Resistance*, you began the process of planning how to deal effectively with the human impacts of your transformation. Your intention was to design the change in ways that minimized negative dynamics for the people making the change, and agree on how to help the people who were adversely affected. Back then, your planning was based on how you *thought* people would react. Now, with implementation about to begin, you can make more realistic plans to support people through the *actual* changes impacting them. With the information you now have from people's reactions to the effort so far, you will be better able to create specific, tangible strategies to meet their current needs and maximize support for them.

Some organizations recognize that the degree of acceptance a change gets from the workforce is directly dependent on how their middle managers deal with the change and address their people's reactions to it during implementation. In the worst cases, middle managers criticize the change as a disruption or bad decision, thereby increasing resistance in their people. In the best cases, the leaders provide middle managers training to understand their role as key supporters of the change and to learn how to deal directly with people's reactions and resistance. We have supported many organizations—including financial institutions, health care systems, utilities, manufacturing, and federal government agencies—in providing this type of training in how to lead people through change in a more proactive, conscious manner. In these cases, the middle managers played a significant role in easing implementation and added to their permanent repertoire for supporting and engaging their people to contribute their best to the organization.

Most organizations have a variety of pre-existing employee assistance services and policies for providing support. Consider these services and policies in your plans. The following sidebar lists several to consider. Tailor them to fit your situation. They can help reduce some of the stress induced by the change, as well as help shift the organization's culture by demonstrating leadership's concern for people. Communicating these policies and services in advance of implementation adds to management's credibility, company loyalty, and positive morale at a time when they are needed most.

Be cautious about how you communicate and monitor these support mechanisms. Too often, employees and managers avoid using them because they fear being

SUGGESTED WAYS TO SUPPORT YOUR WORKFORCE

- Employee assistance counseling
- Career development counseling
- Outplacement services, job placement
- Personal empowerment training
- Coaching
- Training on managing stress and handling emotions
- Training on dealing with difficult people and conflict
- Job request system
- "Grandfathering" or "red-lining" salary policy
- "No demotion" policy
- "Guaranteed job with training provided" policy
- Skills training (technical or professional)
- Mindset and behavior training, management development
- On-the-job training
- Team building for new teams
- Financial assistance counseling and training
- Support groups

labeled as weak or inadequate and therefore less valuable to the organization. These approaches must be encouraged and made easy to pursue and receive. Consider the power of instituting the value that people are human beings with legitimate reactions and needs when impacted by change, and they deserve to be supported by the organization causing that impact. If employees could believe that leaders truly support them when they need it most, their commitment to the success of the business would skyrocket. And at this phase of the change, they just might need it most.

Review your Implementation Master Plan to identify actions or events that may be the most difficult or challenging for people to accept or embrace. Review any assessments you made of people's core needs, their emotional readiness, and their capacity to take on the change. Ask your OD or change management specialists or HR people for input. Or, as a developmental exercise, have the change leaders scan the plan for their predictions about people's reactions. They can review if the actions planned are designed in ways that will *consciously minimize negativity*, and if need be, redesign them. This work is well worth the time and effort. It is now that people's genuine reactions to making the transformation will emerge and now that your earnest efforts at engaging people, minimizing trauma, and supporting people emotionally will pay off. If necessary, alter your Implementation Master Plan to incorporate required changes that ensure support of the majority of your target groups' and stakeholders' core needs.

Letting Go of the Past

In Task I.F.6, we presented Adams' Stages of Personal Adjustment to Transition Model of the emotional cycle people experience when undergoing change. One critical phase is the "pit," which requires people to let go of the past to move into more productive phases. Creating strategies to assist employees to let go of their old ways of operating and providing assignments to take on and succeed at the new ways are essential to supporting people through the inevitable "pit." It is through this stage that they turn from resistance to commitment. The following sidebar lists several strategies for letting go. As you consider them, plan to do more than you think people need.

Be sure that most of the required letting-go work occurs in intact work teams. The heart of this process must occur among people who work together on a daily basis. Letting-go rituals can be a collective rite of passage when done as a shared experience. Be cautious not to rely solely on the organization's formal or en-masse letting-go rituals. Those driven by the executives can be beneficial, but should not be thought of as replacing more intimate events during which workmates directly connect with one another about what they are going through.

- "Roast" the old ways of doing things
- A final meeting of a group or team to acknowledge their ending and celebrate their past
- Team debriefings and "post-op" learning sessions
- A ritual "wake" or burial of the old ways
- A museum to honor the old; putting the old products under glass or in display cases to be respected but not touched
- Videos or slide shows commemorating the past
- Counseling
- A bonfire, with speeches and mementos
- A "final edition" newsletter
- A televised ritual to tear down or dismantle old equipment, factories, or products
- Published stories of individual successes and breakthroughs to the new ways
- Extra time for people to practice, learn, and gain confidence in new state practices
- Behavioral and skill training for new state requirements
- Celebration events of the new ways of working

Task VI.B.3: Communicate Implementation Master Plan

After the communication of your case for change, vision, and change strategy, and your desired state design, this communication is the next most critical of your entire change process. Here you will highlight the important aspects of your Implementation Master Plan. You will describe the relevant elements of your infrastructure and the conditions you designed to support the transformation. Reference your original change strategy or announce how it has been course-corrected. It is important to demonstrate and reinforce that the organization is in the "process" of carrying out the transformation and that this communication marks a major milestone in the journey.

This communication is a primary opportunity for the change leaders to demonstrate their commitment to the transformation, the workforce's well-being, and the future. The leaders' ability to walk the talk of the transformation will become

We helped to create a letting-go strategy for two organizations that were being merged. We planned a dramatic event for both groups with the intention of demonstrating that their old organizations were "a thing of the past" and that they were becoming a part of something completely new.

The leaders asked all of management from both organizations to come to a very large open field and bring with them all of their old organization's paperwork and artifacts that showed their old company name and logo. People came with letterhead, mugs, business cards, binders, door signs, hats, and manual forms. In the middle of the field, in a fire pit, was a huge rectangular box adorned to look like a coffin. Each organization's attendees were asked to file past the box and throw their artifacts in. When all of the people had tossed in their offerings, the box was closed and the newly announced president ignited it.

A huge bonfire ensued, symbolically cremating the old organizations. While it burned, the new executives of the merged company talked about the value of each old organization and the vision for the new one that all of the attendees would create together. Plans were communicated about the change strategy and timeline. People were asked to talk about their memories of working together in the past. They honored their history, and the future was born.

To end the session, the people from both organizations were asked to mingle together. They were given pens and IOU's for new business cards with the name of the new company on them. People felt valued and supported for their past efforts. Moreover, the message was very clear about moving into the future.

Such rituals should be emotionally uplifting. This one certainly was.

evident in what they communicate and how they come across to people at this important juncture. Review your communication strategy for input to this task.

Ensure, again, that you treat this communication as a series of multiple, reinforcing opportunities for people to explore what the core messages mean for them personally because this is likely where you are informing people of the "extra" work the change requires of them. Consciously design this process to support people to move through and out of the "pit" and on to making a positive contribution to the future. Be aware of where people currently are in their cycle of reaction and what you are asking them to do while they continue their normal work.

SUMMARY

You have now planned for implementation, created a realistic pace for the change, and put in place key support mechanisms to enable the transformation to roll out smoothly. This completes the midstream stage of the process. Having communicated how everything is designed to work, you are ready to enter the downstream stage and implement the transformation.

CONSULTING QUESTIONS FOR ACTIVITY VI.A: DEVELOP IMPLEMENTATION MASTER PLAN

Task VI.A.1: Design Process to Develop Implementation Master Plan

- How will you develop your Implementation Master Plan?
- Who will do this work?
- What information will your plan capture?
- What format and software will you use to map your Implementation Master Plan?
- How will you ensure that your impact solutions and actions are optimally integrated so that implementation is most expedient?

Task VI.A.2: Identify Impact Solutions and Action Plans

- What impact resolution process will you use to determine the best solutions to your impact issues?
- How will you determine which impacts need to be combined to generate the best solutions? How will you handle doing this?
- Will the impact group leaders do this work or their entire teams?
- How will you determine the actions needed to put your solutions into place? What level of detail do you want in your action plans?
- Do any of your solutions need further approval? If so, how will you obtain it?

Task VI.A.3: Integrate Solutions and Action Plans and Compile Implementation Master Plan

- What process will you use to share solutions and action plans so they can be considered by others for integration opportunities?
- Who will represent and describe the solutions and action plans?
- After optimal integration has occurred, how will you compile all of this work into your Implementation Master Plan?
- How will you review the details of your plan to ensure the best and most expedient implementation?

Task VI.A.4: Design Strategies to Sustain Energy for Change

- What strategies will you use to sustain people's energy for the change? How will you renew people's focus on the change?
- How will you determine when to use your strategies?
- How will you know if people need more support to stay focused until implementation is complete?

Task VI.A.5: Determine Resources, Pacing Strategy, and Timeline

- How will you determine an accurate projection of the resources you need to implement your plan? Who will do this projection work?
- How will you determine the best pacing strategy?
- How will you analyze the Implementation Master Plan for the realistic amount of time required to carry it out effectively? How can you use your capacity review results to influence your determination?
- How will you handle any differences in timeline from what you originally estimated in your change strategy? If you have to renegotiate this initial timeline, how will you do this?
- How will you align your Implementation Master Plan to reflect your pacing strategy and timeline?
- Who has to approve the Implementation Master Plan? How will that be handled?

CONSULTING QUESTIONS FOR ACTIVITY VI.B: PREPARE ORGANIZATION TO SUPPORT IMPLEMENTATION

Task VI.B.1: Establish Infrastructure and Conditions to Support Implementation

▶ Which conditions, temporary support structures, systems, policies, and technologies will you use to help deliver a successful implementation? How will you put each into place?

▶ How will you communicate them to the organization engaged in making the change?

Task VI.B.2: Support People Through Implementation

▶ How will you ensure that your Implementation Master Plan is designed to minimize negative impacts on the people who must make the change?

▶ How will you support people to manage their reactions to the implementation in real time?

▶ Is further training or coaching required for the change leaders and management to be able and willing to support people as implementation rolls out? Are they adequately skilled in consciously leading their people through the change?

▶ Do you need to create "letting-go" strategies? If so, what will they be?

Task VI.B.3: Communicate Implementation Master Plan

▶ How will you communicate your Implementation Master Plan so that the people making the change feel ready and willing to take on implementation?

▶ How will you use this communication to further demonstrate leadership's commitment to a successful outcome as well as people's well-being during the rollout?

Downstream Change

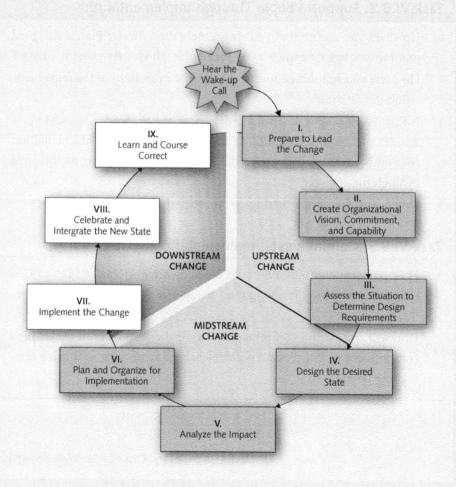

Hear the Wake-up Call

IX.
Learn and Course Correct

I.
Prepare to Lead the Change

VIII.
Celebrate and Intergrate the New State

II.
Create Organizational Vision, Commitment, and Capability

DOWNSTREAM CHANGE

UPSTREAM CHANGE

VII.
Implement the Change

III.
Assess the Situation to Determine Design Requirements

MIDSTREAM CHANGE

VI.
Plan and Organize for Implementation

IV.
Design the Desired State

V.
Analyze the Impact

PHASE VII

PHASE VIII

PHASE IX

PHASE VII
Implement the Change

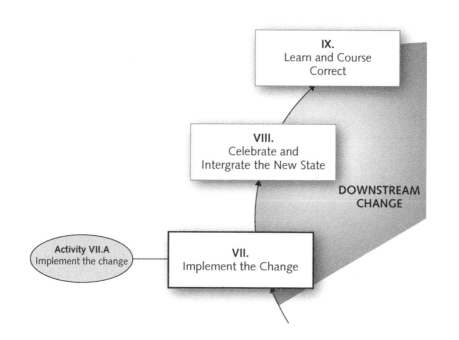

PHASE VII: TASK DELIVERABLES

VII.A.1: The Implementation Master Plan is being rolled out. Leaders and key stakeholders are modeling the new mindset, behaviors, and relationships of the desired state as they carry out change activities.

VII.A.2: Implementation is being course-corrected as required.

VII.A.3: The desired state is being course-corrected as required.

With the initial planning and preparation behind you, you now enter the downstream stage of change implementation. It is time to roll out your plan to create your content solution in reality. The organization will now take on the tangible form of your desired state, and you will continue to refine both your change process and your desired state as you go. To complete this stage, you will tie up your change process, hopefully having achieved your intended results.

The purpose of this phase is to carry out your Implementation Master Plan and course-correct it and your future state as the needs of the organization require. During implementation, the bulk of activity takes place to dismantle the organization's old ways of working and thinking, to learn the new ones, and to monitor whether everything is on the right track. Many of the people dynamics for which you so diligently prepared will now play out. Keep all quadrants and levels of the Conscious Change Leader Accountability Model in mind as you go because there will be many interdependent dynamics at play in the process as you implement.

There is no formula for how implementation should occur. Every transformation is different. Implementation will inevitably go differently than you planned. Hopefully, all of the preparing, analyzing, and designing you have done will create an efficient and effective implementation. You must rely on your supporting infrastructures and conditions for success, and you must actively use your course correction system to respond immediately when things need to be adjusted.

Your most important work in this phase is to consciously attend to what is happening in the organization as it is changing. This is your opportunity to accept that you can't "force the river." Your toughest personal work starts here—allowing implementation to take on its own character, learning from what occurs, influencing appropriately, and course-correcting intelligently.

ACTIVITY VII.A: IMPLEMENT THE CHANGE

Task VII.A.1: Roll Out Implementation Master Plan

Your organization now makes your desired state design a reality. It is always eye-opening to look back at all of the preparation you have done; it has been a long runway until takeoff! So many leaders jump into implementation immediately after announcing that they are going to make a change. Imagine all of the confusion and disruption that would happen if you had not planned for your implementation so thoughtfully, and prepared the leaders, the organization, and all of your stakeholders for its rollout!

Because your Implementation Master Plan is your guide, we cannot speak to how it will or should go. However, we will discuss some of the people and process dynamics to be aware of as the action unfolds.

Dealing with Resistance

Many change models emphasize the need to overcome people's resistance during implementation. This focus becomes necessary because these models put so little attention on the upfront work that The Change Leader's Roadmap covers in Phases I, II, and VI, which prepare the leaders and the organization for the transformation. If you are using this methodology for the first time, and you do the upfront work to minimize negative impacts on your stakeholders and target groups, you likely will see much less resistance in people than you might have expected.

Even with good upstream and midstream planning, however, some resistance is inevitable. It is a natural phenomenon and should be embraced as a normal part of change, along with people's other emotional reactions. Review the overview of resistance in Task I.F.6, and keep an open mind to it when it happens. Keep asking, listening to, and engaging your resisters!

Attend to People's Reactions

During implementation, people will be realizing the full impact of letting go of their old ways of operating and thinking. If they are committed to the overall transformation, this reaction will be manageable. If they are not, the reality of the change will come crashing in on them now. We hope that you have put sufficient strategies in place in Phases I through VI to deal with the emotional roller coaster that implementation may unleash. Because this part of the process is so unpredictable, be prepared to give additional attention to the human dynamics during implementation.

This applies equally to the leaders and managers, who are not exempt from their own personal reactions during this volatile time. Change consultants should be prepared to spend significant time coaching leaders and counseling key players. Actively add to your communications and engagement strategies to help reduce the reaction. If you have only used content consultants to plan your change process, be prepared to catch the many emotional and cultural balls that may be falling in between your content-related implementation actions!

Walk Your Talk and Support People's Change in Culture, Mindset, and Behavior

During implementation, the leaders must actively walk their talk, modeling the new cultural imperatives, mindset, and behaviors that they publicly espoused during earlier phases of the transformation. Employees will be highly critical of leaders who are not acting in the new ways. There are many tough people and process questions to keep in mind at this phase of your change. For instance, when transformational change requires significant culture, mindset, and behavioral change in people, how fast can this personal transformation reasonably occur? Is the implementation phase long enough to *complete* this process? How do you make personal and cultural change coincide with the organizational changes during implementation? How do you really engage busy and stressed leaders to do what is needed for this essential part of the transformation to succeed?

There are no easy answers to these important questions. Let's look at some of the dynamics at play to understand better how to address these issues. Specific cultural norms, articulated in specific work practices, are the easiest to address. Mindset and behavior are more challenging.

It is to be expected that not everyone will have fully integrated the new ways of thinking and acting during implementation, even when this work begins in Phase I. In their own ways, everyone who has committed to the transformation will be attempting new behaviors and trying hard to function successfully according to desired state expectations, culture included. Inevitably, however, people will unintentionally slip back to their old behavior, again and again, long after implementation. *This is normal.*

To address this dynamic, the change leaders must create public understanding of the process of *personal transformation* and how to consciously support it. Tolerance, patience, and personal awareness are essential. Otherwise, when people revert to old behavior, blame and distrust will follow, rather than constructive feedback and support.

When people, especially the leaders, fall back into old habits, quick and overt course correction is essential to maintain credibility and sustain the "walk the talk" requirement. Leaders have a valuable opportunity to model learning, human vulnerability, and the importance of personal change, no matter how long it takes.

Deep personal change cannot be "scheduled" to coincide with the formal organizational shifts that occur during implementation. The leaders must understand this reality and allow both to occur in their rightful time.

This dynamic provides important learning about conscious process thinking, which we discuss in depth in our companion book, *Beyond Change Management*. Given the process nature of change, we know that the personal aspects of transformation, so critical to success, occur over time. In more control-oriented and reactive organizations, it is logical to assume that when leaders announce their intention for a certain type of new behavior, people—leaders included—should then act that way immediately and exclusively. *This doesn't happen.* Mindset changes, reflected in behavior, words, and interpersonal skills, take time to integrate and master. Although these changes begin the moment people choose to change, they take much practice to become the norm—two steps forward, one back. Deep personal change can actually take years for leaders and employees.

It is one thing to know this intellectually. It is another to create this understanding overtly in the organization, as everyone is collectively undergoing his or her own transformation, and the organization is being changed as a result. It is important that you take the time to recognize and publicize this critical aspect about how transformational change—on the individual, relationship, and team levels—takes place. Any assumption otherwise causes unnecessary turmoil. People must be encouraged and supported for making this effort on behalf of the organization's, and their own, transformation. It is not easy, and it is absolutely essential.

If you offer breakthrough training to your leaders or employees early in the transformation, you can clarify this notion then, or do it as you prepare the organization for implementation in Phase VI. Then have the leaders model it openly during implementation, and give them a lot of support and coaching.

Task VII.A.2: Monitor and Course-Correct Implementation

No matter how well you prepared for implementation, it will go differently than you planned. In Phase I, you developed a course correction process and system for overseeing your change process and outcome. Ideally, you established the expectation that everyone in the organization participates in the course correction process, monitoring how the transformation is going, recognizing problems early, and offering recommendations for improvement.

However, change is commonly seen as the "leaders' thing" and is rarely presented as everyone's responsibility. Traditionally, the leaders do their planning and announce the change. Then people either help or hinder its progress, depending on what they think about it. In this scenario, employees view change as something that is done *to* them. This circumstance creates a reactive, autopilot orientation, fraught with unnecessary difficulties and obstacles.

By doing your early Phase I and II work, hopefully you have established the change effort as a *conscious* and *collective* endeavor. We have a motto for how the conscious and collective effort works: "Everyone is responsible. No one is to blame." If you have actively engaged your project community and created a critical mass of support for the transformation, everyone shares responsibility for making the change a success. Make sure your course correction strategy is clear to everyone, and clarify what they should look for and how to give this input.

Remember that you want everyone to pay attention to the *change process* dynamics, the *human* factors at play, as well as any issues about the *content* of what you are changing. The next task pays particular attention to content, monitoring your desired state as it is being implemented. To cover these bases, there are many topics to monitor during implementation. Exhibit 10.1, Change Process Topics to Monitor during Implementation, offers a checklist of people and process issues to observe. Use the checklist to hone your focus for this task. Make sure to look for things that are going right as well as things that require adjustment, at all levels of the organization.

Task VII.A.3: Monitor and Course-Correct Desired State

Like your implementation process, your desired state will inevitably take shape somewhat differently than you intended. During implementation, you must watch for new information indicating that your desired state design needs to be altered. Likely, these alterations will be at the managerial and operational levels of design. For the most part, you are better off making these modifications now while implementation is underway, rather than later when people are trying to adjust to the new state after it is in place. Exhibit 10.2, Desired State Topics to Monitor during Implementation, provides another checklist of content issues, plus some relevant people issues, to assist your planning of this work. Tailor it to your needs.

Exhibit 10.1. Change Process Topics to Monitor During Implementation

- Change governance
- Implementation Master Plan
- Communication delivery and impact; rumor management
- People's reactions and how they are being dealt with
- Mindset and behavior changes: successes or failures among leaders and/or target groups
- Need for more training and coaching
- Cultural norms that need to be changed, values that are not being respected
- Stories that effectively demonstrate the new culture and future state
- Commitment to the transformation from the leaders or key stakeholders
- People's capacity to engage in the transformation as well as perform their ongoing responsibilities
- Opportunities to celebrate and recognize milestones, best practices, and new behaviors
- Political dynamics that hinder progress
- Needs for additional bold actions
- Unforeseen relationship issues
- Operating problems in sustaining the ongoing business; interface issues between operations and the change effort
- Conditions for success
- Additional resources needed
- Pacing and timetable
- Metrics met or missed
- Team effectiveness
- Information generation and how new information and feedback are being handled
- Effectiveness of decision making and decision follow-through
- Needs of your project community
- Appropriateness of your temporary support structures, systems, policies, and technologies
- Handling of new impacts that show up
- Leaders' ability to walk the talk of the desired state
- Use of rewards to support the change process
- Effectiveness of your employee engagement strategies
- Ease and ability to course-correct the change process

In our experience, there are two common factors driving the need to alter the desired state. The first is the recognition that some people dynamic has been missed and must be incorporated formally into the new state if it is going to succeed. As much as The Change Leader's Roadmap stresses attention to people's needs at all levels, inevitably during implementation, unforeseen people requirements show up.

The second factor is that some design requirement or boundary condition is not being met by the new state design. It may have been known and thought

---

Exhibit 10.2. **Desired State Topics to Monitor During Implementation**

- Fulfillment of design requirements and respect of boundary conditions
- Fulfillment of customer and marketplace requirements
- Performance metrics for the desired state
- Completion of the operational design
- Effectiveness and alignment of each aspect of the new organization (structure, business processes, work practices, management systems, policies, technology, facilities, culture, skills, etc.)
- How well the new organization works as an integrated system; operating efficiencies; indicators of optimization or sub-optimization
- Changes needed in customer or vendor relationships
- Forays into innovative new state solutions
- How well the new organization manifests its vision and Big Win
- Competencies of management and the workforce to succeed in the new organization
- Effectiveness of decision-making, knowledge management, and information systems
- Fit of the new culture with the requirements of the operation
- Ability to integrate and model the new mindset and culture
- Cross-boundary relationships and interactions
- Leadership capacity
- Workload realities
- Resource requirements
- Ability to continuously improve

A health care system was implementing several new patient safety practices. As the various protocols were being implemented, it became very clear that the procedures as defined on paper were not reflective of the relational norms among doctors, nurses, and support staff. Nobody felt safe enough to mention to the doctors in charge any factor they thought put the patient at risk. The doctors, by habit, perpetuated the expectation in all others that they did things the way they thought best and were not to be questioned. Unfortunately, many of the adverse events that occurred did so because a physician was unaware of a change in some aspect of the patient's condition or some small change in technology or procedure.

The design of the new protocols needed to spell out required culture change as well as mindset and behavior change on everyone's part. These personal and relationship changes were not a side show to the procedures. The success of the patient safety practices depended on the formalization of new ways of relating and communicating, all in support of better quality care.

The change team added the required training, coaching, and team building to their implementation plans to ensure that these human factors were accounted for in the new state. This enabled an essential alteration to both the change process and the new state design.

to have been handled, and reality is not behaving according to plan, or it may have been missed. Either way, adjustment to the design is required, now rather than later. Acknowledge getting smarter by the minute, and make the needed changes.

SUMMARY

You have now carried out your Implementation Master Plan—and all of its adjustments—and put your desired state into place. Most likely, operational implementation will continue as you further establish your desired state. This brings you to the next phase, *Celebrate and Integrate the New State.*

CONSULTING QUESTIONS FOR ACTIVITY VII.A: IMPLEMENT THE CHANGE

Task VII.A.1: Roll Out Implementation Master Plan

▶ How will you ensure that the change leaders remain committed to modeling the new mindset, behaviors, and relationships during implementation?

▶ How will you build understanding that behavioral and mindset changes take time and support to occur?

▶ How will you establish the expectation that all stakeholders are responsible for the successful implementation of the desired state, including all of the content, people, and process elements?

▶ Does everyone know what to look for to support success? Have you established adequate monitoring and course correction protocols?

▶ How will you communicate to the organization necessary course corrections to your change process and desired state during implementation?

Task VII.A.2: Monitor and Course-Correct Implementation

▶ How will you oversee the implementation process and course-correct it in real time? What aspects of the process will you observe?

▶ How will you engage the organization in active monitoring of the implementation process while the operation continues?

▶ Who will you involve in hearing and integrating feedback about how the change process is proceeding?

Task VII.A.3: Monitor and Course-Correct Desired State

▶ How will you assess the appropriateness of the desired state as it is implemented?

- What aspects of the desired state will you monitor? How will you ensure attention to the required human dynamics?

- How will you engage the leaders to expect improvements to the desired state design as it is being implemented?

- How will you engage the organization to seek improvements to the desired state design as it is being implemented?

CHAPTER

11

PHASE VIII
Celebrate and Integrate
the New State

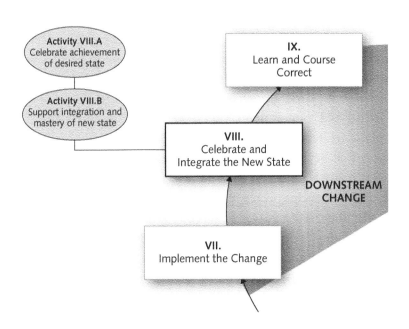

PHASE VIII: TASK DELIVERABLES

VIII.A.1: • The achievement of your desired state has been declared and celebrated.

• People throughout your project community have been recognized and rewarded for supporting the successful creation of the desired state.

VIII.B.1: Individuals and intact work teams understand how best to work together and how they fit into the big picture of the new state.

VIII.B.2: A critical mass of the organization understands how the overall new state operates and how to support its optimal performance.

Congratulations! Your desired state—now the organization's "new state"—is largely up and running. It may look like what you originally planned, or you may have course-corrected it several times during implementation. In either case, to address the dynamics of this phase, assume that the organization has begun to operate in ways that will likely produce your intended outcomes.

Having reached this point, your organization needs and deserves to know that it has officially entered its "new state." The purpose of this phase is to celebrate the great milestone of achieving your desired state and to support people's integration and mastery of the new culture, mindsets, behaviors, skills, and work practices that make their new state work. This phase allows people to settle in, learn about, and gain competence and comfort in their new ways of working and relating.

This phase creates an essential psychological and physical "pause" that nurtures people's well-being, as well as giving them an energy boost through celebration. This phase is not a vacation, however; you accomplish very important work here. This work helps people reorient more quickly to their new reality and appreciate what they have achieved while continuing to improve it. This outcome expedites their ability to produce quality results and be ready for the next evolution of change.

If you determined a specific level of success in Task I.B.8 as a part of your desired outcomes for the change, review it here to ensure that you have actually achieved that level of success, or have put in place the conditions that will ensure its achievement over the course of time. To refresh your memory, the levels are (1) New State Design Determined, (2) New State Design Implemented, (3) Business Outcomes Achieved, (4) Culture Transformed, and (5) Organizational Change Capability Increased.

ACTIVITY VIII.A: CELEBRATE ACHIEVEMENT OF DESIRED STATE

Task VIII.A.1: Celebrate Achievement of Desired State

In the first activity of this phase, the change leaders officially declare that the organization is now functioning in its new state. Consider sponsoring a celebration of all the hard work up to this point, rewarding the people and teams who most directly supported the transformation and, in particular, modeled its new mindset, culture, and desired behaviors. Celebrating the new state allows people to enjoy the fruits of their efforts and is an opportunity for the change leaders to reinforce the new culture further. You may have been hosting mini-celebrations of milestone events during each of the prior phases of the change, which is a good way to sustain people's energy for the transformation. This celebration, however, is your landmark celebration, and it should be given extra attention.

Because so many organizations are traditionally too busy to celebrate, you have an opportunity to change this norm. When planning your celebration strategy, design it so that it clearly reinforces your vision and desired outcomes. You can also use this strategy to recognize best practices for conscious change leadership.

Celebrations can take many forms. Consider the following:

- Celebration party
- Festive dinner or luncheon; can be prepared or served by senior executives or change leaders
- Written announcement or special edition newsletter
- Electronic or video celebration address
- Personalized appreciation letters
- Large group awards meeting (serious and/or humorous)
- Gifts, engraved mementos such as hats, mugs, T-shirts
- Bonuses
- Tickets to sporting or cultural events
- Photo shoot for publicity; media coverage
- Promotions and/or high-visibility job placements
- Family gatherings at work to show off the tangible changes

There are two specific risks inherent in celebrating the achievement of your new state to be aware of. The first risk is communicating that "the change is over"

In a manufacturing facility located in Louisiana, the plant manager wanted to reward his entire organization for its efforts in transforming its structure from a functional, compartmentalized one to a completely integrated production process. The culture of the plant was undergoing a radical shift to support this new structure, requiring people to play many roles and serve many masters.

To celebrate the achievement of the new structure, the plant manager decided to invite the entire organization to a Monday breakfast "fish fry," which was a very fun and rowdy event. The plant manager spent his weekend catching and preparing fish for the event and was the lead cook at the breakfast. His intention was to demonstrate his willingness to serve his people and to reinforce that working together could be a lot of fun. The event was the first of many such uplifting gatherings used to energize the new culture.

and that the organization has arrived where it ultimately wants to be. Given the continuous nature of transformational change, this is *never true*. People have to understand that, even though they have attained a major milestone, change is ongoing and everyone is expected to improve the organization as it strives to reach its vision.

The second risk is that the leaders may want to celebrate completion of a change effort that has had significant emotional impact on various stakeholder groups in the organization. Where the leaders may fully think they are doing something positive, their efforts to celebrate may actually cause further animosity. This is particularly true if the leaders did not address the negative people dynamics triggered by the change effort in constructive ways for those impacted. In these cases, the best strategy is to create an "acknowledgment" communication that recognizes that progress was made, and, at the same time, the journey was a difficult one for many people and the organization. This is far more authentic than pretending to celebrate out of guilt or relief that a change effort is over.

ACTIVITY VIII.B: SUPPORT INTEGRATION AND MASTERY OF NEW STATE

We are at times astounded by leaders who assume that when their organization's new state is finally in place, their people should immediately be able to function at full capability within it. When you were old enough to drive, even after taking a driver's education class, you were not a fully competent driver. Driving takes practice; competent driving takes experience. People have the same needs when they are required to operate in new and different ways at work. With conscious attention, this activity is the rite of passage where the change you have been implementing becomes the normal way of operating. If you are so motivated, you can also pave the way for high performance, where the work is actually taking place at the optimal level.

This activity supports individuals, intact teams, and the organization as a whole to further integrate and master the new state and how it operates. It reflects all of the levels in the Conscious Change Leader Accountability Model.

What do we mean by "integration" and "mastery"? By *integration*, we mean assimilating change so that it becomes the norm. Integration occurs when a person moves from their "discomfort zone" of *trying* to function in new ways to their "comfort zone" of being *competent* to perform effectively. Learning, trial and error, and course correction are essential to people integrating the new state.

By *mastery*, we mean fully understanding and being competent to fulfill the needs of the new state, continuously developing your skills to new levels of excellence, both individually and collectively. Mastery is a way of being, not a destination. You can also describe mastery as consistently being able to perform at peak levels and able to produce breakthrough results. These advanced states of mastery take a conscientious effort from leaders to create the conditions where this is possible and fully supported.

The following list describes an ideal state of integration. Consider how productive and satisfying the work experience will be when any or all of these items are *clear and mutually understood* by all who are involved in the new state! Consultants, change leaders, and organizational managers can target any of these outcomes to improve their group's or organization's effectiveness.

Integration has occurred when you have:

- Clarified work goals, metrics, and expectations for all involved
- Completed an operational impact analysis and worked out operational issues and kinks
- Ensured every individual has adequate skills and knowledge, and the appropriate mindset and attitude, to function effectively and make his or her expected contribution to the new state
- Initiated adjustments and course corrections to your new state

- Identified and shared best practices and behaviors
- Identified the optimal way of interfacing with others in the organization, especially cross-boundary relationships
- Established positive working relationships
- Created and accepted new concepts and terminology
- Assimilated new working norms
- Established new power, influence, and support norms
- Clarified how to communicate with one another
- Agreed on how to manage knowledge and information as work proceeds
- Agreed on how decisions are made and who has authority for what
- Determined and secured appropriate resource requirements
- Clarified how conflicts are handled
- Fully explored the appropriate use of technology
- Created mechanisms for monitoring and course correcting the mindset, behaviors, and work practices of your new state
- Identified further support needed and figured out how to obtain it
- Left behind all nonrelevant old state practices

This next list presents several indications of mastery. Again, consider how responsive and resilient your new organization will be when these are living characteristics of how it operates in real time!

Mastery is occurring when you are:

- Fully competent in your current state, yet committed to improve continuously
- Able to perform routinely at "best-in-class" levels
- Continuously learning and pushing the next edge of innovation or breakthrough
- Inquiring about different ways to do things; thinking creatively
- Taking on new challenges
- Mentoring and supporting excellent performance in others
- Embracing different people's ideas and approaches
- Achieving new, more advanced levels of performance

First, we will address integration and mastery of the new state at the individual and intact team level and then address it for the organization as a whole.

Task VIII.B.1: Support Individuals and Teams to Integrate and Master New State

Metaphorically, this task is the bridge between a couple's honeymoon and actually being able to live happily together in the marriage. This task focuses on clarifying roles and straightening out the kinks of working together in a new way. Carrying the metaphor further, you will be figuring out who cooks and who cleans, whether you push the toothpaste from the bottom or the middle, how to handle disagreements, and how to make financial decisions.

In this task, individuals, intact teams, and even whole departments talk about how to operate most effectively to make their contribution to the larger organization. They work out their own snags and figure out what they must know and do, and how they have to behave and relate, to succeed in the new state. Dispersed or virtual teams also undertake this work but in a way that enables them to engage in the dialogue and then operate optimally from their own locations.

When change leaders provide overt attention and encouragement for this kind of conversation and learning at the local level of the organization, they directly accelerate integration and mastery of the new state. Everybody needs to know where he or she fits in and adds value to the organization. This work meets those needs. Enabling quality and thorough conversation about how best to work together and do things will clarify people's assumptions and inevitably improve how they work. Your overt support for integration dialogue should also enable people to continue their personal change work and embrace the new culture and mindset more fully. Competent OD and change management practitioners can offer invaluable assistance.

There are two main requirements for individuals and teams to integrate and master their roles in the new state. First, they must fully understand what it takes to make their part of the organization function effectively at the day-to-day, pragmatic level. No doubt, people will have different opinions, so alignment is essential. The steps for accomplishing this are listed here:

1. Identify new ways of thinking and behaving, new work practices and relationships, and supportive norms that are essential to making this part of the new state work at peak performance level.
2. Practice, test, and fine-tune these new ways.

3. Share best practices about these new ways among those involved or impacted by the person's or group's work.

4. Achieve and celebrate competence in these new ways.

There are many ways to accomplish these steps. Exhibit 11.1, Integration and Mastery Strategies, offers a checklist of options for this work. Review it to shape your thinking.

The second requirement of this activity is for individuals and work units to understand how their part of the organization fits into and contributes to the larger organization. This brings us to the second task of this activity.

Task VIII.B.2: Support Whole System to Integrate and Master New State

Learning to drive a car requires more than knowing how to steer and how to press the gas pedal or the brake pedal. Every part of the car—inside the engine and in its body—is required for the smooth functioning of the vehicle. As the driver,

Exhibit 11.1.   **Integration and Mastery Strategies**

- Dialogue and learning groups
- Classroom training and follow-up application sessions
- Coaching and mentoring by experts or "super users"
- Identifying and rewarding best practices and desired behaviors
- Appreciative inquiry sessions to fortify what is going well
- Further impact analysis and working sessions to resolve issues
- Job, project, and skill clinics, or online learning programs
- Further benchmarking of other organizations
- Process or quality improvement work
- Computer conferencing to support learning, questions, and resolution of issues
- Check-in meetings to bring up operational, cultural, and emotional needs
- Relationship/partnership contracting
- Counseling to reinforce mindset and behavior changes
- On-the-job training
- Ensuring the right people are in the right jobs

you must know how to operate the car as well as learn the laws and etiquette for competent driving. All of this comes together as "systemic requirements" for excellent and safe driving. The same is true in learning how your entire new state operates in order for it to achieve its vision and business goals. System-wide integration of the new state is essential to establish the big picture of success in your organization. It also sets the expectation for strengthening any aspect of your new state so that it better supports the effectiveness of the whole. This notion is reinforced by the Conscious Change Leader Accountability Model.

This task designs and carries out a process to ensure that all of the key players in your organization, and certainly in the change you have just undertaken, understand how the overall organization now has to operate to meet the needs of its marketplace and changing environment. You are actually making people smarter about how to support the new state by expanding their view of the organization, beyond the change. Even if the scope of your change effort was only a piece of your larger organization, you began the change with initial desired outcomes that were going to somehow contribute to the larger enterprise. If yours was an enterprise-wide change, then your goals were clearly in support of the whole. In this task, you ensure the whole system benefits optimally from the change by ensuring system integration and mastery. (See Premium Content: Elements of a Whole System Integration and Mastery Strategy, www.pfeiffer .com/go/anderson.)

Through this task, each part of the organization—functional groups, divisions, product or service lines, or geographical regions—gains a greater appreciation for how the whole system now functions and how each part contributes to the greater good. In addition, the change leaders discover what aspects of the new state still need fine-tuning, where the gaps and redundancies in its operation are, and where there are opportunities for further breakthrough in system dynamics or performance.

The ideal outcomes for this task are that everyone involved must understand the following:

▶ How your new state is a fulfillment or a major advancement toward the organization's vision (both operations and culture).

▶ The interdependencies and relationships among the various components of your new organization.

A manufacturing company revamped its business strategy, functional structure, management processes, culture, and decision making to create strategic business units. After the majority of the organization's changes were in place, we designed a system-wide integration strategy to unify the whole and fortify the leaders' collective understanding of how the new organization worked.

Every functional leader in the new design was asked to prepare a creative presentation of his or her function's purpose, contribution, responsibilities, and assets. In addition, they presented their views of what services or resources they offered to other key functions and what they needed from others to carry out their roles effectively. They also identified the relationships they had with the other leaders that were in good working order and those that were in need of clarification or support. Everyone was encouraged to engage their staff in preparing this work to expand the organization's involvement.

All of these leaders participated in a two-day Business Integration meeting. In the logical sequence of business workflow, the leaders presented their input. As the organization's total functioning was pieced together like a complex puzzle, the beauty of the whole picture began to take shape. Rather than understanding just the theory behind the new design, the leaders saw how each of them was essential to the success of the whole. They saw that the total organization needed their individual functions to work optimally. And they pinpointed where new relationships were required, how to improve their effectiveness, and how the culture of shared responsibility, cross-boundary relationships, and teamwork was essential to the company's new business direction.

The senior leaders used the meeting to reinforce their new expectations of management, to put some old negative political and behavioral patterns to rest, and to reward examples of breakthrough thinking and acting. The participants went away with a much broader perspective and much sharper directives to share with their staffs. Every manager was tasked with sharing the outcomes of the meeting with their entire functional organizations and how their thinking had evolved to more clearly contribute to the good of the whole organization.

- How newly installed organization-wide IT systems, management systems, or processes will work.
- What each area of the organization contributes to the larger system and enterprise goals.
- How all areas of the organization work co-creatively together to form an integrated whole. Your employees, as well as your executives, must be aware of what is happening across organizational boundaries and why.
- How everyone interfaces with customers and vendors.

One critical human dynamic to be attentive to in this process is the return of old state political battles. Even though leaders may be in entirely new roles and have very different relationships and positions of influence in the new organization, their old behavior patterns may not have been resolved. If you have established ground rules for how to deal with these dynamics in advance, you can avert much of this. If you haven't, give some thought to how to address these issues if they show up as the new organization refines its optimal way of performing. This work is yet another culture change leverage point, as well as direct reflection of conscious change leadership.

The preceding Case-In-Point focused on middle management and upper management, but ideally, you will accomplish this task throughout your entire organization. The more people understand how the new organization operates as an integrated whole, the more people you have who can intelligently course-correct and improve it over time. By definition, you have completed this task when a critical mass of the organization has attained this big picture understanding and their behavior and working relationships reflect it.

SUMMARY

At this point, you have truly succeeded in implementing your new state. You have celebrated the achievement of your intended outcomes and supported individuals, teams, and the entire organization to function effectively and to understand how each contributes to the greater good of the organization. From this place, you can now "close" this chapter of change.

CONSULTING QUESTIONS FOR ACTIVITY VIII.A: CELEBRATE ACHIEVEMENT OF DESIRED STATE

Task VIII.A.1: Celebrate Achievement of Desired State

▶ How will you announce to the organization that your desired state is now in place?

▶ What methods will you use to celebrate and reward people's efforts to create the new state?

▶ How can you use your announcement and celebration to further reinforce the mindset, values, norms, and behaviors required for the success of your new state?

▶ How will you ensure that your organization understands the need for further changes, even though the new state has been achieved?

CONSULTING QUESTIONS FOR ACTIVITY VIII.B: SUPPORT INTEGRATION AND MASTERY OF NEW STATE

Task VIII.B.1: Support Individuals and Teams to Integrate and Master New State

▶ What strategies will you use to support individuals and teams to dialogue about and master their part of the new state?

▶ How will you handle this work within dispersed or virtual teams?

▶ How will you ensure that individuals and teams consciously model the new mindsets, behaviors, culture, and relationships after "go live" has occurred? How can you make this *their* work to proactively manage?

Task VIII.B.2: Support Whole System to Integrate and Master New State

▶ How will you make the case to your change sponsor to invest in a "whole system" or large group integration and mastery process or event?

▶ What strategies will you use to support the whole organization to learn and master its new state?

▶ Who are the appropriate attendees for organization-wide integration meetings?

▶ Should you invite customers or vendors to such meetings? What outcome would you want?

▶ How will you present the purpose, content, and norms of these meetings to the attendees when you invite them?

▶ What topics will you ask the participants in this process to prepare and present as their contribution to how the overall system works (e.g., their role, responsibilities, deliverables, relationships, assets, resources, services, products, needs, etc.)?

▶ How can you ensure that the senior leaders model the new culture and behaviors they want to reinforce in the organization during their integration and mastery process?

▶ How can you use this work to establish the expectation for continuous course correction?

▶ How will you keep old political dynamics from creeping back into the new state at these gatherings?

▶ What strategies will you use to deepen front-line employees' understanding of how the new state functions as an integrated, whole system?

CHAPTER

12

PHASE IX
Learn and Course-Correct

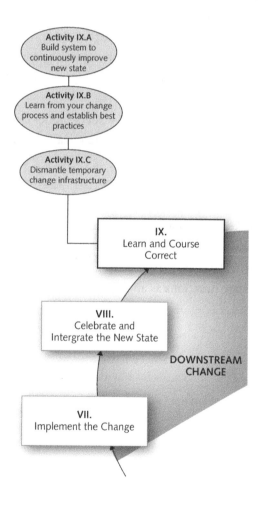

Activity IX.A
Build system to
continuously improve
new state

Activity IX.B
Learn from your change
process and establish best
practices

Activity IX.C
Dismantle temporary
change infrastructure

IX.
Learn and Course
Correct

VIII.
Celebrate and
Intergrate the New State

DOWNSTREAM
CHANGE

VII.
Implement the Change

PHASE IX: TASK DELIVERABLES

IX.A.1: A system to refine and continuously improve the new state has been designed and implemented.

IX.B.1: Key learnings and best practices about how to lead the people and process dynamics of change have been identified, communicated, and integrated into the organization's way of leading change.

IX.C.1:
- The temporary change governance, support structures, management systems, policies, and technology that are no longer relevant have been dismantled and communicated as complete.
- The support structures, management systems, policies, and technology employed in the change process and useful in the new organization have been tailored, formalized, and communicated as continuing.
- The target groups of your change understand that this current iteration of change is now complete.

You should never consider your new state the "be all and end all" guarantee of success for your organization. Your environment and marketplace continue to change, as do the dynamics inside your organization. Although your reality remains dynamic and you may already have started the next wave of change, people have a need for completion. It is a natural human desire. Your attention to the "ending" of this round of transformation is a requirement of the process.

There are three activities of this final phase. Always, we are looking to raise leaders' conscious awareness, and this phase is critical to this. Its meta-purpose is to reveal to the organization's leaders what they do and don't yet see about how they lead their most important changes so that they can continuously build their capability to lead their organizations more effectively. Specifically, the goals of this phase's three activities are the following:

- Create mechanisms for continuous improvement of the new state.
- Evaluate and learn from how your change strategy and process were designed and implemented, and how best to handle the human dimensions of change.
- Initiate actions to improve your organization's readiness and ability to facilitate future changes successfully.
- Close down your existing change effort by dismantling the temporary infrastructure and conditions that no longer serve the needs of the new organization.

This task is essential to supporting the organization as it evolves in a balanced and healthy way. Endings leave a lasting impression that will impact the beginning of the next iteration of change. What you do here to prepare for the future and put closure on the past will influence the degree of readiness, willingness, and capacity in the organization for continued transformation. This is an important responsibility of the change leaders, who must continue to pave the way to the future.

ACTIVITY IX.A: BUILD SYSTEM TO CONTINUOUSLY IMPROVE NEW STATE

Note that this task focuses on *improving* what you have already implemented as your content solution. It does not address the formal evaluation you will likely do to test how well this new state works and whether or not it fulfills your business or financial goals. We assume this evaluation will occur, and the data it reveals will cause more improvement. For now, we want to make sure that you have the conscious means to make all improvements to your new state.

Task IX.A.1: Build System to Continuously Improve New State

This task formalizes how your organization will continue to improve its new state and, therefore, ensure its ongoing success. The expectation for continuous improvement must be made overt as the normal way of doing business. Your goal here, from a process perspective, is to create an organization that remains viable over time, responsive to new demands as a matter of course. Do not leave this attitude to hope. It is a part of both transforming your organization's mindset and culture, and the way the organization operates and evolves. Make it conscious!

In this task, you design a system or method to engage people in monitoring and refining your new or now "current" state. The system and methods you create need to focus on the operational and technical aspects of the business, as well as the human and cultural aspects. There is a process challenge in this work. Your operational and technical changes have already been implemented, and yet your desired culture is still a work in progress. Therefore, your culture improvement strategy has to ensure continued conscious attention to culture and mindset.

Your system needs to ensure responsiveness to any change in requirements of your organization's stakeholders—its customer base, industry, workforce, and community. It should include how the organization will scan its external and internal environments for new wake-up calls, as well as how it will keep the vision alive and evolving.

We describe this work as the creation of a system and method for continuous renewal. Another approach is to embed the "renewal theme" as the modus operandi for your entire organization. Consider this Case-In-Point.

Exhibit 12.1. **Mechanisms to Continuously Improve the New State**

- Stretch goals to search out worthy opportunities for course correction
- Public recognition or rewards for people who have suggested valuable ideas; wake-up call recognition system
- Online information generation network
- Leave the change process leader in place to oversee ongoing learning and course correction
- "Office of the Future" to research new trends or technologies
- Customer input Internet site
- Stakeholder input intranet site
- Appreciative Inquiry, World Café, or Future Search conferences
- "Skip level" dialogues about how to course-correct, or organization-wide teleconferences with the CEO to offer ideas for improvement or ask questions
- Periodic visioning for new renewal processes
- "Barrier busters" group
- Quality improvement tools and teams

For those of you who will create a system and method for continuous improvement, Exhibit 12.1 provides a checklist of options. Review these with the leaders of the organization, and tailor them to fit your situation.

ACTIVITY IX.B: LEARN FROM YOUR CHANGE PROCESS AND ESTABLISH BEST PRACTICES

Task IX.B.1: Learn from Your Change Process and Establish Best Practices

Inasmuch as you have monitored and course corrected your change process in every phase, this task *formally* looks back at your entire transformation process with "20/20 hindsight" and identifies both people and process learnings from the experience. It is based on two assumptions: (1) change is continuous, and (2) you are committed to strengthening your organization's capability to successfully lead its future changes, transformation or other types of change.

This task focuses on identifying an array of best practices for change, including strategies, skills, knowledge, mindsets, behaviors, tools, and techniques. It is a high-gain effort to determine how you would design and facilitate your next transformation—what you would do similarly and what you would do differently. This is for both how well you planned and led the process of change and how well you handled all of the human dynamics of the change.

Some organizations have used the results from this task as input to their executive and management development programs for strengthening change leadership. Others use the information to influence the competencies they look for in new hires. Some have used it to further embed The Change Leader's Roadmap methodology as their organization's common change model. Each of these strategies delivers a substantial return on investment.

Depending on the time, resources, and commitment you have available to do this work, you can select any number of approaches for learning and evaluation. Organizations that are committed to creating a learning-oriented culture typically emphasize this task and plan a comprehensive and formal change process audit strategy. Others take a less formal tactic and design a self-reflective, qualitative approach to evaluate how well they did. Consider using an Appreciative Inquiry approach to focus on what worked especially well in this change.

Whose input will you seek? Be sure to include the key members of your project community—the change process leader, sponsor, change leadership team, executive team, union leaders, employee groups or change advocates, and other key target groups and stakeholders. Also consider including the consultants and trainers who supported the effort, and representatives from the organization's external constituents, such as customers, clients, patients, and vendors.

In selecting what to study about your change process, consider using the relevant measurements that you identified for the change process in Task I.F.8, *Determine Measurements of Change*, and your conditions for success. In addition, Exhibit 12.2 offers a checklist of many more options. Select and add items that fit your learning needs and the goals for your change leadership development strategy. Use the results of this study to determine best practices for change for your organization.

After you have identified your best change practices, it is worth considering a strategy to further embed them into the organization. Many organizations are establishing a Change Leadership Community of Practice or Center of Excellence. Most design these strategies to support their internal change consultants and service providers. However, some also invite the participation of line leaders who are keen to improve their skills in change leadership.

Exhibit 12.2. Topics to Assess Your Change Process to Identify Best Practices

- How well you met the expectations for the change process as set by:
  - Your vision for the transformational experience
  - Your overall change strategy
  - Conditions for success
  - Engagement strategies
  - Change communications effectiveness (Evaluate for attention to all five levels of communication.)
  - Measurements of the process
  - Desired culture
- How well your change strategy balanced speed with thoroughness
- How well the deliverables of each phase and each task were communicated and achieved (Be sure to assess each phase and/or activity independently.)
- Clarity of roles among your change leaders, and their performance—change process leader, change team members, and change consultants, including how well they modeled and walked the talk of the transformation
- How well you modeled your values and guiding principles
- How well you set up and used your conditions for success
- How much trauma was created for people adversely affected by the process, and how well the leaders assisted people through their reactions and resistance
- How effective your strategies were for building readiness and ensuring adequate capacity to make the change
- How clear and effective your decision-making processes were
- How well you were able to determine and secure adequate resources
- How effectively the leaders dealt with political dynamics
- How well new information was handled and used for course corrections
- Responsiveness to the needs of the organization as it changed; balancing ongoing business requirements and stakeholder needs with the emerging requirements of the transformation
- Ability to course-correct the process quickly and effectively
- How well you handled changing the mindset and behavior of your leaders and stakeholders
- How much more capable the organization is in keeping itself on the cutting edge and continuously adapting than it was before this change
- Effectiveness of your temporary change structures, management systems, policies, and technologies
- How much more capable the executives are as change leaders after building their capability to lead the transformation individually and as a team

(continued)

- How flexible, responsive, and sensitive the change leaders were to unpredicted disruptions, conflicts, or changes in direction
- What condition the people of the organization are in as they "conclude" this change effort

ACTIVITY IX.C: DISMANTLE TEMPORARY CHANGE INFRASTRUCTURE

Task IX.C.1: Dismantle Temporary Change Infrastructure

Now that you have "completed" this particular change effort, it is time to dismantle your temporary infrastructure, including your support structures, systems, policies, and technologies. This task identifies which of these have served their purpose and have to end, and which might need to continue. All too often, project teams and committees meet long after their mission is accomplished and their value has been realized. This "bureaucratization" of change structures justifiably creates a negative perception among employees and must be avoided.

In reviewing your infrastructure, look for any temporary mechanisms that have actually made life in the organization much easier and more effective and, with some tinkering, can be valuable additions to your organization's normal governance or operations. Realign the structures or systems that still serve a useful purpose as official parts of your new state.

A part of this task is to end the special roles people have played to support the transformation. Many of the people who have served on special teams or in temporary roles will now go through their own emotional transitions as they settle back into their old roles. For those moving into new state positions, this is still somewhat true, but less so, especially if their new roles are attractive to them.

Special attention may be required for both categories of people, particularly if they became engrossed in their temporary assignments, as many do. They are not the same people they were before the transformation; their views of both the organization and their individual contribution to it have been expanded, and you must recognize this. Be sure to celebrate their successes overtly and create formal closure to their participation with their teams. Be especially cautious of

Exhibit 12.3. Designing Your Dismantling Strategy

- How will you determine which of your structures, management systems, policies, and technologies have to be dismantled and communicated as complete?
- How will you determine if any of these should be continued to serve the new organization?
- How will you tailor, formalize, and communicate those you want to embed into your new state?
- How will you provide a formal ending and celebration for your change teams?
- How will you communicate that this change is now "complete"?

placing people who have thrived in these dynamic and influential change leadership roles back into more static, routine jobs. We have often seen talent leave the organization because their post-change jobs lack the thrill and challenge of leading transformation.

There are many things to consider when designing your strategy for this task. Exhibit 12.3 offers a list of questions to answer as you plan. Think through the outcomes you want in completing this change effort and the types of support you have to give to the organization as it readies itself for its next round of changes.

SUMMARY

Phase IX completes the downstream stage of change and brings you around to the beginning of The Change Leader's Roadmap once again. You have implemented your transformation, supported your organization to build its understanding and capability to succeed in its new state, and completed this particular transformation in preparation for the next. If you haven't already heard them, new wake-up calls await you.

We hope that this descriptive journey through the process of transforming your organization has prepared you to take on your next real transformational challenge.

The last section of the book explores how people typically respond to The Change Leader's Roadmap and how you can best leverage its value to your organization.

CONSULTING QUESTIONS FOR ACTIVITY IX.A: BUILD SYSTEM TO CONTINUOUSLY IMPROVE NEW STATE

Task IX.A.1: Build System to Continuously Improve New State

▶ How will you ensure that your new organization continues to stay current with the ever-changing needs of its environment and marketplace?

▶ What system and methods will you use to support the continuous improvement of your new state? Whom will you engage in this work?

CONSULTING QUESTIONS FOR ACTIVITY IX.B: LEARN FROM YOUR CHANGE PROCESS AND ESTABLISH BEST PRACTICES

Task IX.B.1: Learn from Your Change Process and Establish Best Practices

▶ What aspects of your change process will you study?

▶ How will you ensure attention to both the process and people dynamics of your change?

▶ Who will evaluate the effectiveness of your change process and identify your best practices for change?

▶ How will you measure the effectiveness of your change process? Will you attempt to quantify it? In what ways?

▶ How will you document, communicate, and educate your organization about your best practices for change? Who needs to use and master them?

- Will you incorporate the results of your assessment into your existing or new executive or management development programs to build greater change leadership capability?
- Will you embed them into a Change Leadership Community of Practice or Center of Excellence?

CONSULTING QUESTIONS FOR ACTIVITY IX.C: DISMANTLE TEMPORARY CHANGE INFRASTRUCTURE

Task IX.C.1: Dismantle Temporary Change Infrastructure

See Exhibit 12.3 for these questions.

Leveraging The Change Leader's Roadmap

Putting The Change Leader's Roadmap into Practice

Now that you have read through The Change Leader's Roadmap in its entirety, you may have a number of questions about it. This chapter addresses several common questions about the model, as well as the developmental stages of learning it. Where people are in their professional development as change agents or change leaders impacts their reactions to the methodology, as does their ability to use it to their advantage in real time. We will be discussing this further. We hope this chapter provides guidance to help you use the methodology to it full potential.

This chapter explores four areas influencing how people respond to the model:

1. The model as a customizable thinking discipline versus an instruction manual of prescribed sequential actions
2. Developmental stages of learning to master The Change Leader's Roadmap
3. Common reactions to the model and how people's reactions influence their ability to take advantage of it
4. Misperceptions that the model recommends a "top-down" approach to change versus a more organic, multi-directional approach

THE MODEL AS A THINKING DISCIPLINE

The nine-phase Change Leader's Roadmap model has an appealing logic and flow. Some leaders and consultants may inadvertently assume that this logic implies that transformation is controllable and predictable, and that the model is meant to be adhered to rigidly and followed sequentially. They also assume that they must do all of the tasks in it. These assumptions would be neither wise nor beneficial. As we noted in the Introduction to this book, The Change Leader's Roadmap is not a cookbook for how to orchestrate transformational change. The model is designed as a *thinking discipline*, a guidance system for navigating the complexity and chaos of transformation in a conscious and thoughtful way. The structure and depth it provides are meant to support your thinking, not necessarily to order or dictate your actions. You will never do all of the tasks in it; you must always select the most important tasks for your current needs—*as few as possible and only what you need to ensure your success.* We encourage you to revisit this discussion in the Introduction now that you have read about the model in its entirety. Also, the next chapter provides an outline of the thirty tasks we believe to be the most critical and always worthy of your consideration.

As you read about the nine phases, no doubt you were thinking through the relevance of the CLR's tasks applied to your current change effort or to a past case. In working with change leaders and consultants, we have discovered that a person's level of professional experience as a change agent influences his or her reactions to the model. We identify four levels or stages of development that can be a useful guide to learning the model and understanding your reactions to it.

DEVELOPMENTAL STAGES FOR LEARNING THE CLR METHODOLOGY

We have identified four stages of growth for practitioners of change—novice, proficient, expert, and master. These apply both to consultants and to change leaders. We recognize that the stage of development a change practitioner is in influences his or her perception of the methodology and ability to readily use it. The four stages, shown in Figure 13.1, nest *within* each other rather than replace each other sequentially. A brief description of each stage follows, with general characteristics of each. As we overview the stages, we encourage you to find yourself within them, both where you are today and where you hope to be to gain the greatest value from the CLR. The stages are intended to raise your level of conscious awareness—of yourself and your use of the methodology. Later in this chapter, we review the common initial reactions people have to the methodology, which are often reflections of their stage of development and awareness. We also encourage you to find yourself there.

Figure 13.1. Developmental Stages for Learning the CLR Methodology

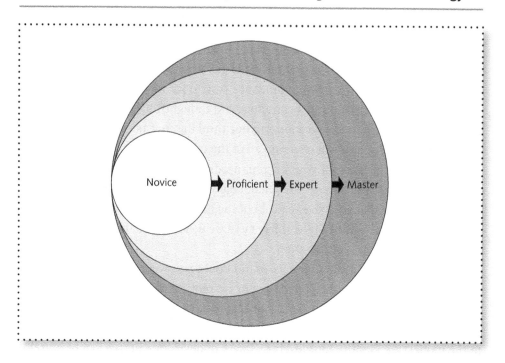

Novice practitioners are new to change leadership and consulting, and they need guidance and encouragement when first delving into the breadth of the CLR resources online. It is best for novice practitioners to work directly with a change consultant or leader more experienced and familiar with the CLR. Frequently, novice practitioners take in everything they are learning with equal enthusiasm. Absorbing a comprehensive approach such as the CLR can often overwhelm them or make them anxious about not "getting it right" or not doing it "by the book." They often assume they have to do everything suggested in the model, in the right order, for fear of missing something important. Their ability to discern what is needed, what can be skipped, and what should be tailored to the reality of a particular situation is not yet fully developed. Novices should be careful to not view the CLR as their cookbook for success, as it is not intended to be used that way.

Novices appropriately look to the methodology continually to help guide their planning and ensure they are "on track." Novices will test their newly acquired understanding of what to do as they work, eyes open to discovery and validation. They are looking to become more aware and knowledgeable. Although they may naturally fear making mistakes, they can also enjoy the latitude of trial-and-error if they make their experience and comfort level known to the people they are supporting. This latitude for experimentation can help accelerate their learning process and is far better than pretending that they are more advanced than they are. Of greatest importance to the development of a novice is that "no question is a dumb question!" Ask away!

Proficient practitioners have more experience with change and less concern than novices about doing everything in the CLR. They exercise more conscious choice about how best to apply it to unique situations, accessing its resource materials regularly. Although they may have been introduced to the principles and foundations underlying the design of the CLR, they have not yet fully integrated them into their worldview or approaches. Proficient practitioners are most comfortable working with expert or master practitioners at their sides, especially if they are working on a complex transformational change effort. They only venture out alone in settings where they feel the risk is minimal or where a plan for action has already been developed. They often seek out opportunities to test their wings and appreciate having the safety net that the model offers.

Expert practitioners understand the entire methodology and are familiar with how to navigate the breadth of resources within it to guide a major change effort through to fruition. They are comfortable selecting the best, and fewest, tasks and tailoring the work as different situations demand. They are comfortably aware of what the methodology offers and how and when to use its resources. Expert practitioners know the CLR well enough to teach and coach others. They can integrate it with other models and competencies in their consulting and management repertoires, yet still reference CLR resources periodically to check their thinking and course-correct. Expert practitioners are competent in the most complex of change efforts and like the challenge of transformation. They can be good models of the conscious mindset, behavior, and strategies the CLR promotes if they have developed their personal awareness capabilities as much as their knowledge and expertise. They are very familiar with the Conscious Change Leader Accountability Model and have invested in their own personal development process to be able to use it effectively to guide their work.

Master practitioners have all of the experience and comfort of their expert counterparts, with the additional capability of easily changing and evolving the resources within the methodology as the situation indicates. They regularly observe emergent patterns in the transformational process and the people involved in it, and test new hypotheses and approaches that may better serve the achievement of real results from change. They actively coach others and may present or write about their theories and experiences for the consulting profession or at leadership conferences.

Achieving mastery, and the breakthrough results that it makes possible, requires practitioners to develop themselves mentally, emotionally, and spiritually; acquiring change skills is simply not enough for mastery. Without considerable personal transformation, the subtle yet significant nuances of organizational transformation go unseen or unappreciated. Their personal development gives masters the gift of being authentic models of the conscious approach to change leadership. They demonstrate their own learning, course correction, and personal breakthrough when they encounter live opportunities to do so. Their personal presence in these situations is always a powerful illustration of how people's consciousness is always evolving, at both the individual and organizational levels. Their beings are more their guides, not their egos.

Our intent here is only to overview these developmental stages, not to address how to advance from one stage to another. Further support for building capability in consultants and change leaders is available through Being First's Conscious Change Leadership Development curriculum. (See Premium Content: Upgrade Your Organization Development and Project Management Staff to Strategic Change Consultants, www.pfeiffer.com/go/anderson.)

Keep the four developmental stages in mind when considering how to teach and mentor people in the CLR methodology. When adding to your organization's change leadership capacity, hire people—employees or external consultants—who actually have the level of expertise you need. This often requires an expert or master-level practitioner to participate in your interview process because they will know what to look for in candidates. Many efforts have failed due to staffing at too low a level of competence for the complexity of the changes required. Most importantly, hire people who are devoted—first and foremost—to their own personal development and conscious awareness. These people always make better change leaders and consultants.

As we noted earlier, people's different levels of expertise in leading change influence their impressions about The Change Leader's Roadmap. Let's explore the various reactions we encounter.

REACTIONS TO THE CHANGE LEADER'S ROADMAP MODEL

Through teaching thousands of people this methodology over three decades, we have observed a range of reactions to it. These reactions either support or hinder people's use of the model. Some people's reactions cause them to adopt the model in its entirety, almost as the "savior" of their change effort, while others' reactions cause them to reject it outright, even if portions of it serve their needs.

As a consultant or leader who has chosen to read this book, you are more than likely looking for insight, tools, and techniques to help guide your efforts. If you have not used a change process model before, after reading through the description of all nine phases of this process, you are likely experiencing one of three reactions—or something similar.

Reaction 1: "Thanks for the Structure and Security"

"Finally! A structure I can follow! I knew a lot of this had to be done, I just didn't know how to get it all organized. Now it is all in one place, in sequence! I'm relieved to know I am on the right track."

This first reaction infers that the model provides a sense of security in its organization and comprehensiveness. For individuals who have a novice level of experience in leading change, the reaction expresses relief that their strategies are sound. We often hear this, even from proficient and expert practitioners.

This reaction is common in organizations that value a clear and structured approach to things, such as engineering, utilities, traditional manufacturing, healthcare, or other organizations that are largely regulated in their operating practices. The people in these settings appreciate the structure of the methodology and its all-inclusiveness. It provides a comprehensive roadmap for planning their change process and guiding their decisions along the way.

There is a downside to this reaction, however. These consultants or leaders put themselves at risk in believing that the model is a "silver bullet"—the answer to the discomfort and chaos of transformation. If these people rely too heavily on the model for lockstep instructions, they are in danger of thinking that they really are in control. Worse yet, they may think that following everything the model suggests will guarantee their success. Clearly, this is not true.

As a consultant or change leader, your reality will always dictate how to proceed and should supersede your strict adherence to this or any model. Be cautioned. No change model takes the place of your own experience and expertise, conscious perception, and intuitive evaluation about the situation you face. If you try to use any change model as a formula or cookbook, including this one, you are making a strategic mistake. Use the structure here as your guidance system! You still need to navigate the actual terrain of change!

Reaction 2: "I Want Simple!"

"This is far too complicated for me. I had no idea that all of this work was required! I'd rather go back to my simple view of change and struggle through like I always have."

This reaction, which is very understandable, is an example of an "ignorance is bliss" orientation to life. It is interesting to observe how many people have a genuine aversion to the complexity of transformational change and resent discovering that transformation is so "messy," let alone that they have to be conscious of so many dynamics as they lead it, especially in themselves. In our view, these people's resentment causes them to reject the model and its thoroughness, as if *not* using it will diminish the complexity of the reality they actually face. They throw the baby out with the bath water and succumb to an autopilot mindset.

Transformational efforts all have some degree of complexity—some more than others. Your change effort will possess the complexity it has, no matter what approach you take. The choice to use a simpler change model will not alter the actual dynamics you must address to succeed. Instead, it may cause more messiness if you overlook critical activities as you proceed.

This aversion to complexity is most common when The Change Leader's Roadmap model is viewed as a rigid prescription for *required action* rather than a *template* for consciously thinking about your options for how to proceed. The CLR is intended to describe most of what *might* have to be addressed in your transformation, allowing you to consciously decide exactly what actions are required for your particular situation. The model can assist you to streamline the activities of your change process to be the most impactful and help you avoid complications that result from neglecting mission-critical actions.

Most people who have used simpler change models discover that the nine-phase model offers essential additional guidance, often what is needed to remedy costly issues they face. Rather than forcing a choice between models, consider integrating the parts of each model that fit your organizational culture and change needs. This is a particularly useful strategy when project management specialists learn the CLR. It expands on the tried-and-true project management tools that have their rightful place in change but do not cover all of the required bases, especially for transformation. No one model has to be the "be-all-and-end-all," and the CLR ought not replace or compete with sound practices your organization already has in place.

Reaction 3: "How Can We Go Faster?"

"I don't begin to have the time or patience to do all of this. This will take way too much time. I want something that will accelerate the change, not slow it down with all of this activity."

If leaders assume that all of what is detailed in the nine phases is necessary, the model could appear as a work-generating, time-consuming burden that is impossible to overlay on an already overwhelmed organization. Parts of this worry are sometimes true; the organization is too burdened to undergo transformation. However, this has nothing to do with The Change Leader's Roadmap model.

The capacity of the organization and the complexity of the transformation process itself—not the comprehensiveness of the model—create enormous discomfort and anxiety for people who feel a deep need to have their change happen lightning fast. Often, these organizations are moving at warp speed. Change is happening everywhere in them, and there is no end in sight. In these settings, the leaders typically make the assumption that they can mandate the pace of transformation despite its complexity or people's capacity, readiness, or stamina. They believe that the transformation must be made immediately, no matter what approach they use. When these leaders establish and sustain high-pressure conditions inappropriately, employee morale usually goes down, resistance goes up, and implementation flounders, all of which slow progress. This is classic in autopilot leaders, an approach explained in depth in *Beyond Change Management*.

Even if the organization has a change model, autopilot leaders in these harried organizations believe that the best way to speed things up is to skip or abbreviate steps in the process; to set urgent, if not impossible, timelines for change; and to mandate action under some real or imagined threat. Such actions carry risk and cost because the organization is not a machine with a gas pedal but a living system with human needs.

Much to the frustration of these pressured leaders, the transformation process always seems to have its own clock. Change can sometimes be accelerated, but not merely by someone's will. Leaders must make sound strategic choices about which change activities to do and which to skip, and then use effective methods to accomplish the actions they select. Helping make these conscious choices is the role and benefit of a comprehensive guidance system such as the CLR.

The right actions and conditions, carried out with intention, build speed and momentum by delivering what the organization needs and by positively impacting people's commitment, readiness, and ability to act. People have to understand the case for change and vision. They must have frequent communication and engagement. They need time to develop new skills and, mostly, to assimilate the impact the transformation has on them personally and emotionally. You must account for the human dynamics in your change strategy and plans; they are not just complicating factors to ignore.

Then how do you speed up your change process? Establish upfront conditions for success that enable you to move expeditiously. This means investing time to set up these conditions correctly in the beginning and then sustain them throughout the process. This investment always brings a significant return. The upstream stage of the change process is worth its weight in gold!

Having said this, there is merit to the "I want to go fast" orientation of reducing planning time and adopting an act first, "ready—fire—aim!" orientation, but only if leaders overtly build rapid, continuous learning and course correction into their change strategy. When leaders rigidly demand that the transformation be done right the first time, they are setting up the organization, and themselves, for failure. The best solution seems to be equal parts of consciously planning a streamlined roadmap, "ready—fire—aim," real-time learning from mistakes, and the ability to course-correct rapidly as you go. The CLR, when used properly, delivers both speed and results from change.

Let it be stated for the record that we do not have "the answer" about this dichotomy of desired speed versus required action. However, we are experimenting with different ways to solve this dilemma, which we discuss in the next chapter. One of them is offered in the CLR Critical Path.

A TOP-DOWN VERSUS A MULTI-DIRECTIONAL APPROACH TO CHANGE

Because we use the language "change leaders" throughout the CLR, some people may make the faulty assumption that the CLR is designed as a top-down approach to driving change. Most of our discussion in this book makes reference to the leaders of the change determining their change strategy and the importance of the executives being sponsors and models of the organization's transformation. The CLR clearly focuses on the important role of leaders in how transformational change is handled. This does not mean we recommend a "top-down" approach. Rather, we acknowledge the vital role senior leaders play and focus intently on supporting them to play it well. They have the power of decision making, direction setting, and resource allocation. There is no doubt that change happens more easily when senior leaders are on board and providing what is required to succeed, let alone being models of what they are asking of the organization.

Let's explore some of the dynamics regarding where change originates, why we focus Phase I on leaders, who the "change leaders" of the organization are, and what transformation demands of "top" leaders.

First and foremost, we believe that transformation will only succeed if the whole system transforms. It can be initiated anywhere and mobilized in any direction—top-down, bottom-up, or middle-out. The work of each phase of the CLR, theoretically, must be accomplished in a critical mass of the organization for the transformation to occur. Where this work is initiated is less important than the fact that it is done consciously to influence how the transformation is designed and facilitated across the entire system.

Phase I of the model, *Prepare to Lead the Change*, specifically addresses the *top leaders* of the change effort, who are the right people to establish the initial infrastructure and conditions for success after they recognize that a transformational change is needed. The process begins with these leaders hearing the wake-up call for change—even if it comes from a lower level of the organization—and initiating the transformation by clarifying change leadership governance and roles, creating the case for change and initial desired outcomes, and building the change strategy. However, all of this work can include mid-managers and select expert contributors, through engagement or as part of the change leadership team. Then in

Phase II, the model recommends that the change leadership team take the change effort out to the organization. Even if Phase I work is done in parallel with Phase II work, the majority of Phase I needs to be done by, or at least known by, the organization's leaders. This helps the leaders manage impact on operations, capacity, and resources. It enables them to organize the multitude of change activities, achieve leadership alignment, and set up conditions for success early, which greatly accelerates the change process.

In Phases II through IX, you *could* construe that the change process design work is the responsibility of the top change leaders, along with their change teams. You could construe that the leaders ask their managers and employees to be involved in design, impact analysis, and implementation as the top leaders see fit. This would be an easy interpretation of the structure and language of the model.

This interpretation would be accurate if the change leaders designing the change strategy and process were all selected from the *top* of the organization being changed. However, we do not recommend that change leaders only come from the top. We believe that both design and implementation are best accomplished with representatives of the whole system being involved in both of these activities. That is why we emphasize high-engagement strategies. Therefore, when we speak of change leaders in Phases II through IX, we do not mean only the change leaders at the top of the organization but throughout the organization. Many tasks in the CLR are best accomplished by representatives of various levels of the organization.

Our discussion has focused on organization-wide transformation, assuming that the "organization" in question is, in fact, the whole system. However, often, transformation is occurring or starting in some part of the whole system—a business line, division, or plant. In these cases, the "leaders" we reference in Phase I are those in charge of the organization undergoing the transformation. The change leaders referenced in Phases II through IX can and should include top leaders, as well as mid-managers and front-line employees who are key stakeholders in the change.

A change leader, from our perspective, is anyone who has a positive influence on the transformation—be they executives, employees, or consultants. If a person is intentionally making a contribution to the effort, we consider that person a change leader.

We also emphasize top leaders in Phase I because transformation can be squelched most easily by top leaders, especially if they have not heard the wake-up call, resist the requirements of the transformation, or operate on autopilot without much conscious awareness of what is needed. Therefore, we focus significant attention on their role. This does not negate a bottom-up or middle-out approach; it simply ensures that the top leaders engage in the transformation in ways that are critical to the effort's success, especially at the beginning. Otherwise, the effort gets derailed from the start.

In situations in which the leaders are operating on autopilot or in traditional command-and-control fashion, they often do not understand or support the requirements of transformation. Even if they give a lip-service head nod to it, they do not know what they are agreeing to, and their behavior remains unchanged. Beware of the "empty head" nod! To overcome this, Phase I work has to focus on bringing leaders to conscious awareness of what they are about to do through well-facilitated discussion, leadership breakthrough, and change education. These help leaders "wake up" to the real requirements of the transformation, including whole-system engagement and mindset and behavior change, especially for the leaders.

We have seen—100 percent of the time—that when the entire system must transform, even if the change ignites in the middle or bottom of the organization and then spreads out, if the senior executives do not eventually get on board with the shift in consciousness and behavior required for the transformation to succeed, the transformation eventually dies on the vine or goes underground. It is put aside until the top leaders get a painful enough wake-up call that they finally recognize the need to change. Historically, U.S. automakers were an example of failed change because top leaders did not understand what was required of them, even when others in the organization did.

We have seen and assisted successful efforts that begin at the grass-roots level of the organization or in a discrete segment of the business before spreading to other parts of the system. It is not uncommon for lower levels of the organization to get a wake-up call much sooner than the executives. We have supported several transformational pilot efforts in divisions that were ready and excited to pioneer their future and pave the way for the larger organization. Most of these efforts were successful ventures in and of themselves, and they all applied The Change Leader's Roadmap at their level of the organization, including addressing their mindset change work. A key enabler in each was top leader support, which sometimes came only after the true value of the change was clearly demonstrated to them.

Sadly, we have also witnessed countless examples where conscious, proactive, upper or middle managers and supervisors courageously engaged their own parts of the organization in a well-designed transformation, only to hit the wall of a resistant mindset in the top echelon when the content or personal changes required extended beyond the managers' sphere of influence. The managers' mindsets had evolved, but the executives' mindsets had not. In every one of these cases, the transformation eventually aborted. For transformation to succeed, there must be conscious awareness where the power resides.

Mindset can be either the key that opens the door of transformation or the key that keeps it locked shut. Mindset change is best accomplished through simultaneous efforts throughout the whole organization. From our experience, this whole-system effort has the best chance of succeeding when it is sponsored by a senior executive who can pave the way and keep less "conscious" leaders from stifling the transformation. Acknowledging this, we emphasize that the top leaders of the organization that is transforming must become models of the mindset and behavior change required for the whole organization to transform as early as possible in the effort. They are the ones who set up the safe conditions for the rest of the organization to engage in the personal work required for the transformation to succeed. It is interesting to reflect: Is this not at the core of the quality of sponsorship that transformational change requires? The top leaders *must* walk the talk of what they are asking of the organization.

SUMMARY

In this chapter, we reinforced the guideline that the CLR must be customized and that you use it as a thinking discipline rather than a prescription for rigid action. We discussed four stages of development that influence people's effectiveness in using the CLR model to their advantage. We explored how people's reactions to the methodology impact their ability to apply it, and we addressed the issue of tailoring the model to engage the right change leaders at all levels of the organization, depending on where your change effort lives.

Now that you are familiar with The Change Leader's Roadmap, ask yourself how you can use it to ensure that your change process reflects the right balance of structure, order, and speed to match the real people and process dynamics of your transformation as it is happening. From that awareness, build your roadmap accordingly.

We will now turn our attention to various strategies for using The Change Leader's Roadmap to your organization's greatest advantage.

Opportunities for Leveraging The Change Leader's Roadmap Methodology

After you decide to use The Change Leader's Roadmap methodology, you must decide how to gain the greatest value from it. We recommend several ways to use and leverage the unique attributes of the CLR methodology:

1. Apply the CLR Critical Path, which consists of the thirty most important tasks in the methodology, to streamline your project planning process.
2. Use The Change Leader's Roadmap as your organization's common change methodology on all change initiatives.
3. Increase your organization's change capability.
4. Use the CLR to transform your organization's culture.
5. Use the CLR as a "just-in-time" consulting strategy.
6. Find ways to accelerate the change process.
7. Use the CLR as a phase gate process.

We will first look at the best way to begin your project planning process on each change effort you lead.

THE CLR CRITICAL PATH

After you become fully versant in the CLR methodology, you will be able to decipher which of the seventy-seven tasks to do on each new change effort you lead or support. To expedite your learning and planning, we have identified the CLR Critical Path. The CLR Critical Path consists of the thirty most important tasks in the methodology. We selected the tasks based on our thirty years of experience observing the work most critical to client success. This does not mean that you must always do the thirty tasks in every change effort. It means that being familiar with this list can help you more quickly determine which tasks you might select as your starting place. Review the list in Exhibit 14.1 to understand why these tasks are on the list. Always keep in mind that other tasks in the CLR might also be required work for any of your change efforts.

In the Introduction, we mentioned the strategy to use the CLR as your organization's common change methodology. After your key change leaders and consultants have learned about the methodology and how to tailor it, this strategy can greatly reduce time, confusion, and the cost of change across the organization.

USING THE CHANGE LEADER'S ROADMAP AS YOUR COMMON CHANGE METHODOLOGY

At any point, most organizations have many change efforts underway. These initiatives may or may not appear to be related or integrated. In fact, most often, they compete with each other for time, attention, and resources. Almost all are run using different and inconsistent methods, producing confusion in the organization and slowing down progress and results. No wonder the workforce resents the "flavor of the month" syndrome and loses faith in leadership's ability to lead change! Imagine if your leaders all used different accounting methods, performance management systems, or compensation formulas!

The most value-added application of the CLR is using it as your common change methodology, the *operating system* for how all existing and future change efforts are led. Much like Microsoft's Windows™, or the MAC-OS™ systems that support the consistent running and cross-referencing of myriad software programs, using The Change Leader's Roadmap as the operating system for all change initiatives ensures that they all run in a manner that promotes integration across business

Exhibit 14.1. The CLR Critical Path

THE CHANGE LEADER'S ROADMAP CRITICAL PATH TASKS

PHASE 1: PREPARE TO LEAD THE CHANGE

Activity I.A—Start Up and Staff Change Effort

Task I.A.2–Clarify and Staff Initial Change Leadership Roles

Task I.A.4–Identify Project Community

Activity I.B—Create Case for Change and Determine Initial Desired Outcomes

Task I.B.2–Assess Drivers of Change

Task I.B.3–Clarify Type of Change

Task I.B.5–Perform Initial Impact Analysis

Task I.B.6–Clarify Target Groups and Scope

Task I.B.8–Determine Desired Outcomes and Compile Case for Change

Activity I.C—Assess and Build Organization's Readiness and Capacity

Task I.C.2–Build Readiness and Capacity

Activity I.D—Build Leadership's Capability to Lead the Change

Task I.D.2–Ensure Leaders Model Desired Mindset and Behavior

Task I.D.3–Build Leader Commitment and Alignment

Activity I.E—Clarify Overall Change Strategy

Task I.E.2–Define Values and Guiding Principles

Task I.E.3–Clarify Governance and Decision Making

Task I.E.6–Create Multiple Project Integration Strategy

Task I.E.8–Clarify Engagement Strategy

Task I.E.9–Design Overall Communication Plan

Task I.E.12–Identify Milestones and Timeline, and Compile Change Strategy

Activity I.F—Build Infrastructure and Conditions to Support Change Effort

Task I.F.2–Create Conditions for Success

Task I.F.5–Initiate Course Correction Strategy and System

Task I.F.6–Initiate Strategies for Supporting People Through Emotional Reactions and Resistance

PHASE II: CREATE ORGANIZATIONAL VISION, COMMITMENT, AND CAPABILITY

Activity II.B—Increase Organization's Capability to Change

Task II.B.1–Build Organization's Change Knowledge and Skills

Task II.B.2–Promote Required Mindset and Behavior Change

(continued)

content, people, and process issues. Without a common way of leading, your various initiatives cannot be integrated to serve the overall good of the organization. Having a common change methodology provides great leverage for monitoring how major changes are being planned and led. It enables projects to share work products, integrate tasks, and share resources. Having shared language, strategies, and tools greatly expedites your oversight and review process. See *Beyond Change Management* for a complete discussion.

Who needs to use your common change methodology? In today's fast-paced, ever-changing world, influencing the success of change is inevitably the job of every line leader in your organization. Your executives will need a high-level understanding, as will all of your sponsors of change. Your line leaders—in position to champion your organization's major changes—ought to have at least a conceptual understanding of The Change Leader's Roadmap as a required process methodology and navigation system. Your in-house consultants would, of course, be trained in it in greater depth to consult, accelerate, and enable effective change leadership, but line leaders must ultimately be accountable for producing results from their change efforts. All project leads and project management experts must be familiar with the CLR at a minimum, and optimally, know how their tools and approaches fit against it.

If you decide to implement the CLR as your change operating system, be aware that there is a serious risk in asking an already overloaded organization to learn a new methodology for leading change. The initiative leaders may view the methodology as yet another change program, something to be added on top of all of the other change initiatives underway. In fact, The Change Leader's Roadmap is not something else to be done *on top of* existing efforts and must not be positioned that way. Instead, it should *support* the way in which you are setting up and accomplishing all existing efforts. Of course, learning the change methodology does take additional time on the part of change leaders and consultants who will apply it. If they recognize in advance, however, that the organization is serious about improving its change leadership track record, then this learning needs to take place. Let's explore the benefits of a common change methodology and a case example.

The benefits of having a common change methodology include the following:

- Increases speed in project launch, design, and implementation
- Sets a standard for best change practices
- Reduces resistance and confusion
- Establishes a common expectation for change governance, including clear roles, decision making, and temporary structures, systems, policies, and technologies
- Builds protocol for quickly establishing conditions for success that expedite planning, design, and implementation

- Makes integration of change efforts and information sharing across initiatives easier for acceleration and course correction
- Consistently and effectively handles the human dynamics of change
- Creates common language for effective change communications and stakeholder engagement

CASE-IN-POINT

We worked with one organization that had more than thirty "priority" change efforts underway simultaneously. People were exhausted and frustrated with their leaders. The executives engaged us to help organize, prioritize, and coordinate their many initiatives into one unified approach and build the organization's understanding of its transformation.

Consistency and integration of the discrete efforts were desperately needed because many of the initiatives were competing with each other when their outcomes could only be achieved through working synergistically together. Nearly every initiative was being run using a different change model, if one could even be deciphered. This made collaboration nearly impossible. Like different computer platforms, the initiatives could not "talk" to each other. They needed a common language and approach.

We established, with the backing of the CEO, that one change methodology would be used in the organization. We helped the change leaders prioritize their top initiatives and educated them and their internal consultants in The Change Leader's Roadmap. The training was all "live case-based," and the change leaders applied the model to each of their top initiatives as they learned it. Those that had used different change models were supported to map their work to the CLR to make the transition to it easier. Having a change process operating system became a strategic advantage that provided a basis for consistency, integration, and flexibility. With this approach, their multiple changes could coexist, work in collaboration, and be communicated as one overarching transformation. The methodology allowed them to lead all of the changes in a coherent yet customized fashion. With continuous follow-up, application clinics and coaching, the leaders learned and established a system that met the majority of their needs as well as accomplishing their transformation.

- Enables better progress monitoring using similar criteria and process milestones
- Accelerates start-up of change teams, and eases shifting change team members to other change projects as needed
- Reduces resource needs
- Enables better management of capacity and understanding of the impact on operations

Should you decide to use The Change Leader's Roadmap as your common approach to change, consider the guidance in Exhibit 14.2, Strategies to Implement the CLR as Your Common Change Methodology.

Increasing the Organization's Change Capability

Conscious change leaders embrace building change capability as an outcome of their work. Strong change capability is vital to their organizations' near- and long-term success. Defined simply, change capability is the ability of an organization to plan, design, and implement all types of change efficiently with committed stakeholders, causing minimal negative impacts on people and operations so that desired business and cultural results from change are consistently achieved and integrated seamlessly into operations to deliver maximum ROI. A key strategy for doing this is to view change as a strategic discipline, much like we view finance, HR, IT, and supply chain. This means not only building your leaders', managers', and internal consultants' change leadership knowledge and skills but also the organizational systems and infrastructure that will enable change to be led more effectively and consistently. *Beyond Change Management* discusses change capability and the strategic disciplines for change in more detail, but here is an overview. (See Premium Content: Building Change Capability: Leading Change as a Strategic Discipline, www.pfeiffer.com/go/anderson.)

We have identified five key strategies so far to creating change as a strategic discipline: (1) identifying and managing an enterprise change agenda; (2) having one common change *process* methodology—ideally the CLR; (3) establishing a change infrastructure; (4) building a strategic change center of excellence for all change practitioners, and (5) creating a strategic change office.

An enterprise change agenda names the most important change initiatives required to execute your organization's business strategy. Its purpose is to capture and integrate the major changes underway or planned in your organization, ensuring

Exhibit 14.2. **Strategies to Implement the CLR as Your Common Change Methodology**

1. Secure the Right Sponsor

a. Ideal: Senior "C-Suite" Executive. If you have them, your Chief Change Officer (CCO) or your strategic change office (SCO) (see *Beyond Change Management* for more information on these concepts)

b. Positioned to influence the strategy, rollout, and use of the CLR

c. Fully commits to achieving the desired outcomes and benefits of the CLR as the organization's change operating system

d. Able to model and sustain the use of the CLR

2. Clarify Who "Owns" the CLR Methodology

a. Where the CLR methodology will "live" in the organization

b. Who will steward its use once implemented

c. Who will be responsible for building the organization's capability in its use, including all of your various "user groups"

d. Who will maintain and evolve it

e. Who will manage access to it, especially if you subscribe to Being First's online CLR software

3. Ensure the CLR Will Work for You

a. Determine what aspects of the CLR methodology you will feature:

   ▸ Process tasks (e.g., CLR Critical Path tasks)

   ▸ Tools

   ▸ Templates

   ▸ Information sheets, articles, and online guidance

   ▸ Leadership style, cultural norms, and mindset parameters

   ▸ Metrics

b. Determine how to access the CLR resources (e.g., via subscription to Being First's online CLR software)

c. If you have done a change audit and know what hasn't worked in the past, clarify how to position the CLR as the remedy to these issues.

d. Ensure that the CLR builds on what already works well.

e. Clarify if you need to integrate it with other existing processes (e.g., project management, LEAN, Six Sigma, OD, change management, strategic planning, leadership development, culture change).

f. Decide if you will add existing or other preferred tools that support good change leadership.

(continued)

4. Develop Your Rollout Strategy

a. Consider the best approach:

- General Offering: "Use as you wish; here is how to access it; come to a training on it if interested."
- Mandate: "This is our change methodology; use it enterprise-wide."
- "Soft Launch":
  1. Apply the CLR and consult using it on selected projects; build momentum and scale after its value is demonstrated.
  2. Make CLR expertise known and available: create a resource pool of OD/OE/change management/project management experts; use the CLR as the guide for just-in-time consulting.
  3. Make CLR/Leading Transformation trainings available for key audiences.

b. Determine your user groups and develop appropriate launch/training strategies for each:

- Senior leaders
- Project leads
- Internal OD/PM/change management consultants
- Managers
- HR professionals/HR business partners
- Include CLR training in your executive and management development curriculum
- Certify internal "super users"

c. Secure resources for rollout.

d. Prepare required infrastructures.

5. Identify and Ensure Conditions for Success

a. Senior leaders and key project leads agree to use this as their core approach.

b. External consultants cannot bring in other change models.

c. All internal change-related resources understand how to use the CLR in sync with their own expertise and approaches.

d. Ensure deep confidence and comfort in your internal change consulting experts so you have masterful CLR super users ready to assist line leaders in real time.

e. Design strategy and incentives for continuous improvement and sustained use over time.

6. Roll Out

a. Communicate.

b. Train.

(continued)

    c. Consult/coach to your various user groups or projects.

    d. Make access to the CLR tools and knowledge *easy*.

    e. Set up methods to monitor for consistency of use, evaluation, expansion, and course corrections.

    f. Leverage cultural and leadership alignment.

7. Evaluate Use and Build Best Practices

    a. Determine/use meaningful metrics.

    b. Identify best change practices.

    c. Continue to tailor and demonstrate CLR's adaptability to the organization's real needs.

    d. Position the CLR as a lever for culture change.

    e. Keep CLR visible in supporting business outcomes and aspired culture and leadership.

8. Create a CLR "Users" Community of Practice or Center of Excellence

    a. Identify appropriate user groups to participate.

    b. Hold periodic Learning Clinics on live projects and high leverage topics/skills/tools.

    c. Determine how users can best be used on major change efforts.

    d. Use to do the following:

        ▸ Add/tailor new tools and resources.

        ▸ Expand capability and brand awareness.

        ▸ Build critical mass and cultural alignment.

---

their strategic relevance to business success. We have already discussed the benefits of using the CLR as your common change methodology. It can also be used to guide your creation of organizational change capability. Change infrastructures support your organization to deliver results from change by establishing and using overt, commonly used structures and practices that optimize change execution, accelerate time to results, and build capacity. Once established, these infrastructures become the baseline for people to increase their change leadership effectiveness. They provide a foundation for ensuring your organization's change capability.

A Strategic Change Center of Excellence is comprised of the organization's major change support resources, such as project management, change management, and quality improvement. Likely, your organization has all of this consulting expertise in place at its headquarters and in its business lines. The Center is a way of organizing, networking, and training them for the best and highest use. It need not house all of these resources; rather, it is a function and service that supports them, accesses them for priority change efforts, and develops them as a unified pool of resources.

The strategic change office (SCO) is a senior executive function that oversees the success of change across the entire enterprise. It is led by the Chief Change Officer (CCO), who sits on the executive team. This enables the SCO to be positioned to ensure that major change initiatives are the right ones to drive the business strategy, advocating for what is needed to maximize results on these mission-critical initiatives, and ensuring strong change capability in the organization. The SCO is the primary vehicle for making change a strategic discipline, including the effective use of the CLR to support the success of change overall.

Using the CLR to Change Your Organization's Culture

Culture change is one of our core specialties. In *Beyond Change Management*, we describe seven key strategies for culture change, called the Being First Approach to Transforming Culture. We customize these strategies and their application to each client's needs and use the CLR to guide their implementation. This organizes the work and ensures that all vital tasks get attention.

Although the entire CLR supports culture change, various tasks specifically drive this work. Throughout this book, we have referenced special guidelines in these tasks to use when you are transforming your organization's culture. Figure 14.1 shows the nine phases of the CLR as a flow chart that calls out these tasks in terms of the work required for culture change. If you are working to change culture, study this flow chart, as well as the seven strategies offered in *Beyond Change Management*.

Culture permeates everything in the organization: your structure, systems, business processes, and technology, as well as individual, team, and organizational behavior. Each needs to be addressed as a part of transforming your culture. Similarly, consciously design and implement your organization's content initiatives to reflect your *desired* culture, not your current culture, as they will inevitably affect your cultural outcomes. You will need to establish a legitimate role on these initiatives to be the spokesperson—and integrator—for the organization's overall culture change.

The CLR makes a strong case that individual mindset and behavior are foundational to the organization's collective culture. We strongly recommend that you provide some form of Leadership Breakthrough Training to shift mindset and behavior so that it overtly aligns with and supports your desired culture. See Tasks I.D.2 and II.B.2 for further guidance on this work.

Figure 14.1.   Using the CLR for Culture Change

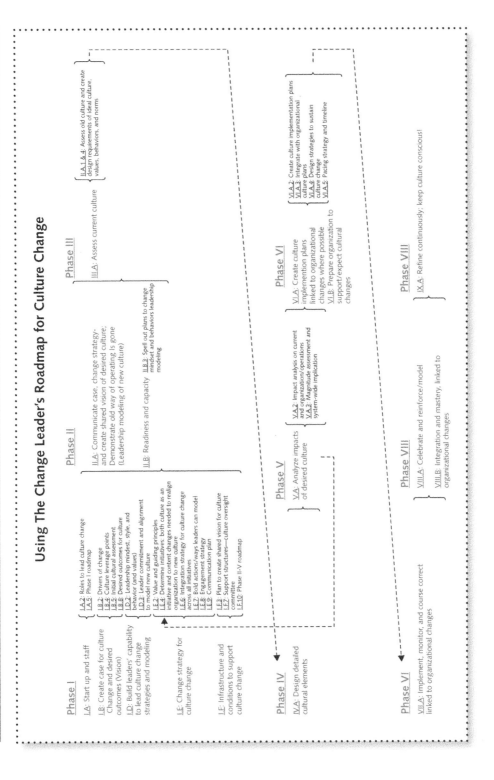

Using The Change Leader's Roadmap for Culture Change

Phase I

I.A: Start up and staff

I.B: Create case for culture Change and desired outcomes (Vision)

I.D: Build leaders' capability to lead culture change strategies and modeling

I.E: Change strategy for culture change

I.F: Infrastructure and conditions to support culture change

I.A.2: Roles to lead culture change
I.A.5: Phase I roadmap

I.B.2: Drivers of change
I.B.4: Culture leverage points
I.B.5: Initial cultural assessment
I.B.8: Desired outcomes for culture
I.D.2: Leadership mindset, style, and behavior (and values)
I.D.3: Leader commitment and alignment to model new culture
I.E.2: Value and guiding principles
I.E.4: Determine initiatives: both culture as an initiative and content changes needed to realign organization to new culture
I.E.6: Integration strategy for culture change across all initiatives
I.E.7: Bold actions/ways leaders can model
I.E.8: Engagement strategy
I.E.9: Communication plan
I.E.3: Plan to create shared vision for culture
I.E.7: Support structures—culture oversight committee
I.E.10: Phase II-V roadmap

Phase II

II.A: Communicate case, change strategy- and create shared vision of desired culture; Demonstrate old way of operating is gone (Leadership modeling of new culture)

II.B: Readiness and capacity

II.B.3: Spell out plans to change mindset and behaviors leadership modeling

Phase III

III.A: Assess current culture

III.A.1 & 4: Assess old culture and create design requirements of ideal culture, values, behaviors, and norms

Phase IV

IV.A: Design detailed cultural elements

Phase V

V.A: Analyze impacts of desired culture

V.A.2: Impact analysis on current and organization/operations
V.A.3: Magnitude assessment and system-wide implication

Phase VI

VI.A: Create culture implementation plans linked to organizational changes where possible

VI.B: Prepare organization to support/expect cultural changes

VI.A.2: Create culture implementation plans
VI.A.3: Integrate with organizational culture plans
VI.A.4: Design strategies to sustain culture change
VI.A.5: Pacing strategy and timeline

Phase VII

VII.A: Implement, monitor, and course correct linked to organizational changes

Phase VIII

VIII.A: Celebrate and reinforce/model

VIII.B: Integration and mastery, linked to organizational changes

Phase VIII

IX.A: Refine continuously; keep culture conscious!

The CLR Just-in-Time Consulting Strategy

The CLR just-in-time consulting strategy is an approach for using the Roadmap to serve fast-paced organizations that would otherwise never reap its benefits, although they urgently need them. Often, the leaders of these organizations do not understand the complexities of transformation and unknowingly make critical assumptions about how to lead change that end up being costly to their results and people. The CLR just-in-time strategy can help raise these leaders' awareness in small, value-added doses and relatively painless ways. This is also a viable strategy for use when leaders are not interested in building their own change leadership capability but rather want focused and expert help from consultants. What follows is a composite of recommendations that can assist these leaders to succeed in change.

The CLR just-in-time strategy can be used when companies recognize that they (1) don't have management's time or interest to stop, learn, and master a methodology; (2) need better change leadership and greater results from their change efforts; (3) are undergoing large-scale change; and (4) have a cadre of in-house change consultants who can learn the CLR as their common change methodology and be used to support this effort. This strategy goes deep with the few, typically proficient change consultants who can be trained to offer competent advice to line leaders on an as-needed basis.

There are three required steps in this strategy. A fourth, when done upfront, can help the organization master its transformation exponentially. However, not all organizations as yet are willing to take on the upfront work. We will discuss it last. The three steps that must be done are (1) adoption of the CLR as the organization's common change methodology; (2) in-depth CLR training of the in-house consultants who will serve as the source of its use in real-time application; and (3) line leader use of these trained resources on live projects, starting at the onset of change.

To begin this strategy, you must make the decision to use the CLR as your change operating system. This can be done in the OD department if they "own" change; in the change management function; in HR; in a Project, Program, or Portfolio Management Office; or by the executives who recognize that a consistent best-practice approach is required to improve their track record in change.

Next, you must select the people who will be trained in the CLR methodology in depth. Ideally, you will select a majority of senior practitioners who have tangible experience in the people, process, and perhaps even the needed content elements of the changes they will support. We highlight the selection of at least a majority of senior practitioners because junior consultants will realistically spend more time learning than delivering sound change advice. They can, however, be mentored by the proficient practitioners as they work.

This team becomes the organization's primary "change agent" resource team. These consultants would be in charge of mastering, owning, and customizing the CLR methodology to best serve the initiatives the organization is undertaking. External CLR master consultants can support the team's learning process and work. With skill in the CLR, the consultants can better support the needs of their line leader clients, demonstrate the value of the CLR guidance in real time, and educate the rest of the organization when appropriate.

The key to this group's success is that they be used by change leaders on live efforts, beginning ideally at the start-up of the initiatives. Their primary mode of consultation is *just-in-time advice*. The consultants would be the keepers of the entire methodology and only use what is needed with their clients to plan for and respond to challenging issues during the course of consultation. For instance, if the change leader needs to establish clear change leadership roles and decision-making authority, the consultants would assist with this particular work using those tasks' resources from the CLR. If the client is ready to do an impact analysis, the consultant would become familiar with the work required of those tasks and provide tailored impact analysis guidance to the client. The clients never have to know that they are in Task I.A.2 or Phase V. They only need to receive the help they require in the moment. The CLR is invisible to them, unless they inquire about the source of the expertise their consultants are providing.

Where a project has a need and the change leaders have the willingness, the change agents would also support them to attend to the personal development, culture, and mindset work essential to making transformational changes conscious. The consultants could facilitate this personal work with their clients themselves if they have the experience, organizational trust, and capability, or they could bring in external expertise to assist at the right time in their clients' efforts. Rather than doing the mindset and culture work at the organization-wide scale, it would be brought out in individual initiatives when needed, and thereby be most relevant and valuable.

It is important that the consultants stay close enough to their clients' change efforts to assess what work is needed when, because the client will not always know. As the consultant in-the-know about all of the potential change work provided within the CLR, you need to be able to stay one step ahead of the action. This requires clear contracting and partnering agreements between the consultants and the leaders they serve. Just-in-time consulting support might always provide value to clients when activated, but having an ongoing, consistent means to engage in the work of the project is far more effective than the "Don't call me, I'll call you" basis of the consulting relationship.

In addition to supporting individual clients, consultants from this group might also work with the executives on organization-wide change leadership requirements in a number of ways. The following list describes several functions that CLR-proficient consultants can play. These functions are among those described in Chapter Five of *Beyond Change Management*, as representative of being a strategic change consultant responsible for building the organization's change capability.

- Facilitate the executives to build an enterprise-wide change strategy for transformation, including both the organizational/technical and the human/cultural components of change.
- Integrate the multitude of initiatives that may be ongoing in the organization.
- Address culture change across initiatives.
- Coordinate the many external consultants who may be engaged throughout the organization.
- Keep an active eye on the capacity of the workforce for handling the transformation—emotionally, culturally, and physically—and coach the executives to alter their change process and pace, as required.
- Design large group interventions when major segments of the organization, or the organization as a whole, must address change issues through widespread engagement.
- Continually evolve the organization's use of the CLR and building organization-wide best practices and infrastructures, for change.

The CLR just-in-time strategy offers the organization a choice about whom to expose to The Change Leader's Roadmap and to what extent. Organizations that want to embed the CLR as their change operating system would choose to involve and expose more people to it throughout the organization. Consider the guidance provided earlier in this chapter for embedding the CLR as your common change methodology. The just-in-time consulting strategy is one vehicle for demonstrating the value of the CLR in a "soft launch" approach.

At the beginning of this discussion, we mentioned a potential fourth step in the just-in-time strategy, which involves the executives of the organization. This step is a highly leveraged one for enterprise-wide transformation because it engages the leaders in their own understanding of change and their personal impact on its success. It is their gateway to leading change consciously and being full and active players in the transformation. This work is ideally done at the beginning of the process when the leaders are willing to look more deeply at their effectiveness in leading change. In it, the leaders engage in discussion about how they think they have been leading change and may review actual assessment data about the organization's track record in achieving results from change. If their data suggests, they must recognize that their traditional ways of leading change and their old mindsets about change are a part of the problem. There is no way around the mindset issue. They must agree to address their mindsets about how they view transformation and how they have reacted to the dilemmas it presents.

This strategy of raising leaders' awareness and engaging them in building their change leadership skills requires one or both of the following: (1) initial change education for executives about the CLR and the human dynamics of transformation, and (2) a breakthrough training experience to drive home the requirement that leaders must walk the talk of the transformation from its inception, in both their thinking and their behavior. The value of both of these activities is fully explored in *Beyond Change Management*.

If these two initial interventions are successful, the leaders will come away with new perceptions about the changes that are happening in their organization. They will have been introduced to the strategic level of The Change Leader's Roadmap and be in active dialogue about how it can be used to drive the success of their most important changes. Because they typically will not have the time or need to become masters of the CLR themselves, these two initial executive-level sessions set the stage for supporting just-in-time change consulting so that the leaders can reap the benefit of the CLR without having to learn it in depth. Imagine how different the use of the methodology would be when the executives are full players in setting up their change efforts for success rather than being potential—albeit inadvertent—impediments to it. It is so much easier to be open and candid about the issues of transformation when the senior leaders are fully engaged in it, as well as their own personal transformation. As we said earlier, this step is best done at the beginning, so it can have the greatest impact on leveraging the use of the CLR in the organization.

The conditions required to support the CLR just-in-time consulting strategy include the following:

- (Ideally) Executive understanding and commitment to the strategy and The Change Leader's Roadmap model being proposed
- Enough capable in-house change agents (representing both staff and line)
- Sufficient resources and time to support the change agents' initial and continued development toward mastery, including a community of practice
- Visibly positioning and sponsoring the change agents as dedicated, available, and competent to assist with major change efforts
- External consultants understand that *your* change methodology, *not theirs*, is the operating system to be used and they are willing to have your in-house resources partner with them to create the strategy for how their work will be carried out

The following Cases-In-Point describe two experiences that helped us formulate how to set up the just-in-time consulting strategy for success. The first case illustrates the need for the strategy to have a comprehensive development plan for all of the consultants engaged in it. One-size CLR training does not fit all because consultants come to the CLR with vastly different levels of expertise and openness. The second case describes both the development process and a change leadership toolkit offering to all of management.

Accelerating the Change Process

The conscious approach to leading transformation is the fastest accelerator of the process we know. We designed the CLR to create the greatest possibility for breakthroughs in people's mindsets, behavior, and abilities—early, fast, and frequently throughout the entire process.

Traditional leaders have very different ideas of what it takes to speed up change, such as mandating a more urgent pace or skipping critical activities, neither of which works. We recommend that leaders explore their assumptions about what causes change to go *slowly* in their organizations and what they think would accelerate it. Our own research has uncovered many causes of slowdown. The causes are largely reflections of the autopilot approach to transformation, which

We worked with one global manufacturing organization to develop in-house change leadership capability worldwide. We were able to use some aspects of the just-in-time strategy but not all of what we have just described. The company was not undergoing an enterprise-wide transformation, but many of its businesses were engaged in transformational change. The client's request to us was to educate a group of ten change consultants they had previously selected from around the world in The Change Leader's Roadmap and conscious change leadership approaches, and to coach them as they offered just-in-time CLR support to their line clients. During start-up, some of their change leader clients were also introduced to the methodology, which generated some very important learnings for everyone on how to set up their change efforts for success.

During the consultant development process, it quickly became obvious that the consultants were at very different levels of expertise with the content, people, and process dynamics of complex change. Some of the consultants were open to their own personal and mindset change; others were not. Some had a greater bias for the content of change and less awareness of the people and process dynamics. Those who had a better understanding of the people dynamics and engaged in their own personal work were most adaptable and effective in using the CLR with their line clients. The more proficient consultants were able to recognize the complexities of people and process issues and were able to provide focused, valuable advice. Their internal work enabled them to more fully understand how to address the most difficult issues inherent in the complex changes they consulted to.

Those who were new to whole-systems dynamics were intimidated by the challenging requests coming from their clients. Those who chose not to focus on the people issues or do the personal work struggled with how to get their clients to see that the clients' strategies for planning their change processes and dealing with the people impacted were inadequate to deliver desired results. These consultants' habitual and unconscious ways of relating and intervening with their clients got in their way. Because these

(continued)

consultants were unsuccessful in conveying these foundational messages to their clients, their advice often fell on deaf ears, and their projects took a toll.

A flaw in the overall effort was that the client's budget and time constraints prohibited the less experienced consultants from being mentored by or partnered with the more proficient consultants. Budget also placed limitations on our ability as external consultants to support these people over time.

From this experience, we learned that the CLR just-in-time strategy has to be designed as a comprehensive approach, fully supported and funded by leadership, and tailored to the actual level of skill and awareness in the participant consultants. A piecemeal approach can add some real value, as it did here, but not nearly what we have seen by setting up this approach for system-wide success from the beginning, complete with proficient consultants, mentoring of novices, and a long-term development and coaching plan.

we covered in depth in *Beyond Change Management*. A few of the major drags on the transformation process include the following:

- Unclear case for change and competing outcomes, which denotes a lack of leadership alignment
- An inadequate process map for the actual activities required, including both the content changes and the people changes
- No clear governance for the change effort or governance that is superimposed over the existing management structure and therefore competes with the demands of running current operations
- Leaders who do not walk their own talk, which causes employee distrust and resistance
- Inadequate resources, capacity, and unrealistic time pressures
- Operational and HR systems that are unable to accommodate the additional demands of change

- Leadership resistance to engaging in personal development and learning about the human dynamics of transformational change
- Lack of recognition of the need to course correct the process continuously, or the inability to do so

---

CASE-IN-POINT: JUST-IN-TIME PLUS GENERAL TOOLKIT OFFERING

In a global financial organization, we worked with a broad spectrum of consultants and advisors to build their internal change leadership and consulting capability. The strategy was supported by the vice presidents of the relevant staff experts, who committed to be introduced to the CLR but then delegated the in-depth training to their staff. The consultant team was made up of representatives from OD, learning and development, quality improvement, HR business partners, project managers, and change management specialists.

The organization licensed the CLR methodology, and in a series of trainings, explored its guidance and breadth of resources through application to the live efforts the participants were consulting to. Most of their projects were priorities for the organization's business strategy and highly visible, so the participants' commitment to gain skill was very high.

The team selected a preferred set of CLR methodology resources that they wanted to offer to all of management as their best practices. They added these to other tools and techniques that were already familiar and held value for the organization. All of these tools were housed on a company-wide Change Intranet site. The site was launched as a general offering to improve change leadership and increase global consistency.

The team created an in-house Community of Practice and met virtually each quarter to exchange experiences and share best practices. They consulted to each other on live issues and engaged Being First over time to deepen their understanding of additional CLR resources they wanted to master. In addition, the CLR and their best practices were taught as an integral part of relevant management development programs. All of this led to a significant increase in their change leadership capability and support to their executive leaders and change projects.

So the acceleration question is "How do you resolve these conditions if they exist or prevent them in the first place?" Our answer is by using The Change Leader's Roadmap as a vehicle for *conscious* change leadership. Our recommendations for accelerating transformation include five strategies that you will recognize from our discussions of the model. They are all direct actions that result from taking a conscious approach to planning and leading change. The five strategies are listed here:

1. Create the conditions for success upfront, and sustain and course-correct them throughout the process.
2. Design a change strategy and streamlined process plan that maximizes parallel and concurrent actions.
3. Build and sustain collective commitment and alignment early among all change leaders, members of your project community, and the various change initiatives required by your transformation.
4. Build a critical mass of commitment through organization-wide engagement, including large group working sessions.
5. Provide change-relevant personal transformation opportunities for both leaders and employees throughout the change effort, and celebrate the behavioral and cultural changes.

One last point about the pace and timing of transformation: Although we wish we had the power to make transformation happen faster than is humanly possible, and we continue to search for ways to speed it up, the truth—plain and simple—is that *transformation takes the time it takes*. Winter lasts as long as it does. A human fetus takes nine months to develop, no matter how fast the mother wants the baby to be born. It is a sign of masterful change leadership to accept this reality and design change strategies that support the change to occur as fast as *is humanly* possible and not to expect more. Make a full commitment to creating the optimal conditions and resourcing to achieve breakthrough results. As we discussed in *Beyond Change Management*, this level of upfront investment can catapult your outcomes.

Using the CLR as a Phase Gate Process

Our last high-leverage strategy for gaining the greatest value from the CLR is to use it as a phase gate process to drive the expectation and consistency in how your change efforts are being planned and led. This is best done in organizations

Our most shining example of using the CLR as a phase gate approach was co-created with PeaceHealth, a large U.S. healthcare delivery system that was undergoing a five-year transformation. PeaceHealth has trained 250 leaders and managers in the CLR and developed the phase gate model to shape how leaders use the CLR to drive every transformational initiative on its agenda. The PeaceHealth model shows the planning and deliverables required for CLR Phases I through III (upstream) as Phase Gate One, Phase IV and V (midstream) as Phase Gate Two, and Phase VI as Phase Gate Three. The remaining phases follow (downstream). All transformational initiative leaders use this model to drive their preparation for each phase gate review, supported by standard templates called for by the CLR to address the content, people, and process requirements for success. The PeaceHealth System Transformational Leadership Team, composed of key senior executives, serves as the review board for every initiative's three phase gates. After each project's change leadership team demonstrates clear and adequate completion of the requirements of each phase gate, the executives give the "green light" for that initiative to proceed to prepare for the next phase gate.

PeaceHealth has also trained its initiative teams in the CLR and provides internal change coaching to initiative leaders as they prepare for each phase gate. Their investment in the CLR as their change operating system, change leadership development, live application on their most strategic changes, and in-house consulting support enables them to ensure greater consistency, more thorough planning, realistic oversight, better management of capacity, and ultimately, more successful results.

that are already familiar with phase gates as a planning strategy. The phase gates, applied to the CLR, give structure, preparation guidelines, deliverables, and reality to what it takes to see a transformation through from start to finish, through all nine phases. It is one of the most profound strategies for ensuring leaders' conscious awareness of what success requires. Figure 14.2 shows the CLR designed as a phase gate process. The Case-In-Point describes its use. Note that each phase gate addresses three phases of the CLR. To pass a phase gate, project leaders and

Figure 14.2. The CLR as a Phase Gate Process

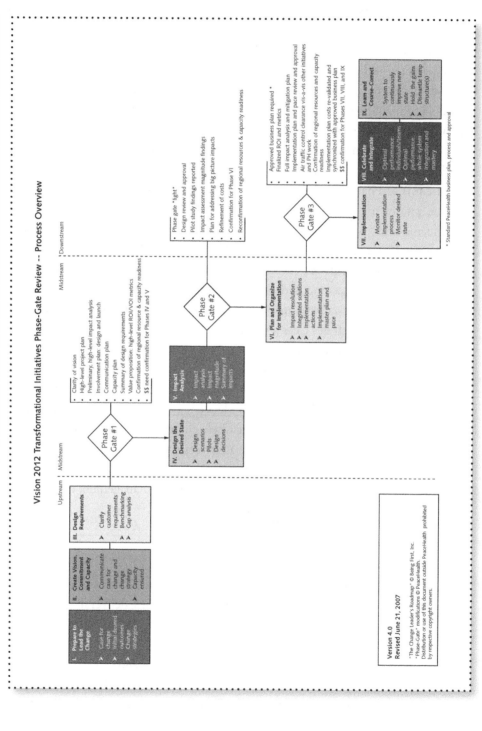

Vision 2012 Transformational Initiatives Phase-Gate Review -- Process Overview

Upstream | Midstream | Midstream | Downstream

I. Prepare to Lead the Change
> Case for change
> Initial desired outcomes
> Change strategies

II. Create Vision, Commitment and Capacity
> Communicate case for change and change strategy
> Capacity ensured

III. Design Requirements
> Clarify customer requirements
> Benchmarking
> Gap analysis

Phase Gate #1
- Clarity of vision
- High-level project plan
- Preliminary, high-level impact analysis
- Involvement plan, design and launch
- Communication plan
- Capacity plan
- Summary of design requirements
- Value proposition: high-level ROI/VOI metrics
- Confirmation of regional resource & capacity readiness
- $$ need confirmation for Phases IV and V

IV. Design the Desired State
> Design scenarios
> Pilots
> Design decisions

V. Impact Analysis
> Impact analysis
> Impact magnitude
> Summary of impacts

Phase Gate #2
- Phase gate "light"
- Design review and approval
- Pilot study findings reported
- Impact assessment magnitude findings
- Plan for addressing big picture impacts
- Refinement of costs
- Confirmation for Phase VI
- Reconfirmation of regional resources & capacity readiness

VI. Plan and Organize for Implementation
> Impact resolution
> Integrated solutions
> Implementation actions
> Implementation master plan and pace

Phase Gate #3
- Approved business plan required *
- Finalized ROI and metrics
- Full impact analysis and mitigation plan
- Implementation plan and pace review and approval
- Air traffic control clearance vis-a-vis other initiatives and PH work
- Confirmation of regional resources and capacity readiness
- Implementation plan costs re-validated and synchronized with approved business plan
- $$ confirmation for Phases VII, VIII, and IX

VII. Implementation
> Monitor implementation process
> Monitor desired state

VIII. Celebrate and Integrate
> Optimal performance: individuals/teams
> Optimal performance: whole-system integration and mastery

IX. Learn and Course-Correct
> System to continuously improve new state
> Hold the gains
> Dismantle temp structure(s)

* Standard PeaceHealth business plan, process and approval

**Version 4.0
Revised June 21, 2007**

"The Change Leader's Roadmap" © Being First, Inc.
"Phase-Gate" modifications © PeaceHealth.
Distribution or use of this document outside PeaceHealth prohibited by respective copyright owners.

their teams must fulfill the predetermined requirements of preparation and present the depth of their thinking for discussion and approval. Both the presenters, from the project's perspective, and the executives reviewing the project strategy and status must understand and be able to evaluate conditions for success in real time.

If you adopt the phase gate strategy, design your process clearly, including the information and deliverables you will require of project leaders to pass each phase gate. Provide consistent preparation and presentation templates so that when a phase gate review is presented, executives understand the CLR work that has been accomplished and the upcoming work that will need their approval for giving the project the "go-ahead." Then, design your strategy for rolling out this process, including how you will educate your leaders on the CLR, the phase gate process, and each phase gate's preparation and presentation templates. Review the guidelines for rolling out the CLR as your common methodology noted previously.

SUMMARY

The Change Leader's Roadmap provides significant value in a number of ways. We have described how it can be used to support and accelerate all of the organization's change efforts as a common change methodology, internalized as a change operating system. We offered various scenarios for how to roll out the methodology and described the "just-in-time" approach for making the methodology useful in organizations whose leaders have less tolerance for learning about the complexities of transformational change but need its guidance for their success. We also addressed how consciously designing your transformation process speeds it up more than any other acceleration strategy, and portrayed how the CLR can be structured as a phase gate process. These approaches deliver value-added benefit for serious change leaders.

The next chapter supports your continued journey to conscious change leadership.

Continuing the Journey to Conscious Change Leadership

The process of transformation is continuous, as is the pursuit of greater consciousness about how to lead and consult to it. Rather than conclude the journey here, we would like to offer you some things to think about to keep your development process going. In this chapter, we list three sets of questions and ideas for you to ponder: one about your general reactions and insights about using the CLR, one for change consultants, and one for change leaders. We encourage you to think about these questions and suggestions, and talk about them with like-minded colleagues.

- What are your reactions to The Change Leader's Roadmap? What conclusions have you drawn about its use and value to you and the organizations you support?

- In reading through the CLR as one pathway to conscious change leadership, in what ways has your thinking about leading transformation changed?

- What are the most important insights you have had about how you have been leading or consulting to large systems change? How will each insight affect your leadership or consulting practice and your way of being from this point on?

- If you could position and use the CLR in any way in your organization, what would that be? What outcomes or benefits would you want to accomplish from your strategy? How could you use the Conscious Change Leader Accountability Model to frame this work?

- Are you currently in a role to use a methodology such as this effectively? If not, what would have to be different in your situation to enable you to use it to its greatest advantage? Who else would you need to work with to accomplish this?

- What do you have to do to develop mastery as a conscious change leader or consultant? What obstacles or factors do you need to overcome to move your development process forward? What support do you require? How can you obtain that support?

- What natural strengths and ways of being do you have that support your effectiveness as a conscious change leader or consultant? Are you using these assets in your work and life? What would have to happen for you to be able to bring them more fully into your normal way of working and living?

- How can you get the support you need to continue to think about and act on your responses to these questions after you close this book?

SOME THOUGHTS FOR CONSULTANTS

Becoming masterful at consulting to large-scale transformational change requires serious professional and personal growth for change consultants in organization development, organization effectiveness, change management, and project management. As we personally evolve this body of work, we continue to grow ourselves; the work, in fact, "grows us."

We see several key leverage points for building your consulting proficiency. Some of these may be relevant to you, especially if you are interested in becoming a masterful strategic change consultant—and being used that way! Here is our overview, for your consideration:

- View yourself as a full-fledged partner with executives in charge of change. You cannot do the work of helping build change strategy for the full lifecycle of a transformation from the sidelines or behind the scenes. In our experience, until you embrace this fact, you will not be able to enter a client engagement properly positioned to do the work that is required. Creating a viable partnership with your clients is at the heart of strategic change consulting.

▶ If you are a consultant who has a content specialty, learn about how to apply it to organizations from a *change process* perspective. Learn the CLR, and use it to integrate the people and process components into your content contribution. You will contribute far more to your clients.

▶ Learn how to become the bridge between dealing with the comfortable challenges of the "external" world (the environment, business strategy, organizational configurations) and the more subtle realms of the "internal" world (culture, mindset, emotions, and relationships). Position yourself to serve as a translator and integrator of these two worlds in creating integrated change strategy and facilitating transformational change.

▶ Commit to doing the personal work on your own mindset and behavior to better serve your clients as a model and mirror of the personal development that transformational change requires of leaders.

▶ Further develop your skills in building change strategy for transformational change, addressing enterprise transformation in global organizations, and effecting real change in mindset and culture.

▶ Rebrand yourself as a specialist in change leadership so that you can focus your development and services on supporting the critical changes your organization or clients are undergoing. If your time is taken up with other more tactical work requirements than change, you will not be able to do this. Create the intention and find ways to be seen and valued for your contribution to the organizations' most strategic changes.

SOME THOUGHTS FOR LEADERS

Having consulted with leaders for more than thirty years, mostly on designing and implementing transformational change strategy and cultural/personal transformation, we have experienced tremendous satisfaction when making a significant contribution to the success of their efforts and their development as change leaders. We have also had times of extreme frustration at not being able to get leaders' attention about what was required to make a profound difference in their work and organizations. Older and wiser, we accept this, as we see leaders in one of three different places. Some leaders (growing in numbers!) are visionaries, traveling in the same boat of exploration with us, pioneering and testing breakthroughs in how transformation can best be consciously supported, catalyzed, and led. Some are on the boat launch, with a toe or a foot on the conscious transformation boat, intrigued by the possibilities of this "mysterious" yet compelling journey. And others, quite frankly, are firmly rooted on dry land, operating on autopilot, and either not aware of the journey being made by their peers or not believing that it is necessary, worthy, or possible. Harsh economic times exacerbate this as leaders turn to how to survive the short term rather than thrive in the long term. Operating consciously will enable you to handle both.

For those in the first two places, we offer these thoughts. Perhaps they will help you bring those on dry land to the conscious transformation boat.

- Learn as much as you can about what transformation entails. Partner with conscious, process-oriented consultants, in-house or external, who are committed to their own transformations, and make this journey together. If you haven't already, read *Beyond Change Management* to more deeply understand conscious change leadership and the internal dynamics it requires of you as you lead change in your organizations.

- Learn to use your consultants in ways that enable them to support you, your personal work, and the organization as it transforms. Use them to help you observe the internal and external dynamics that occur during the process and to map the subtleties of the organization's culture that can make or break your transformation. Let them be your coaches to expand your conscious awareness of all that demands your attention as you lead the organization through its transformation. Be curious! Be open!

- Do the personal work to become the change leader that your organization needs to succeed in its transformation. Look in the mirror at your mindset's fundamental assumptions and beliefs and how they impact your change leadership performance, relationships, and results. Contemplate your needs for influence, control, reputation, advancement, security, money, and political affiliations. What are they gaining you, and what might they be costing you—and others—as you strive to lead change?

- Accept that the organization is made up of human beings—people who are devoting much of their lives to its success. The organization is a living, dynamic human system. All of its members want and deserve to be treated with respect, concern, and gratitude for their contribution to the organization's continuing viability. They want to be accepted, as you do, for having physical, emotional, mental, and spiritual dimensions that, whether or not they like it, are impacted by *your* leadership and the realities at play in the organization, including the necessary changes you are making. Observe and take responsibility for the impact you and the change efforts you are leading have on others. Make those changes, and do it in a way that demonstrates your understanding of how to truly lead *people*.

▸ In doing this, know that when you are fully present with people and genuinely ask for what they think and how they feel, you are creating one of the highest conditions for breakthrough results. Having a say gets people into the transformation boat, and engaging them in ways that allow them to make a real difference fuels the right action!

▸ If you are leading a transformation, accept that you do not have all of the answers and will not get it right the first time. Consciously leading your organization's transformation requires you to acknowledge that transformation must be co-created by the entire organization, not just you. Letting go of control, having faith, and setting up conditions for the whole system—at least a critical mass of its people—to engage in re-creating itself require strength of character and an evolved mindset. Try this on for size. Ask your stakeholders for input about both the outcome your organization needs to produce and the best process for getting there. And then be willing to course-correct, course-correct, course-correct. *That* is your safety net!

▸ Instead of getting swept up in the tidal wave of "faster, faster, faster," we encourage you to discover the art of "right timing for leveraged action." In this book, we spoke of discovering the strategic leverage points for change that can catalyze profound shifts with efficient effort. We spoke of appropriate pacing of change activities. "Right timing for leveraged action" integrates these two strategies. Together, they enable the breakthrough in speed and performance that is possible in the transformation.

▸ You cannot control or mandate breakthrough; you can only facilitate the conditions for it to occur. Often, this is intuitive. When faced with urgency and complexity, before getting sucked into the vortex of "do-mode," ask yourself where the leverage is that can deliver maximum gain for minimum effort and when is the right time to pull the lever. The answer you come up with may not match your original plan, yet it may be the very catalyst you need for transformational breakthrough. To access these catalysts, learn to *listen to your intuition*. Learn to master conscious process thinking and the human dynamics of change, and put their true requirements at least on par with, if not before, speed.

▶ Consider teaching others in your organizations about your insights on leading change from a conscious perspective. This teaching might be in a training classroom, but more likely, it is on the job, in real time. Use every opportunity you have to communicate, engage, and model what you are learning, striving to achieve, and who you are becoming.

SUMMARY

Our life's work is helping people and organizations transform to generate a more positive future. Our primary method is supporting the development of conscious change leadership and providing the training, coaching, consulting, methodology, and tools that enable it. In this pursuit, we place ourselves on a lifelong path of personal and professional development. We believe wholeheartedly that expanding conscious awareness facilitates human evolution. In our worldview, learning about and mastering the process dynamics of all levels of our reality—beginning with ourselves—is the greatest leverage for leading the transformation of our organizations, in all quadrants and all levels. All transformational leadership skills derive directly from this increased insight and capability.

Assisting organizations to transform and developing transformational change leaders give us the vehicles through which to bring the benefits of conscious awareness and mindset into the open. Consciousness must become a legitimate, sought-after leadership and consulting focus if our organizations and the world are going to transform successfully.

The Change Leader's Roadmap is an overarching guidance system through which conscious change leadership can be expressed and catalyzed in organizations. In writing this book, we have attempted to provide you with both a well-balanced experience of conceptual models and pragmatic guidance for leading transformation consciously. Our goal has been to offer potent, user-friendly tools and processes to increase your awareness and your transformational leadership capability for both the process of change and the human dynamics within it. Through what you have learned, we hope you will choose to be more than a leader; we hope you will choose to be a *conscious change leader* and continue to explore and evolve this expanding role and work. We encourage you to create the strategic disciplines for change that your organization needs to thrive in this rapidly changing world. We hope the CLR has broadened your view of the territory of transformation, and that it serves you and the people you serve well. Above all, we hope you will choose to intentionally help evolve our world in the ways we must for a more positive future, made possible by conscious change leadership.

APPENDIX: PHASES, ACTIVITIES, AND TASKS OF THE CHANGE LEADER'S ROADMAP

PHASE I: PREPARE TO LEAD THE CHANGE

Activity I.A—Start Up and Staff Change Effort

Task I.A.1–Obtain Project Briefing

Task I.A.2–Clarify and Staff Initial Change Leadership Roles

Task I.A.3–Create Optimal Working Relationships

Task I.A.4–Identify Project Community

Task I.A.5–Determine Phase I Roadmap

Activity I.B—Create Case for Change and Determine Initial Desired Outcomes

Task I.B.1–Design Process for Creating Case for Change and Initial Desired Outcomes

Task I.B.2–Assess Drivers of Change

Task I.B.3–Clarify Type of Change

Task I.B.4–Identify Leverage Points for Change

Task I.B.5–Perform Initial Impact Analysis

Task I.B.6–Clarify Target Groups and Scope

Task I.B.7–Determine Degree of Urgency

Task I.B.8–Determine Desired Outcomes and Compile Case for Change

Activity I.C—Assess and Build Organization's Readiness and Capacity

Task I.C.1–Assess Readiness and Capacity
Task I.C.2–Build Readiness and Capacity

Activity I.D—Build Leaders' Capability to Lead the Change

Task I.D.1–Assess Leaders' Capability to Lead the Change
Task I.D.2–Ensure Leaders Model Desired Mindset and Behavior
Task I.D.3–Build Leader Commitment and Alignment
Task I.D.4–Develop Leaders' Change Knowledge and Skills
Task I.D.5–Develop Executive and Change Leadership Teams
Task I.D.6–Support Individual Executives and Change Leaders

Activity I.E—Clarify Overall Change Strategy

Task I.E.1–Design Process for Building Change Strategy
Task I.E.2–Define Values and Guiding Principles
Task I.E.3–Clarify Governance and Decision Making
Task I.E.4–Determine Required Initiatives and How to Unify Them
Task I.E.5–Determine Fit and Priority of Change Effort
Task I.E.6–Create Multiple Project Integration Strategy
Task I.E.7–Identify Bold Actions
Task I.E.8–Clarify Engagement Strategy
Task I.E.9–Design Overall Communication Plan
Task I.E.10–Determine Change Acceleration Strategies
Task I.E.11–Secure Commitment for Resources
Task I.E.12–Identify Milestones and Timeline, and Compile Change Strategy

Activity I.F—Build Infrastructure and Conditions to Support Change Effort

Task I.F.1–Initiate Strategies for Dealing with Political Dynamics
Task I.F.2–Create Conditions for Success
Task I.F.3–Identify Process for Creating Shared Vision

Task I.F.4–Design Information Generation and Management Strategies

Task I.F.5–Initiate Course Correction Strategy and System

Task I.F.6–Initiate Strategies for Supporting People Through Emotional Reactions and Resistance

Task I.F.7–Initiate Temporary Support Mechanisms

Task I.F.8–Determine Measurements of Change

Task I.F.9–Initiate Temporary Rewards

Task I.F.10–Determine Phase II Through Phase V Roadmap

PHASE II: CREATE ORGANIZATIONAL VISION, COMMITMENT, AND CAPABILITY

Activity II.A—Build Organizational Understanding of Case for Change, Vision, and Change Strategy

Task II.A.1–Communicate Case for Change and Change Strategy

Task II.A.2–Roll Out Process to Create Shared Vision and Commitment

Task II.A.3–Demonstrate That Old Way of Operating Is Gone

Activity II.B—Increase Organization's Capability to Change

Task II.B.1–Build Organization's Change Knowledge and Skills

Task II.B.2–Promote Required Mindset and Behavior Change

PHASE III: ASSESS THE SITUATION TO DETERMINE DESIGN REQUIREMENTS

Activity III.A—Assess the Situation to Determine Design Requirements

Task III.A.1–Assess Relevant Aspects of Your Organization

Task III.A.2–Benchmark Other Organizations for Best Practices

Task III.A.3–Clarify Customer Requirements

Task III.A.4–Write Statement of Design Requirements

PHASE IV: DESIGN THE DESIRED STATE

Activity IV.A—Design Desired State

Task IV.A.1–Create Process and Structure to Design Desired State
Task IV.A.2–Design Desired State
Task IV.A.3–Pilot Test
Task IV.A.4–Communicate Desired State

PHASE V: ANALYZE THE IMPACT

Activity V.A—Analyze Impacts of Desired State

Task V.A.1–Design Process for Conducting Impact Analysis
Task V.A.2–Identify and Group Impacts
Task V.A.3–Assess Magnitude of Impacts and Prioritize
Task V.A.4–Refine Desired State

PHASE VI: PLAN AND ORGANIZE FOR IMPLEMENTATION

Activity VI.A—Develop Implementation Master Plan

Task VI.A.1–Design Process to Develop Implementation Master Plan
Task VI.A.2–Identify Impact Solutions and Action Plans
Task VI.A.3–Integrate Solutions and Action Plans and Compile
Implementation Master Plan
Task VI.A.4–Design Strategies to Sustain Energy for Change
Task VI.A.5–Determine Resources, Pacing Strategy, and Timeline

Activity VI.B—Prepare Organization to Support Implementation

Task VI.B.1–Establish Infrastructure and Conditions to Support
Implementation
Task VI.B.2–Support People Through Implementation
Task VI.B.3–Communicate Implementation Master Plan

PHASE VII: IMPLEMENT THE CHANGE

Activity VII.A—Implement the Change

Task VII.A.1–Roll Out Implementation Master Plan
Task VII.A.2–Monitor and Course-Correct Implementation
Task VII.A.3–Monitor and Course-Correct Desired State

PHASE VIII: CELEBRATE AND INTEGRATE THE NEW STATE

Activity VIII.A—Celebrate Achievement of Desired State

Task VIII.A.1–Celebrate Achievement of Desired State

Activity VIII.B—Support Integration and Mastery of New State

Task VIII.B.1–Support Individuals and Teams to Integrate and Master
New State
Task VIII.B.2–Support Whole System to Integrate and Master New State

PHASE IX: LEARN AND COURSE-CORRECT

Activity IX.A—Build System to Continuously Improve New State

Task IX.A.1–Build System to Continuously Improve New State

Activity IX.B—Learn from Your Change Process and Establish Best Practices

Task IX.B.1–Learn from Your Change Process and Establish Best
Practices

Activity IX.C—Dismantle Temporary Change Infrastructure

Task IX.C.1–Dismantle Temporary Change Infrastructure

BIBLIOGRAPHY

Ackerman Anderson, L. (1986). Development, transition or transformation: The question of change in organizations. *OD Practitioner, 18*(4).

Ackerman Anderson, L., & Anderson, D. (1996). *Facilitating large systems change participant manual.* Durango, CO: Being First, Inc.

Ackerman Anderson, L., & Anderson, D. (2001). *The Change Leader's Roadmap.* San Francisco: Jossey-Bass/Pfeiffer.

Adams, J. (1984). *Transforming work: A collection of organizational transformation readings.* Alexandria, VA: Miles River Press.

Adams, J. (1986). *Transforming leadership: From vision to results.* Alexandria, VA: Miles River Press.

Adams, J., & Spencer, S. (2002). *Life changes: A Guide to the seven stages of personal growth.* New York: Paraview Press.

Alban, B., & Bunker, B. (1997). *Large group interventions: Engaging the whole system for rapid change.* San Francisco: Jossey-Bass.

Anderson, D. (1986). *Optimal performance manual.* Durango, CO: Being First, Inc.

Anderson, D., & Ackerman Anderson, L. (2001). *Beyond change management: Advanced strategies for today's transformational leaders.* San Francisco: Jossey-Bass/Pfeiffer.

Argyris, C. (1985). *Strategy, change, and defensive routines.* Marshfield, MA: Pitman.

Argyris, C. (1993). *Knowledge and action: A guide to overcoming barriers to organizational change.* San Francisco: Jossey-Bass.

Ashkenas, R., Ulrich, R., Jick, T., & Kerr, S. (1995). *The boundaryless organization: Breaking the chains of organizational structure.* San Francisco: Jossey-Bass.

Axelrod, R. (1992). *Terms of engagement: Changing the way we change our organizations.* San Francisco: Berrett-Koehler.

Balthazard, P. A., Cooke, R. S., & Potter, R. E. (2006). "Dysfunctional Culture, Dysfunctional Organization: Capturing the Behavioral Norms the Form Organizational Culture and Drive Performance." *Journal of Managerial Psychology,* 21(8), 709–732.

Beck, D., & Cohen C. (1996). *Spiral dynamics: Mastering values, leadership and change.* Cambridge, MA: Blackwell.

Beckhard, R. (1997). *Agent of change: My life, my practice.* San Francisco: Jossey-Bass.

Beckhard, R., & Harris, R. (1987). *Organizational transitions.* Reading, MA: Addison-Wesley.

Bennis, W. (1989). *Why leaders can't lead: The unconscious conspiracy continues.* San Francisco: Jossey-Bass.

Bennis, W. (1995). *On becoming a leader* (audio). New York: Simon & Schuster.

Bennis, W., & Nanus, B. (1985). *Leaders: The strategies for taking charge.* New York: Harper & Row.

Blanchard, K. (2006). *Leading at a higher level: Blanchard on leadership and creating high performing organizations.* Upper Saddle River, NJ: Prentice Hall.

Blanchard, K., & Hersey, P. (1982). *Management of organizational behavior: Utilizing human resources.* Upper Saddle River, NJ: Prentice Hall.

Blanchard, K., & O'Connor, M. (1997). *Managing by values.* San Francisco: Berrett-Koehler.

Block, P. (1999). *Flawless consulting: A guide to getting your expertise used* (2nd ed.). San Francisco: Jossey-Bass/Pfeiffer.

Block, P. (2003). *The answer to how is yes: Acting on what matters.* San Francisco: Berrett-Koehler.

Block, P. (2009). *Community: The structure of belonging.* San Francisco: Berrett-Koehler.

Bohm, D. (1980). *Wholeness and the implicate order.* New York: Routledge.

Bridges, W. (1980). *Transitions* (2nd ed.). New York: Perseus Publishing.

Bridges, W. (1991). *Managing transitions: Making the most of change.* Reading, MA: Addison-Wesley.

Bridges, W. (1994). *Jobshift: How to prosper in a workplace without jobs.* Reading, MA: Addison-Wesley.

Bridges, W. (2001). *The way of transition: Embracing life's most difficult moments.* New York: Perseus Publishing.

Bridges, W. (2003). *Managing transitions: Making the most of change* (2nd ed.). Cambridge, MA: Da Capo Press.

Briggs, J., & Peat, F. D. (1989). *Turbulent mirror: An illustrated guide to chaos theory and the science of wholeness.* New York: Harper & Row.

Briggs, J., & Peat, F. D. (1999). *Seven life lessons of chaos: Spiritual wisdom from the science of change.* New York: HarperCollins.

Brown, J. & Isaacs, D. (2005). *The World Café: Shaping our futures through conversations that matter.* San Francisco: Berrett-Koehler.

Bunker, B., & Alban, B. (eds.). (1992/December). Special issue: Large group interventions. *Applied Behavioral Science, (28)*4.

Cady, S., Devane, T., and Holman, P. (2007). *The Change Handbook: The Definitive Resource on Today's Best Methods for Engaging Whole Systems* (2nd ed.). San Francisco: Berrett-Koehler Publishers, Inc.

Canter, L., Ulrich, D., & Goldsmith, M. (eds.). (2004). *Best practices in leadership development and organization change: How the best companies ensure meaningful change and sustainable leadership.* San Francisco: Pfeiffer.

Capra, F. (1983). *The turning point: Science, society, and the rising culture.* New York: Bantam.

Capra, F. (1991). *The tao of physics: An exploration of the parallels between modern physics and eastern mysticism.* Boston: Shambhala.

Capra, F. (1996). *The web of life.* New York: Anchor Press.

Case, J. (1998). *The open-book experience: Lessons from over 100 companies who successfully transformed themselves.* Reading, MA: Addison-Wesley.

Collins, J., & Porras, J. (1994). *Built to last: Successful habits of visionary companies.* New York: HarperCollins.

Combs, A. (2002). *The radiance of being: Understanding the grand integral vision: Living the integral life.* New York: Paragon House.

Combs, A. (2009). *Consciousness explained better: Towards an integral understanding of the multifaceted nature of consciousness.* New York: Paragon House.

Conger, J., Spreitzer, G., & Lawler, E., III (1999). *The leader's change handbook: An essential guide to setting direction and taking action.* San Francisco: Jossey-Bass.

Conner, D. (1993). *Managing at the speed of change: How resilient managers succeed and prosper where others fail.* New York: Villard Books.

Conner, D. (1998). *Leading at the edge of chaos: How to create the nimble organization.* New York: John Wiley & Sons.

Cooperrider, D., Whitney, D., Stavros, J., & Fry, R. (2008). *Appreciative inquiry handbook: For leaders of change*. Brunswick, OH: Crown Custom Publishing.

Csikszentmihalyi, M. (1990). *Flow: The psychology of optimal experience*. New York: Harper & Row.

Csikszentmihalyi, M. (2004). *Good Business: Leadership, flow and the making of meaning*. New York: Penguin.

Dalai Lama. (2006). *The universe in a single atom: The convergence of science and spirituality*. New York: Broadway.

De Chardin, P. (1962). *Human energy*. New York: Harcourt Brace Jovanovich.

Deal, T., & Kennedy, A. (1982). *Corporate cultures: The rites and rituals of corporate life*. Reading, MA: Addison-Wesley.

Devane, T., & Holman, P. (eds.). (1999). *The change handbook: Group methods for shaping the future*. San Francisco: Berrett-Koehler.

Dowd, M. (2009). *Thank god for evolution: How the marriage of science and religion will transform how you live and our world*. New York: Plume.

Drucker, P. (1999). *Management challenges for the 21st century*. New York: HarperCollins.

Drucker, P. (2006). *The effective executive: The definitive guide to getting the right things done*. New York: Harper Paperbacks.

Drucker, P. (2008). *The five most important questions you'll ever ask about your organization*. San Francisco: Jossey-Bass.

Dym, B. (1995). *Readiness and change in couple therapy*. New York: HarperCollins.

Ferguson, M., & Naisbitt, J. (1980). *The aquarian conspiracy*. Los Angeles: Jeremy P. Tarcher.

Forrester, J. (1961). *Industrial dynamics*. Cambridge, MA: MIT Press.

Francis, D., & Woodcock, M. (1990). *Unblocking organizational values*. Glenview, IL: Scott, Foresman.

Frenier, C. (1997). *Business and the feminine principle: The untapped resource*. Boston: Butterworth-Heinemann.

Friedman, T. (2002). *Longitudes & attitudes: Exploring the world after September 11*. New York: Farrar, Straus, Giroux.

Friedman, T. (2005). *The world is flat: A brief history of the twenty-first century*. Vancouver, CA: Douglas & McIntyre.

Fullan, M. (2008). *The six secrets of change: What the best leaders do to help their organizations survive and thrive*. San Francisco: Jossey-Bass.

Galbraith, J., Lawler, E., & Associates. (1993). *Organizing for the future: The new logic for managing complex organizations*. San Francisco: Jossey-Bass.

Gleick, J. (1987). *Chaos: Making a new science*. New York: Penguin.

Gleick, J. (1999). *Faster: The acceleration of just about everything*. New York: Pantheon.

Goldsmith, M. (2009). *Mojo: How to get it, how to keep it, how to get it back if you lose it*. New York: Hyperion.

Goldstein, J. (1994). *The unshackled organization: Facing the challenge of unpredictability through spontaneous reorganization*. Portland, OR: Productivity Press.

Goleman, D. (1995). *Emotional intelligence: Why it can matter more than IQ*. New York: Bantam.

Greenleaf, R. (1977). *Servant leadership: A journey into the nature of legitimate power and greatness*. Mahwah, NJ: Paulist Press.

Grof, S. (1993). *The holotropic mind: The three levels of human consciousness and how they shape our lives*. New York: Harper Collins.

Gross, T. (1996). *The last word on power: Executive re-invention for leaders who must make the impossible happen*. New York: Doubleday.

Hagberg, J. (1984). *Real power: Stages of personal power in organizations*. Minneapolis, MN: Winston Press.

Hall, B. (1995). *Values shift: A guide to personal & organizational transformation*. Rockport, MA: Twin Lights Publishers.

Hammer, M., & Champy, J. (1993). *Reengineering the corporation: A manifesto for business revolution*. New York: HarperCollins.

Hammond, S. (1996). *The thin book of appreciative inquiry* (2nd ed.). Plano, TX: Thin Book Publishing.

Hammond, S., & Royal, C. (1998). *Lessons from the field: Applying appreciative inquiry*. Plano, TX: Practical Press.

Hawkins, D. (2002). *Power vs. force: The hidden determinants of human behavior*. Carlsbad, CA: Hay House.

Heisenberg, W. (1958). *Physics and philosophy*. New York: Harper Torchbooks.

Henricks, G., & Ludeman, K. (1996). *The corporate mystic: A guidebook for visionaries with their feet on the ground*. New York: Bantam.

Herbert, N. (1985). *Quantum reality: Beyond the new physics*. New York: Doubleday.

Herman, S. (1994). *The tao at work: On leading and following*. San Francisco: Jossey-Bass.

Hesselbien, F., & Goldsmith, M. (2006). *The leaders of the future 2: Visions, strategies and practices for the new era*. San Francisco: Jossey-Bass.

Hesselbein, F., Goldsmith, M., & Beckhard, R. (1996). *The leader of the future: New visions, strategies, and practices for the next era*. San Francisco: Jossey-Bass.

Holman, P., Devane, T., & Cady, S. (eds.). (2007). *The change handbook: The definitive resource on today's best methods for engaging whole systems*. San Francisco: Berret-Koehler.

Huxley, A. (1956). *The doors of perception and heaven and hell*. New York: Harper Colophon.

Jacobs, R. (1994). *Real time strategic change: How to involve an entire organization in fast and far-reaching change*. San Francisco: Berrett-Koehler.

James, W. (1999). *The varieties of religious experience: A study in human nature*. New York: The Modern Library.

Jantsch, E. (1980). *The self-organizing universe*. New York: Pergamon Press.

Jaynes, J. (1990). *The origin of consciousness in the breakdown of the bicameral mind*. Boston: Houghton Mifflin.

Johnson, B. (1996). *Polarity management: Identifying and managing unsolvable problems*. Amherst, MA: HRD Press.

Joiner, W. B., & Josephs, S. A. (2007). *Leadership agility: Five levels of mastery for anticipating and initiating change*. San Francisco: Jossey-Bass.

Jones, J., & Bearley, W. (1996). *360-degree feedback: Strategies, tactics, and techniques for developing leaders*. Amherst, MA: HRD Press.

Jones, Q., Dunphy, D., Fishman, R., Larne, M., & Canter, C. (2007). *In great company: Unlocking the secrets of cultural transformation*. Sydney, Australia: Human Synergistics.

Jung, C. (1963). *Memories, dreams, reflections*. New York: Random House.

Jung, C. (1973). *Synchronicity: An acausal connecting principle*. Princeton, NJ: Princeton University Press.

Kanter, R. (1983). *The change masters: Innovation for productivity in the American corporation*. New York: Simon & Schuster.

Katz, J., & Miller, F. (2008). *Be big: Step up, step out, be bold*. San Francisco: Berrett-Koehler.

Katzenbach, J., & Smith, D. (1993). *The wisdom of teams: Creating the high performance organization*. Boston: Harvard Business School Press.

Katzenbach, J., & Smith, D. (2001). *The discipline of teams: A mindbook-workbook for delivering small group performance*. New York: Wiley.

Kay, B., & Jordan-Evans, S. (2005). *Love 'em or lose 'em.* San Francisco: Berrett Koehler Publishers.

Klein, E., & Izzo, J. (1998). *Awakening corporate soul: Four paths to unleash the power of people at work.* Lions Bay, BC, Canada: Fairwinds Press.

Koestenbaum, P. (1991). *Leadership: The inner side of greatness.* San Francisco: Jossey-Bass.

Kotter, J. (1996). *Leading change.* Boston: Harvard Business School Press.

Kotter, J. (2008). *A sense of urgency.* Boston: Harvard Business School Press.

Kotter, J., & Cohen, D. (2002). *The heart of change: Real-life stories of how people change their organizations.* Boston: Harvard Business School Press.

Kouzes, J., & Posner, B. (1995). *The leadership challenge: How to keep getting extraordinary things done in organizations.* San Francisco: Jossey-Bass.

Kouzes, J., & Posner, B. (1999). *Encouraging the heart: A leader's guide to rewarding and recognizing others.* San Francisco: Jossey-Bass.

Kouzes, J., & Posner, B. (2006). *A leader's legacy.* San Francisco: Jossey-Bass.

Kubler-Ross, E., & Kessler, D. (1997). *On grief and grieving.* New York: Scribner.

Kuhn, T. (1962). *The Structure of Scientific Resolutions* (1st ed.). Chicago: The University of Chicago Press.

Land, G., & Jarman, B. (1992). *Breakpoint and beyond: Mastering the future today.* San Francisco: HarperCollins.

Laszlo, E., Grof, S., & Russell, P. (1999). *The consciousness revolution.* Boston: Element Books.

Lebow, R., & Simon, W. (1997). *Lasting change: The shared values process that makes companies great.* New York: John Wiley & Sons.

Leider, R. (2010). *The power of purpose: Creating meaning in your life and work.* San Francisco: Berrett-Koehler.

Liebau, P. (1985). *Thoughts on relationships.* London, Ontario, Canada: P.S.A. Ventures.

Lipnack, J., & Stamps, J. (1993). *The teamnet factor: Bringing the power of boundary crossing into the heart of your business.* Essex Junction, VT: Oliver Wright.

London, M. (1988). *Change agents: New roles and innovation strategies for human resource professionals.* San Francisco: Jossey-Bass.

Lovelock, J.E. (1987). *Gaia.* London, England: Oxford University Press.

Ludema, J., Whitney, D., Mohr, B., & Griffin, T. (2003). *The appreciative inquiry summit: A practitioner's guide for leading large-group change.* San Francisco: Berrett-Koehler.

Maslow, A. (1964). *Religions, values, and peak experiences.* New York: Penguin.

Maslow, A. (1999). *Motivation and personality* (2nd ed.). New York: Harper and Row.

Maslow, A. (1999). *Toward a psychology of being* (3rd ed.). New York: John Wiley & Sons.

Maynard, H., & Mehrtens, S. (1993). *The fourth wave: Business in the 21st century.* San Francisco: Berrett-Koehler.

McFarland, L., Senn, L., & Childress, J. (1994). *21st century leadership: Dialogues with 100 top leaders.* Los Angeles: The Leadership Press.

McIntosh, S. (2007). *Integral consciousness and the future of evolution.* New York: Continuum.

Miles, R. (1997). *Leading corporate transformation: A blueprint for business renewal.* San Francisco: Jossey-Bass.

Miles, R., Miles, G., & Snow, C. (2005). *Collaborative Entrepreneurship.* Stanford, CA: Stanford University Press.

Mink, O., Mink, B., Downes, E., & Owen, K. (1994). *Open organizations: A model for effectiveness, renewal, and intelligent change.* San Francisco: Jossey-Bass.

Morton, C. (1984). *Managing operations in emerging companies.* Reading, MA: Addison-Wesley.

Nadler, D. (1998). *Champions of change: How CEOs and their companies are mastering the skills of radical change.* San Francisco: Jossey-Bass.

Nadler, D, Shaw, R., & Walton, A. (1995). *Discontinuous change: Leading organizational transformation.* San Francisco: Jossey-Bass.

Nadler, D., & Tushman, M.L. (1977). A diagnostic model for organizational behavior. In J.R. Hackman, E.E. Lawler, & L.W. Porter (eds.), *Perspectives on behavior in organizations.* New York: McGraw-Hill.

Naisbitt, J., & Aburdene, P. (1985). *Re-inventing the corporation: Transforming your job and your company for the new information society.* New York: Warner Books.

Nevis, E., Lancourt, J., & Vassallo, H. (1996). *Intentional revolutions: A seven-point strategy for transforming organizations.* San Francisco: Jossey-Bass.

Oakley, E., & Krug, D. (1994). Enlightened leadership: Getting to the heart of change. New York: Fireside.

O'Donovan, G. (2007). *The corporate culture handbook: How to plan, implement and measure a successful culture change.* Dublin, Ireland: Liffey Press.

Ogle, R. (2007). *Smart world: Breakthrough creativity and the new science of ideas.* Boston: Harvard Business Press.

Oshry, B. (1992). *The possibilities of organization.* Boston: Power & Systems.

Oshry, B. (1995). *Seeing systems: Unlocking the mysteries of organizational life.* San Francisco: Berrett-Koehler.

Pascarella, P., & Frohman, M. (1989). *The purpose-driven organization: Unleashing the power of direction and commitment.* San Francisco: Jossey-Bass.

Peat, D. F. (1987). *Synchronicity: The bridge between matter and mind.* New York: Bantam.

Penfield, W. (1975). *Mystery of the mind: A critical study of consciousness.* Princeton, NJ: Princeton University Press.

Peters, T., & Waterman, R. H. (1982) *In search of Excellence.* New York: Harper & Row.

Pribram, K. (1971). *Languages of the brain: Experimental paradoxes and principles in neuropsychology.* New York: Brandon House.

The Price Waterhouse Change Integration Team. (1995). *Better change: Best practices for transforming your organization.* New York: Irwin.

Prigogine, I. (1997). *The end of certainty: Time, chaos, and the new laws of nature.* New York: The Free Press.

Prigogine, I., & Stenger, I. (1984). *Order out of chaos.* New York: Bantam.

Puccio, G., Murdock, M. & Mance, M. (2006). *Creative leadership: Skills that drive change.* Thousand Oaks, CA: Sage Publications.

Quinn, R. E. (1996). *Deep Change: Discovering the leader within.* San Francisco: Jossey-Bass.

Ralston, F. (1995). *Hidden dynamics: How emotions affect business performance & how you can harness their power for positive results.* New York: American Management Association.

Rapaille, C. (2006). *The culture code: An ingenious way to understand why people around the world live and buy as they do.* New York: Broadway Books.

Ray, M., & Rinzler, A. (1993). *The new paradigm in business: Emerging strategies for leadership and organizational change.* New York: Tarcher/Pergee.

Reder, A. (1995). *75 best business practices for socially responsible companies.* New York: Tarcher/Putnam.

Renesch, J. (ed.). (1992). *New traditions in business: Spirit and leadership in the 21st century.* San Francisco: Berrett-Koehler.

Renesch, J. (1994). *Leadership in a new era: Visionary approaches to the biggest crisis of our time.* San Francisco: New Leaders Press.

Rogers, R., Hayden, J., Ferketish, B., with Matzen, R. (1985). *Organizational change that works: How to merge culture and business strategies for maximum results.* Pittsburgh, PA: Development Dimensions International.

Ross, G. (1994). *Toppling the pyramids: Redefining the way companies are run.* New York: Times Books.

Russell, P. (1995). *The global brain awakens: Our next evolutionary leap.* Palo Alto, CA: Global Brain, Inc.

Russell, P. (2008). *Waking up in time: Finding inner peace in times of accelerating change.* Novato, CA: Origin Press.

Ryan, K., & Oestreich, D. (1991). *Driving fear out of the workplace: How to overcome the invisible barriers to quality, productivity, and innovation.* San Francisco: Jossey-Bass.

Schein, E. (1969). *Process consultation: Its role in organization development.* Reading, MA: Addison-Wesley.

Schein, E. (1999). *The corporate culture survival guide: Sense and nonsense about culture change.* San Francisco: Jossey-Bass.

Schein, E. (2004). *Organizational culture and leadership.* San Francisco: Jossey-Bass.

Schwartz, P. (1996). *The art of the long view.* New York: Doubleday.

Schwartz, T. (1996). *What really matters: Searching for wisdom in America.* New York: Bantam.

Senge, P. (1990). *The fifth discipline: The art and practice of learning organization.* New York: Doubleday.

Senge, P. (2006). *The fifth discipline: the art and practice of the learning organization.* Broadway Business; revised edition.

Senge, P., Kleiner, A., Roberts, C., Ross, R., & Smith, B. (1994). *The fifth discipline fieldbook.* New York: Doubleday.

Senge, P., Kleiner, A., Roberts, C., Roth, G., Ross, R., & Smith, B. (1999). *The dance of change: The challenges of sustaining momentum in learning organizations.* New York: Doubleday.

Senge, P., Scharmer, C., Jaworski, J., & Flowers, B. (2005). *Presence: An exploration of profound change in people, organizations and society.* New York: Broadway Business.

Senge, P., Scharmer, C., Jaworski, J., & Flowers, B. (2008). *Presence: Human purpose and the field of the future.* New York: Doubleday.

Sheldrake, R. (1995). *A new science of life: The hypothesis of morphic resonance.* Rochester, VT: Park Street Press.

Sieler, A. (2007). *Coaching to the human soul: Ontological coaching and deep change: Volume 2: Emotional learning and ontological coaching.* Blackburn, AU: Newfield Austrailia.

Singer, J. (1994). *Boundaries of the soul: The practice of Jung's psychology*. New York: Doubleday.

Smith, H. (1992). *Forgotten truth: The common vision of the world's religions*. San Francisco: HarperCollins.

Spencer, S. A., & Adams, J. D. (1990). *Life changes: Growing through personal transitions*. San Luis Obispo, CA: Impact Publishing.

Stacey, R.(1992). *Managing the unknowable: Strategic boundaries between order and chaos in organizations*. San Francisco: Jossey-Bass.

Stiglitz, J. (2006). *Making Globalization Work*. New York: Norton.

Talbot, M. (1986). *Beyond the quantum*. New York: Bantam.

Tart, C. (1975). *States of consciousness*. New York: E.P. Dutton.

Tart, C. (2001). *Mind Science: Medication training for practical people*. Novato, CA: Wisdom Editions.

Tichy, N., with Cohen, E. (1997). *The leadership engine: How winning companies build leaders at every level*. New York: HarperCollins.

Waldrop, M. (1992). *Complexity: The emerging science at the edge of order and chaos*. New York: Touchstone.

Walsh, R., & Vaughan, F. (1993). *Paths beyond ego: The transpersonal vision*. New York: Penguin/Putnam.

Waterman, R. (1987). *The renewal factor: How the best get and keep the competitive edge*. New York: Bantam.

Watkins, J. M., & Mohr, B. (2001). *Appreciative inquiry: Change at the speed of imagination*. San Francisco: Jossey-Bass/Pfeiffer.

Weisbord, M. R. (1978). *Organizational diagnosis: A workbook of theory and practice*. Reading, MA: Addison-Wesley.

Weisbord, M., & Janoff, S. (1995). *Future search: An action guide to finding common ground for action in organizations*. San Francisco: Berrett-Koehler.

Weisinger, H. (1998). *Emotional intelligence at work: The untapped edge for success*. San Francisco: Jossey-Bass.

Wheatley, M. (1994). *Leadership and the new science: Learning about organization from an orderly universe*. San Francisco: Berrett-Koehler.

Wheatley, M., & Kellner-Rogers, M. (1995). *A simpler way*. San Francisco: Berrett-Koehler.

Wilber, K. (1977). *The spectrum of consciousness*. Wheaton, IL: Theosophical Publishing House.

Wilber, K. (1982). *The holographic paradigm and other paradoxes*. Boston: Shambhala.

Wilber, K. (1996). *A brief history of everything*. Boston: Shambhala.

Wilber, K. (1996). *Up from Eden, new edition: A transpersonal view of human evolution*. Wheaton, IL: Quest Books.

Wilber, K. (1998). *The marriage of sense and soul*. New York: Random House.

Wilber, K. (1999). *One taste: The journals of Ken Wilber*. Boston: Shambhala.

Wilber, K. (2000). A theory of everything. Boston: Shambala, p. 70.

Wilber, K. (2000). Integral psychology: Consciousness, spirit, psychology, therapy. Boston: Shambala.

Wilber, K. (2001). *Sex, ecology, spirituality: The spirit of evolution* (2nd ed.). Boston: Shambhala.

Wilber, K. (2001). *No Boundary: Eastern and western approaches to personal growth*. Boston: Shambhala.

Wilber, K. (2006). *Integral Spirituality: A startling new role for religion in the modern and postmodern world*. Boston: Shambhala.

Williamson, M. (1992). *Return to love*. New York: HarperCollins.

Wilson, J. (1994). *Leadership trapeze: Strategies for leadership in team-based organizations*. San Francisco: Jossey-Bass.

Wolf, F. (1988). *Parallel universes: The search for other worlds*. New York: Touchstone.

Wolf, F. (1989). *Taking the quantum leap: The new physics for nonscientists*. New York: Harper & Row.

Young, A. (1976). *The reflexive universe*. Englewood Cliffs, NJ: Prentice Hall.

Zaffron, S. & Logan, D. (2009). *The three laws of performance*. San Francisco: Jossey-Bass.

Zukav, G. (1979). *The dancing Wu Li master*. New York: Bantam.

ABOUT THE AUTHORS

Linda Ackerman Anderson is a co-founder and principal of Being First, Inc, a consulting, training, and publishing company specializing in facilitating transformational change in Fortune 500 businesses, government, and the military. Over the past thirty years, her work has focused on change strategy development for transformational changes and the development of change consultants and leaders. Linda speaks about leading conscious transformation at national and international conferences and is known as an inspiring model of her message. In the past twenty years, she and her partner, Dean Anderson, have established themselves as thought leaders on leading conscious transformation and changing organizational mindset and culture as drivers of transformational change. She drove the thirty-year development of Being First's renowned change process methodology, The Change Leader's Roadmap. Linda also devotes herself to supporting women as leaders of change.

Ms. Ackerman Anderson was a founding creator of the organization transformation field, and she chaired the Second International Symposium on Organization Transformation in 1984. To help define this field, she has published more than 50 articles, including "Development, Transition or Transformation: Bringing Change Leadership into the 21st Century," "Awake at the Wheel: Moving beyond Change Management to Conscious Change Leadership," "The Flow State: A New View of Organizations and Leadership," and "Flow State Leadership in Action: Managing Organizational Energy." She was one of the first to articulate the notion and use of organizational energy as a tool for transformation.

In 1981 Ms. Ackerman Anderson formed Linda S. Ackerman, Inc., then merged it in 1988 with the Optimal Performance Institute, headed by Dean Anderson, to form Being Fist, Inc. Prior to forming her first business, Ms. Ackerman Anderson spent four years working at Sun Company, Inc. and one of its subsidiaries, Sun Petroleum Products Company, as both an organization development consultant and manager of human resources planning and development.

Ms. Ackerman Anderson's professional education includes Columbia University's Advanced Organization Development and Human Resources Management Program (1978–1979) and University Associates' Laboratory Education Internship Program (1977–1978). She has served on the faculty for the UA Intern Program and other UA conferences and many university professional development programs.

Ms. Ackerman Anderson received her master's degree in interdisciplinary arts from Columbia University's Teachers College and her bachelor's degree in art history and education from Boston University.

Dean Anderson is CEO and co-founder of the consulting, training, and publishing company, Being First, Inc. Mr. Anderson consults to and coaches senior executives of Fortune 500 companies, government, and large nonprofit organizations, specializing in organizational and personal transformation and optimal performance. He helps senior executives achieve breakthrough results from change, release the human potential in their organizations, and build high performing co-creative cultures.

Mr. Anderson has co-authored more than 50 articles on organizational and personal transformation. His first two books, the first editions of *Beyond Change Management* and *The Change Leader's Roadmap*, which he co-authored with Linda Ackerman Anderson, were the second and third best sellers in the Jossey-Bass/Pfeiffer "Practicing Organization Development" Series.

Mr. Anderson's interest in human performance and transformation began at an early age. He was the first ten-year-old boy in the world to swim 100 yards under a minute, and the first to ever swim 200 yards under two minutes. On this foundation, Mr. Anderson founded the Optimal Performance Institute in 1980, where he developed the *Optimizing System for Personal Excellence*, training elite athletes, actors, singers, and other performers, some of whom went on to win Olympic gold medals.

Mr. Anderson is the co-developer of *The Change Leader's Roadmap* methodology, creator of Being First's renowned leadership breakthrough training, *Leading Breakthrough Results: Walking the Talk of Change*, and is the central developer of *The Co-Creating System*.™ He is the co-author of Being First's comprehensive set of change tools and the developer of the *Co-Creative Partnering and Team Development* processes.

Mr. Anderson has two degrees from Stanford University, a bachelor of arts in communications and a master's degree in education, where he was an All-American swimmer and water polo player. His current passions are fly fishing, whitewater rafting, horseback riding, learning guitar, and being in the wilderness with his wife, Linda, and daughter, Terra.

For further information, contact:

Being First, Inc.
1242 Oak Drive, DW2
Durango, CO 81301
USA
(970) 385–5100 voice
(970) 385–7751 fax
www.beingfirst.com
e-mail: deananderson@beingfirst.com
lindasaa@beingfirst.com

INDEX

Acceleration strategies: consulting questions for, 133; determination of, 123, 128; human dynamics and, 308, 310–312. *See also* Timelines; Urgency

Accountability of conscious change leaders, 13–15

Ackerman Anderson, Linda, 3, 148

Adams, John, 149–150

"Aha moments," 38–39

Air Traffic Control, 114–116

Alignment: building of, 95–96, 103; as decision-making style, 112; of leaders, 40; as leadership capability track, 88

Alignment decision-making style, 112

All Quadrants, All Levels (AQAL), 14–15

Analysis of impacts. *See* Impact analysis; Initial impact analysis

Analysis paralysis, 214

Anderson, Dean, 3, 148

AQAL (All Quadrants, All Levels), 14–15

Assessment: of capacity, 79, 81–83, 101–102; change assessment compared to research assessment, 188; of change efforts, 3; of change leadership team effectiveness, 98–101; of culture, 94, 152; of definition of success, 187; of design requirements, 187–190, 192–193; of drivers of change, 56; of initial impact analysis, 61–62, 63–64; of leadership capability, 89, 102, 267–268; of magnitude of impacts, 219; of readiness, 79–81, 101–102; sample technologies for, 156; of team effectiveness, 98–101

Autopilot leaders: defined, 11–13; ego control of, 17; model as too complicated for, 284–285; skipping stages in model by, 285–286; slowdown of change caused by, 308–311

Awareness levels, 11–12

Barrier buster teams, 153

Behavior: communication and change of, 122; consulting questions for, 102, 184; defined, 14–15; as driver of change, 57–58; in drivers of change model, 8; making communication authentic with, 167–168; modeling of mindset with, 92–95; promoting of new, 179–182; rewards for, 157–159, 163

Behavioral imperatives in sample case for change, 69

Being (self), 16–17

Benchmark organizations, 190, 193

Best practices: benchmark organizations for, 190, 193; establishment of, 270–270, 275–276, 301

CCO (Chief Change Officers), 17, 302

Celebration of new state, 255–256, 264

Change: complexity increases in, 1–2; emotional reactivity and, 147–150; failure rate of, 96; inertia and, 175–176; measurements of, 156–157, 162–163, 271; normal versus breakthrough results from, 6; Phase I as foundation for, 39–40; risk of celebrating, 255–256; as strategic discipline, 17, 298; types of, 9–10, 58–61, 75

Change agent resource teams, 305

Change capability. *See* Capability (organizational); Leadership capability

Change capacity. *See* Capacity

Change consultants. *See* Consultants for change

Change initiative leads, 44

Change leaders: defined, 288; development stages for Change Leader's Roadmap, 279–282; mindset of, 47–48; rewards for, 157–159; role in process by, 287–290; as spokespeople, 122; support for, 98, 104. *See also* Conscious change leaders; Leadership capability

Change Leader's Roadmap (CLR): audiences for, 30–31; benefits of, 1; for breakthrough results, 29; as Change Operating System, 24; developmental stages in learning, 279–282; as multi-directional approach, 287–290; overview, 22–25; Premium Content, 31; as process model, 24; reactions to, 283–286; structure of, 25–29; tailoring to specific situation required, 24–25, 27, 137; as thinking discipline, 20–22, 27, 137, 278–279; uniqueness of methodology, 29–31. *See also* Leverage of Change Leader's Roadmap

Change leadership teams: assessment of effectiveness, 98–101; clarifying relationship to executive team, 48–49; consulting questions for, 103; defined, 42–43; development as leadership capability track, 88; development of, 98–101; political

dynamics strategies and, 138–139; wearing two hats by, 47–48

Change management (CM), 9, 201

Change navigation centers, 152–153

Change Operating Systems. *See* Change Leader's Roadmap (CLR)

Change process leaders, 43–44, 46–47

Change process models, 20–22

Change project teams, 44–45

Change strategies: acceleration strategies for, 123; bold actions identification, 116–117; clarification of, 106–107; communication of, 166–171; consulting questions for, 130–134, 182; defined, 125; delegation of, 107; elements of, 126; engagement strategies clarification, 117–119; fit and priority of effort, 113–114; governance and decision-making clarification, 109–112; identifying required initiatives, 112–113; integration of initiatives and, 114–116; process for design of, 108; sample of, 127–129; task deliverables for, 106, 129; template for, 126; timelines as element of, 125; values and guiding principles for, 108–109. *See also* Communication

Change support mechanisms, 150–156

Chief Change Officer (CCO), 17, 302

CLR. *See* Change Leader's Roadmap (CLR)

CM (change management), 9, 201

Coaching, 101. *See also* Learning

Collaboration, common change methodology for, 297

Collective intention, 165–166, 171–175

Command-and-control leadership style, 2, 87. *See also* Autopilot leaders

Commitment: building of, 95–96; consulting questions for, 103, 183; creating shared vision for, 171–175; as leadership capability track, 88; personal influence and, 118; for resources, 124, 133; from stakeholders, 18–19. *See also* Engagement; Engagement strategies

Common change methodology for change efforts case-in-point, 297

Communication: of case for change, 125, 166–171; of change strategies, 166–171; consulting questions for, 132–133; designing plan for, 119–123; of desired state design, 206, 208; dialogue as tool for, 96; engagement vehicles for, 120–121; of Implementation Master Plans, 235–236, 239; kickoff communications, 122–123, 166–171; levels of, 120–122; message sent by selection of change process leaders, 46–47; Phase I completion necessary for, 125; problems from lack of, 120; to reduce negative reactions, 245; resistance and, 147; in sample change strategy, 128; sample technologies for, 155; to support integration and mastery, 259

Competence core need, 18

Conditions for success: consulting questions for, 160; as infrastructure component, 137, 139–140, 141, 300

Connection and inclusion core need, 18

Conscious and collective endeavors, 247

Conscious awareness and change results, 12

Conscious Change Leader Accountability Model, 13–15, 46, 87–88, 109, 141–143, 211, 243, 257, 261, 281, 317

Conscious change leaders: accountability of, 13–16; being (self) controlling of, 17; defined, 11; kickoff communications by, 169–171; learning from change process by, 267–268, 270–270; level of success of, 4; mindset approach and, 12; minimizing resistance by, 18; questions to increase awareness, 316–317; reducing emotional reactions of others by, 147–150; self-mastery by, 16; subjects to be mastered by, 97–97; support for integration by, 259; use of consultants by, 200–201; visioning process design and, 142. *See also* Leadership capability; Modeling

Conscious process thinking, 20, 46–47, 246

Consensus decision-making style, 112

Consultants for change: building change skills by, 178–179; capability, questions for, 101–102; capacity, questions for, 101–102; case for change, questions for, 74–76; change strategies, questions for, 130–134; for change strategy creation, 108; to clarify relationship of executive team to change leadership team, 49; for commitment and alignment, 95–96; desired outcomes determination questions for, 76; development stages for Change Leader's Roadmap, 279–282; just-in-time strategy and, 304–310; leverage points for, 317–318; people and process requirements and, 199–200; readiness, questions for, 101–102; resources and, 124; roles of, 45, 199–201; self-mastery by, 16; start up and staff change questions for, 72–74; Strategic Change Consultant role and, 5; use by leaders of, 318; wake-up calls and, 39; working relationship between, 49

Consulting questions: for acceleration strategies, 133; for alignment, 103; for behavior, 102, 184; for bold actions, 132; for capability (organizational), 182–184; for capacity (organizational), 101–102; for case for change, creating, 74–76, 182; for change leadership teams, 103; for change strategies, 130–134, 182; for commitment, 103, 183; for communication, 132–133; for conditions for success, 160; for course correction, 161–162; for customer requirements, 193; for decision-making, 130–131; for design process, 77, 130; for design requirements, 192–193; for desired outcomes determination, 76; for desired state design, 207–208; for drivers of change, 77; for engagement strategies, 132; for executive teams, 104; for governance structures, 130; for guiding principles, 130; for impact analysis, 220–221; for Implementation Master Plans, 237–239; for implementation of change,

251–252; for information generation strategies, 161; for information management strategies, 161; for infrastructure, 160–161; for initial desired outcomes, 76; for initial impact analysis, 75; for initiatives for change, 131; for knowledge, 103, 183; for leadership capability, 102–104; for leverage points, 77; for milestones, 133–134; for mindset, 102, 184; for modeling, 102; for new state integration and mastery, 264–265; for political dynamics, 160; for project briefings, 72; for project communities, 73–74; for readiness, 101–102; for resistance, 162; for roles, 72–73; for scope of change, 75; for skills, 103, 183; for start up and staff change, 72–74; for target groups, 75; for timelines, 133–134; for urgency, 75; uses for, 32; for values, 130; for vision, 160–161, 183; for working relationship creation, 73

Content, 6–7

Content versus process experts, 46–47

Control and power core need, 18

Cooperation, 115–116. *See also* Engagement; Engagement strategies

Coordination. *See* Integration strategy for initiatives

Core needs, 18

Course correction: conditions for success review and, 140; consulting questions for, 161–162; critical mass and, 247, 263, 320; of desired state, 247, 249–251; desired state design communication and, 206; energy sustaining strategies and, 229; impact analysis and, 213, 219; during implementation of change, 246–248, 251; infrastructure and, 137; metrics and, 157; modeling of, 146; strategy design for, 144–147

Course Correction Model, 145–146

Critical mass: case-in point about, 174; collective intention for, 165–166; course correction and, 247, 263, 320; creating for

support of change, 139; for mindset change, 60, 118; transformational success and, 94, 287. *See also* Engagement; Engagement strategies

Critical path, 293, 294–295

Cultural imperatives, 8, 57, 68–69

Culture: assessment of, 94, 152; defined, 15, 19; values and guiding principles and, 108–109

Culture change: away from fear-based norms, 146; bold actions for, 117; celebrations and, 255–256; conditions of, 19; for continuous monitoring and improving of new state, 268–270; creating shared vision for, 140–141; as driver of transformation, 7–8, 19–20; initiatives and, 113; kickoff communications and, 167, 170–171; to leverage use of Roadmap, 302–303; mindset and, 94; scanning groups or networks for, 152; timeline issues in, 231

Culture scanning groups or networks, 152

Current reality, assessing, 187–190

Customer requirements, 190–192, 193

Daily operations. *See* Running the business

Decision-making, 109–112, 130–131

Deliverables. *See* Task deliverables

Demonstrating old way is gone, 175–176, 183

Design process: for case for change and initial desired outcomes, 56; consulting questions for, 74, 130; for impact analysis, 214–214, 220. *See also* Desired state design

Design requirements: assessing current reality for, 187–190; benefits from clarifying, 187; consulting questions for, 192–193; customer requirements for, 190–192; elements of, 186; identifying benchmark organizations for, 190; statement of, 192, 193; types of, 188–190. *See also* Desired state design

Desired outcomes determination, 66, 70–71, 76

Desired state design: communication about, 206, 208; consulting questions for, 207–208; initiatives for change and, 201–202; Levels of Design model for, 202–204; overview, 197–198; pilot testing of, 204–206, 207–208; process and structure creation, 198–202; refining after impact analysis, 219, 221; vision compared, 197

Desired state (future state): course-correcting and monitoring of, 247, 249–250; customer requirements identification and, 190–192; impact analysis and, 211–214. *See also* New state

Determining What is Driving the Change worksheet, 59

Developmental change, 3, 9, 60

Dial-a-Team, 110–111

Dialogue, 96. *See also* Communication

"Down and in" perspective, 113

Downstream stage of fullstream transformation, 21, 23. *See also* Celebration of new state; Course correction; Implementation of change; New state integration and mastery

Drivers of Change Model: assessment of, 56; consulting questions for, 74; cultural change and, 7–8, 19–20; customers needs as, 191; mindset as, 290; mindset as driver, 8, 58, 290; overview, 7–9, 57–58; in sample case for change, 67–69; scope of change and, 62; worksheet to identify, 59

DTE Energy mindset shift case-in-point, 92–95

Education. *See* Learning

Ego (mind), 16

Emergent re-invention, 20

Emotional reactions to change, 147–150, 162

Employee retention, 270–274

Engagement: audiences for, 119; in change assessment, 188; culture scanning groups or networks for, 152; impact analysis and, 211, 214, 217–218; sample technologies for, 155;

sustaining, 224; types of, 119; vehicles for, 119, 120–121; visioning process design and, 140–142. *See also* Commitment

Engagement strategies: clarification of, 117–119; communication and, 120–121; consulting questions for, 132; information generation and course correction as, 146; kickoff communications and, 167–171; resistance and, 147; in sample change strategy, 128

Enterprise change agenda, 298, 301

Environmental forces, 7, 57

Environmental imperatives in sample case for change, 67

"Everyone is responsible. No one is to blame." motto, 247

Executive teams: assessment of effectiveness, 98–101; Chief Change Officer as part of, 17; clarifying relationship to change leadership team, 48–49; consulting questions for, 104; defined, 42; development as leadership capability track, 88; development of, 98–101; importance of involvement by, 289–290; mindset and, 307; support for, 98, 104; wearing two hats by, 47–48

Expert practitioners, 281

External drivers of change, 8–9

External reality, 14

Failure rate of change, 96

Fairness and justice core need, 18

Feedback. *See* Course correction

Fit of efforts, 113–114, 131

Five Levels of Communication, 120–122, 167–171

"Flavor of the month" syndrome, avoiding, 293

Follow-up sessions, 92–95, 94

Fortune 500 company reward system, 158

Four Quadrants, 14–15

Framework models, change process models compared, 20

Fullstream Transformation Model, 20–22

Process versus content experts, 46–47

Proficient practitioners, 281

Project briefings, 40, 72

Project communities: consulting questions for, 72–74; critical mass and, 139; identification of, 49–53; mapping for, 50–51, 62; purpose of, 49; roles for, 51; strategies for, 51; worksheet for identifying, 52–53

Project community maps, 50–51, 62

Project management, 9, 155–156

Project management methodologies, 26

Project thinking, conscious process thinking compared, 20, 46

Project/process partnerships, 47

Questions for Visioning worksheet, 170

Reactions. *See* Human dynamics

Readiness: assessment, 79–81, 101; building of, 84–85; case-in point about, 82; consulting questions for, 101–102; factors affecting, 80–81; task deliverables for, 78

"Ready-fire-aim" orientation, 286

Renewal, 268–270

Research laboratory infrastructure change case-in-point, 115–116

Resistance: celebration risks and, 256; changing to commitment, 18–19, 234–236; coaching to reduce, 98; consulting questions for, 162; core needs causing, 18; defined, 147; defusing of, 147; engagement of people experiencing, 211; Implementation Master Plans and, 232–235, 236, 244; supporting people through, 147–150

Resources: allocating between operations and change, 83; effect of lack of, 2; Implementation Master Plans and, 229–231, 238; importance of coordination of, 115–116; securing commitment for, 124, 133; timelines and, 229

Results, 12. *See also* Breakthrough results

Rewards, 157–159, 163

Roles of people: of change leaders, 287–290; clarification of, 40, 259–260; of consultants for change, 45, 199–201; consulting questions for, 72–74; design process and, 202; governance structure and, 109–111; as infrastructure component, 136; for project communities, 51; selection criteria for, 41; types of, 41–45

Roll out process: of Implementation Master Plans, 244–246, 251, 300; sequences for, 230; vision and, 171–175

Running the business: clarifying relationship of executive team to change leadership team, 48–49, 98; functional versus change leaders mindsets for, 47–48; governance and decision-making clarification for, 109; resource allocation and, l, 124

Safety core need, 18

Samples: case for change, 67–71; change strategies, 127–129; conditions for success, 141; technologies, 155–156; temporary management systems, 154; temporary policies, 154–155

SCO (Strategic Change Office), 17, 302

Scope of change, 62, 70, 75, 213

Scope of the organization, 230

Self-mastery, 16

Sell decision-making style, 111

Shared vision, 67, 140–142, 160–161

Show stoppers, 215

Skills: consulting questions for, 103, 183; for leadership capability, 97–98; training to build, 178–179. *See also* Learning

Social media technology, 144

Soft launch, 306

Software company impact analysis workshop case-in-point, 217–218

Special project teams, 151–152

Sponsors, 41–42, 170, 299

Urgency: acceleration strategies and, 123; consulting questions for, 75; determination of level, 65–66; priority and, 113–114; timelines compared, 65–66

Utility organization readiness case-in-point, 82

Values, 108–109, 127, 130

Virtual fence for border, 191

Vision: consulting questions for, 160–161, 183; desired state design compared, 197; inertia and, 175–176; interaction with kickoff communications, 167; in Levels of Design model, 202–204; process for creating, 140–142; Questions for Visioning worksheet, 170; role in course correction, 145; roll out process to create, 171–175; in sample case for change, 67; telephone company vision creation case-in-point, 174

Vision statements, 172

Vote decision-making style, 112

Wake-up calls, recognizing, 38–39

Walking the talk. *See* Modeling

Web site for Premium Content, 31

Wilber, Ken, 13–15

Working relationship creation, 48–49, 51, 73

Worksheets: Determining What is Driving the Change, 59; Identifying Your Project Community, 52–53; Initial Impact Analysis Audit, 61–62; Questions for Visioning, 170; Strategies to Add Capacity, 86; Web site for, 32

Pfeiffer Publications Guide

This guide is designed to familiarize you with the various types of Pfeiffer publications. The formats section describes the various types of products that we publish; the methodologies section describes the many different ways that content might be provided within a product. We also provide a list of the topic areas in which we publish.

FORMATS

In addition to its extensive book-publishing program, Pfeiffer offers content in an array of formats, from fieldbooks for the practitioner to complete, ready-to-use training packages that support group learning.

FIELDBOOK Designed to provide information and guidance to practitioners in the midst of action. Most fieldbooks are companions to another, sometimes earlier, work, from which its ideas are derived; the fieldbook makes practical what was theoretical in the original text. Fieldbooks can certainly be read from cover to cover. More likely, though, you'll find yourself bouncing around following a particular theme, or dipping in as the mood, and the situation, dictate.

HANDBOOK A contributed volume of work on a single topic, comprising an eclectic mix of ideas, case studies, and best practices sourced by practitioners and experts in the field.

An editor or team of editors usually is appointed to seek out contributors and to evaluate content for relevance to the topic. Think of a handbook not as a ready-to-eat meal, but as a cookbook of ingredients that enables you to create the most fitting experience for the occasion.

RESOURCE Materials designed to support group learning. They come in many forms: a complete, ready-to-use exercise (such as a game); a comprehensive resource on one topic (such as conflict management) containing a variety of methods and approaches; or a collection of like-minded activities (such as icebreakers) on multiple subjects and situations.

TRAINING PACKAGE An entire, ready-to-use learning program that focuses on a particular topic or skill. All packages comprise a guide for the facilitator/trainer and a workbook for the participants. Some packages are supported with additional media—such as video—or learning aids, instruments, or other devices to help participants understand concepts or practice and develop skills.

- *Facilitator/trainer's guide* Contains an introduction to the program, advice on how to organize and facilitate the learning event, and step-by-step instructor notes. The guide also contains copies of presentation materials—handouts, presentations, and overhead designs, for example—used in the program.

- *Participant's workbook* Contains exercises and reading materials that support the learning goal and serves as a valuable reference and support guide for participants in the weeks and months that follow the learning event. Typically, each participant will require his or her own workbook.

ELECTRONIC CD-ROMs and web-based products transform static Pfeiffer content into dynamic, interactive experiences. Designed to take advantage of the searchability, automation, and ease-of-use that technology provides, our e-products bring convenience and immediate accessibility to your workspace.

METHODOLOGIES

CASE STUDY A presentation, in narrative form, of an actual event that has occurred inside an organization. Case studies are not prescriptive, nor are they used to prove a point; they are designed to develop critical analysis and decision-making skills. A case study has a specific time frame, specifies a sequence of events, is narrative in structure, and contains a plot structure—an issue (what should be/have been done?). Use case studies when the goal is to enable participants to apply previously learned theories to the circumstances in the case, decide what is pertinent, identify the real issues, decide what should have been done, and develop a plan of action.

ENERGIZER A short activity that develops readiness for the next session or learning event. Energizers are most commonly used after a break or lunch to stimulate or refocus the group. Many involve some form of physical activity, so they are a useful way to counter post-lunch lethargy. Other uses include transitioning from one topic to another, where "mental" distancing is important.

EXPERIENTIAL LEARNING ACTIVITY (ELA) A facilitator-led intervention that moves participants through the learning cycle from experience to application (also known as a Structured Experience). ELAs are carefully thought-out designs in which there is a definite learning purpose and intended outcome. Each step—everything that participants do during the activity—facilitates the accomplishment of the stated goal. Each ELA includes complete instructions for facilitating the intervention and a clear statement of goals, suggested group size and timing, materials required, an explanation of the process, and, where appropriate, possible variations to the activity. (For more detail on Experiential Learning Activities, see the Introduction to the *Reference Guide to Handbooks and Annuals*, 1999 edition, Pfeiffer, San Francisco.)

GAME A group activity that has the purpose of fostering team spirit and togetherness in addition to the achievement of a pre-stated goal. Usually contrived—undertaking a desert expedition, for example—this type of learning method offers an engaging means for participants to demonstrate and practice business and interpersonal skills. Games are effective for team building and personal development mainly because the goal is subordinate to the process—the means through which participants reach decisions, collaborate, communicate, and generate trust and understanding. Games often engage teams in "friendly" competition.

ICEBREAKER A (usually) short activity designed to help participants overcome initial anxiety in a training session and/or to acquaint the participants with one another. An icebreaker can be a fun activity or can be tied to specific topics or training goals. While a useful tool in itself, the icebreaker comes into its own in situations where tension or resistance exists within a group.

INSTRUMENT A device used to assess, appraise, evaluate, describe, classify, and summarize various aspects of human behavior. The term used to describe an instrument depends primarily on its format and purpose. These terms include survey, questionnaire, inventory, diagnostic, survey, and poll. Some uses of instruments include providing instrumental feedback to group members, studying here-and-now processes or functioning within a group, manipulating group composition, and evaluating outcomes of training and other interventions.

Instruments are popular in the training and HR field because, in general, more growth can occur if an individual is provided with a method for focusing specifically on his or her own behavior. Instruments also are used to obtain information that will serve as a basis for change and to assist in workforce planning efforts.

Paper-and-pencil tests still dominate the instrument landscape with a typical package comprising a facilitator's guide, which offers advice on administering the instrument and interpreting the collected data, and an initial set of instruments. Additional instruments are available separately. Pfeiffer, though, is investing heavily in e-instruments. Electronic instrumentation provides effortless distribution and, for larger groups particularly, offers advantages over paper-and-pencil tests in the time it takes to analyze data and provide feedback.

LECTURETTE A short talk that provides an explanation of a principle, model, or process that is pertinent to the participants' current learning needs. A lecturette is intended to establish a common language bond between the trainer and the participants by providing a mutual frame of reference. Use a lecturette as an introduction to a group activity or event, as an interjection during an event, or as a handout.

MODEL A graphic depiction of a system or process and the relationship among its elements. Models provide a frame of reference and something more tangible, and more easily remembered, than a verbal explanation. They also give participants something to "go on," enabling them to track their own progress as they experience the dynamics, processes, and relationships being depicted in the model.

ROLE PLAY A technique in which people assume a role in a situation/scenario: a customer service rep in an angry-customer exchange, for example. The way in which the role is approached is then discussed and feedback is offered. The role play is often repeated using a different approach and/or incorporating changes made based on feedback received. In other words, role playing is a spontaneous interaction involving realistic behavior under artificial (and safe) conditions.

SIMULATION A methodology for understanding the interrelationships among components of a system or process. Simulations differ from games in that they test or use a model that depicts or mirrors some aspect of reality in form, if not necessarily in content. Learning occurs by studying the effects of change on one or more factors of the model. Simulations are commonly used to test hypotheses about what happens in a system—often referred to as "what if?" analysis—or to examine best-case/worst-case scenarios.

THEORY A presentation of an idea from a conjectural perspective. Theories are useful because they encourage us to examine behavior and phenomena through a different lens.

TOPICS

The twin goals of providing effective and practical solutions for workforce training and organization development and meeting the educational needs of training and human resource professionals shape Pfeiffer's publishing program. Core topics include the following:

Leadership & Management
Communication & Presentation
Coaching & Mentoring
Training & Development
E-Learning
Teams & Collaboration
OD & Strategic Planning
Human Resources
Consulting

What will you find on pfeiffer.com?

- The best in workplace performance solutions for training and HR professionals

- Downloadable training tools, exercises, and content

- Web-exclusive offers

- Training tips, articles, and news

- Seamless on-line ordering

- Author guidelines, information on becoming a Pfeiffer Partner, and much more

Discover more at www.pfeiffer.com

BEYOND CHANGE MANAGEMENT

How to Achieve Breakthrough
Results Through Conscious
Change Leadership

Second Edition

ISBN: 978-0-470-64808-7 | US $55.00
Available October 2010

Achieving breakthrough results from transformation requires leaders to become conscious of the human and process dynamics that enable and prohibit success. This updated edition reveals those dynamics and provides guidance about how to lead transformation so it delivers superior results.

General themes for the new edition include: raising awareness; recognizing the needs of the entire system in change (individuals, relationships, teams and the organization as a whole; modeling the change; and more. **Beyond Change Management** is written for leaders, OD practitioners, change practitioners, project managers, and consultants.

DEAN ANDERSON is co-founder and president of Being First, a change leadership development and transformational change consulting firm. He is a powerful speaker, writer, coach, consultant and master trainer. He co-authored with Linda Ackerman Anderson of *Beyond Change Management* and *Change Leader's Roadmap*.

LINDA ACKERMAN ANDERSON is a co-founder and vice-president of Being First. She specializes in planning for and facilitating transformational change in Fortune 1000 businesses and the military. Linda has spoken about her work on conscious transformation at national and international conferences, and is known as a thought leader and inspiring model of her message. During the past 25 years, her practice has focused on strategy development for major organizational change using Being First's renown nine-phase Change Leader's Roadmap.

**To order or for more information,
visit www.pfeiffer.com
For bulk orders, e-mail specialsales@wiley.com**

An Imprint of WILEY
Now you know.